BIBLICAL WORLDVIEW RHETORIC I

STUDENT VERSION

SHAUNNA K. HOWAT

To accompany Edward P.J. Corbett's
Classical Rhetoric for the Modern Student

<u>Note</u>: Materials herein may not be reproduced or distributed in any manner without the express permission of the author. Reproducible materials can be found in the document by that title.

The author has made every attempt to obtain permission to reprint the discourses contained in this text book. The copyright of this book only covers the author's own words and does not intend to copyright the words or works of other authors or writers.

This text book is intended to accompany Corbett's text, *Classical Rhetoric for the Modern Student*. This text differs from other "Classical Christian" Rhetoric texts in the respect that it relies on Corbett, which is primarily a college text. Additionally, in order to prepare for college or post-high school, the Christian student needs to strengthen his or her writing ability. This course emphasizes writing skills while learning the Classical technique of Rhetoric. If you take this course independently of a writing instructor, please find a local or online writing tutor who will challenge your ability to write.

Shaunna K. Howat
howat.sk@gmail.com
First edition of this text began in 1994. This has been a work in progress since then. Please direct all questions, comments and concerns to me at the above email address.

ISBN: 1452871779
ISBN-13: 9781452871776

TABLE OF CONTENTS

AUTHOR'S NOTE:

I do not claim to be the originator of these ideas; I have simply put a biblical worldview to this material and applied it to the teaching of Christian high school students. See my **Works Cited page** for other texts I have found valuable in assembling this text.

It must be acknowledged from the outset that this curriculum was not written by me alone. This was written with the daily inspiration and input of the Holy Spirit. I am bold enough to say this, because without submitting myself to His authorship this could not have been completed.

> *The heavens declare the glory of God;*
> *the skies proclaim the work of his hands.*
> *Day after day they pour forth speech;*
> *night after night they display knowledge.*
> *There is no speech or language where their voice is not heard.*
> *Their voice goes out into all the earth,*
> *their words to the ends of the world.*
> —Psalm 19:1-4a

The parent/teacher who decides to use this curriculum to teach his or her Rhetoric course would be well-advised to prayerfully do the following:

- Submit himself to the inspiration of the Holy Spirit, relying on Him to inspire where this curriculum may be lacking;
- Take part in some form of Classical Christian educational training, to be familiar with the methodology used;
- Read as much as possible of primary sources: histories, essays, speeches, letters written by historical figures and leaders;
- Learn as much as possible about the historical context in which these original documents were written;
- Take a course in formal syllogistic logic, including enthymemes, syllogisms, truth tables, the Laws of Thought, and fallacies.

Rhetoric is designed as a two-year course, for Juniors and Seniors (11th and 12th grades) in high school. The ideal situation for a student entering Rhetoric is that he or she has had a complete grammar-school, junior high and at least two years of high school education in English grammar and usage, a class in Logic, and (suggested) one year of Latin. A full background in English includes grammar, writing, and research techniques, with much reading of the classics all along. A good understanding of world history is also important, as we study the background that leads up to, and gives the context for, the discourses we read. Students may consider taking a government class alongside, or at some point during this two-year Rhetoric course.

My students are required to take Logic before they complete the first quarter of Rhetoric. They will either take it the summer before, during summer school, or at home in a guided home-school course, or in night-school sessions during the first quarter. They are also required to submit writing samples to prove their aptitude in English skills. These requirements may seem stiff, but the course of Rhetoric is for those who are adequately prepared beforehand. Those who are not will find it to be a difficult course.

Student Instructions:

You are responsible for adhering to these instructions! Each lesson will be broken down into studies that will cover one week, unless otherwise noted. With the exception of the first week's lesson, one lesson covers a four-day week. Students should spend 1 hour per day for four days each week.

When I instruct you to write 2-3 paragraphs (or whatever length provided), I am looking for an essay. By "essay form" remember that we are talking about all the elements of well-constructed paragraphs, in which you explain the discourse, answer the questions and provide examples. (Examples to support your ideas include quotes with citations from the discourse we are studying.) Paragraphs generally contain 5-12 well-written sentences. If a paragraph has more or less, you may well figure that it does not meet my requirements, and you must reevaluate and rewrite your paragraph.

I will grade you based on your complete thoughts (did you answer the question fully and accurately?) and your use of the English language.

Ground Rules in this Rhetoric class
- When I refer to a discourse, I mean a spoken or written body of work. I could also refer to the piece as an oratory, an article, or an argument. The body of work has many "names," and we could get tied up in trying to understand just to what we refer. A rhetorical piece could just as easily be called a discourse, an essay, a speech, etc.
- When we come across new or difficult terms, we will stop to look them up together. Therefore, we need to have dictionaries on hand as we study rhetoric. Possible vocabulary words will appear in the margin.
- Students must practice being an attentive audience for whoever is speaking.
- There is little understanding in a class whose students do not participate in the discussion. By that I mean: Listen to the speaker, take notes, ask questions, and look for practical ways of applying what you are learning.

Parents of Home school students: Please check your student's notebook every few weeks to make sure he or she is taking notes from the weekly class, is highlighting important words or terms, and studying in advance of quizzes. ALSO make sure that you and your student review the graded assignments that come back from the teacher of this class. If your student is not making changes to future assignments based on teacher comments, he/she will not grow and progress as a student.

Assignments written for this class must follow these requirements: They must be typed in 12-point Times New Roman, with 1-inch margins all around. Your name must be in the upper left-hand side of the page. The title of the assignment (either by assignment number or by title of the discourse being analyzed) must also be in the upper left hand side of the page.
Unless otherwise noted, assignments for this class must adhere to MLA (Modern Language Association) Guidelines.

The following are titles of the works read and/or analyzed during the first year. These can be replaced by the teacher with any other sort of discourse.

Reading for Rhetoric 1 Students (not all-inclusive, in order by author)

Author	Title	Located*
Bauman, M.	Chronicle of an Undeception	App.
Belz, J.	The Lie is Marching On	App.
Bible	Acts 13:16-41	Bible
	Acts 21:39 and 23:1-6	Bible
Bumpers, D.	Closing Defense of Clinton	App.
Burke, E.	Letter to a Noble Lord	App.
Bush, G.W.	Iraq and the Middle East	App.
Chamberlain	1939 Address	App.
Churchill, W.	Blood, Toil, Tears & Sweat	App.
	Be Ye Men of Valour	App.
Cicero	Among Us You Can Live No Longer	Hist.
Colson, C.	A History of God	App.
	Pretty Stones...	App.
Cranmer, T.	I Shall Declare unto you...	Hist.
Cromwell, O.	Let God Judge	Hist.
Douglass, F.	I Hear the Mournful Wail...	Hist.
Eliot, Sir J.	The Exchequer is Empty	Hist.
Elizabeth I	I have the heart...	Hist.
Garrison, W.	For Immediate Abolition	App.
Hamilton, A.	The Cause of Liberty	Hist.
Hancock, J.	The Tremendous Bar of God	Hist.
Harvey, P.	She Did Good	App.
Henry, P.	Give Me Liberty	Hist.
Hitler, A.	Reichstag Speech	App.
	Speech to Germany	App.
Huss, J.	The Church	App.
Jefferson, T.	Inaugural Address	App.
Kennedy, J.F.	Inaugural Address	Hist.
King, M.L.	Letter from Birmingham Jail	App.
	I Have a Dream	App.
Lamb, Charles	Dissertation Upon Roast Pig	App.
Limbaugh, R.	Liberalism's Last Gasp	App.
Lincoln, A.	Gettysburg Address	Hist.
Lindman, D.	They're Smiling in Heaven	App.
Loeffler, J.	Trashing the Planet	App.
Macaulay, T.	Lord Clive	App.
	A Matter of Shame	Hist.
Madison, J.	Federalist No. 10	App.
Marx, K.	Communist Manifesto	App.
Misc.	Fables	App.
Morris, G.	I am an American	Hist.

Nixon, R.	Checkers Speech	App.
Pitt, M.	I Rejoice that America…	Hist.
Reagan, R.	Brandenburg Gate Address	App.
Rooney. A.	This House is Not for Sale	App.
Roosevelt, FD	First Inaugural Address	App.
Sancton, T.	Planet of the Year	App.
Sartre, J.	Republic of Silence	App.
Socrates	Apology	App.
Stalin, J.	Speech on Red Square	App.
Swift, J.	A Modest Proposal	App.
Webster, D.	Liberty and Union	Hist.
Wilberforce	On the Horrors of the Slave Trade	App.
Wycliffe, J.	Condemnation/Answers	App.

* Hist. Refers to The Penguin Book of Historic Speeches (see Bibliography).

* App. refers to the appendix to this text. All works in the Appendix should be easily located on the internet and/or have been reprinted with permission and may be photocopied for classroom purposes only.

Between mediocrity and perfection, there is a very wide interval. There are many intermediate spaces, which may be filled up with honour; and the more rare and difficult that complete perfection is, the greater is the honour of approaching to it, though we do not fully attain it. (*Hugh Blair, in Corbett, Rhetoric of Blair, 128-129*)

LESSON ONE

(WEEK ONE)
INTRODUCTION

Words—why do we study them? The word comes from God. He is the author of the spoken and written word. Read the following verses which include "word" in some way.

John 1:1-4: In the beginning was the Word, and the Word was with God, and the Word was God. He was in the beginning with God. All things came into being through him, and without him not one thing came into being. What has come into being in him was life, and the life was the light of all people.

John 1:14: And the Word became flesh and lived among us, and we have seen his glory, the glory as of a father's only son, full of grace and truth.

Deut. 8:3: He humbled you by letting you hunger, then by feeding you with manna, with which neither you nor your ancestors were acquainted, in order to make you understand that one does not live by bread alone, but by every word that comes from the mouth of the LORD.

"WORD" occurs 651 times in the NIV; 323 times it comes in the phrase "the word of the Lord" or "the word of God." Obviously the Lord placed great emphasis on "Word." He chose to communicate to us in the form of words—spoken and written. He chose to have his law recorded, and many times in the Bible His law was referred to as "word." So we choose to study the written word as well. We know that the written word and the spoken word have power. They are the way in which God chose to communicate with us, so we know that they are important. Words can be used to build up or tear down.

The Greek word is *logos*, indicating "first cause" in Greek philosophy. To Greeks, it indicated the great, unknown Intelligent Reason, Will and Power behind the universe, which the pagans of that day, as well as ours, called "God."

John used this reference of *logos*, infinite wisdom, which helped the Greeks understand the Hebrew concept of God. Here he also gave the Hebrews a way of understanding that God the Creator embodies infinite *wisdom,* as in Proverbs 8:22-31:
"The LORD created me [wisdom] at the beginning of his work, the first of his acts of long ago. Ages ago I was set up, at the first, before the beginning of the earth. When there were no depths I was brought forth, when there were no springs abounding with water. Before the mountains had been shaped, before the hills, I was brought forth—when he had not yet made earth and fields, or the world's first bits of soil. When he established the heavens, I was there, when he drew a circle on the face of the deep, when he made firm the skies above, when he established the fountains of the

deep, when he assigned to the sea its limit, so that the waters might not transgress his command, when he marked out the foundations of the earth, then I was beside him, like a master worker; and I was daily his delight, rejoicing before him always, rejoicing in his inhabited world and delighting in the human race."

Not only does WORD imply wisdom, it is also John's word for Jesus. And if you think about it for very long, you will be amazed at how perfect this is. For the Hebrew mind, knowing that WORD is the reference for God's wisdom and law, and that when God's WORD is spoken great things happen, to understand that Jesus is the WORD is to understand that JESUS IS GOD, the Christ.

In the beginning was the WORD. The WORD of the Lord came (255 times in the NIV - in reference to prophecy). The WORD of the Lord is the source of wisdom (Ps. 33:4, "For the word of the LORD is upright, and all his work is done in faithfulness;" Psalm 33:9, "For he spoke, and it came to be; he commanded, and it stood firm").

Now that we know and understand the Source of all WORDS, and the WORD Himself, let's begin a course that studies words and how they are put together to be understood.

Rhetoric is an <u>ancient study of words and persuasive communication</u>. As long ago as Aristotle, who lived from 384-322 BC, rhetoric has been studied as an art—taken apart, analyzed and practiced. It has thrived since then, used in speech and in writing over the ages. Just in the past fifty years, however, rhetoric has come to mean exaggerated speaking for effect, political doubletalk.

Aristotle said, "Rhetoric may be defined as observing in any given case <u>the available means of persuasion</u>." Quintillian, another ancient rhetorician, commented that "The definition which best suits its real character is that which makes rhetoric the <u>science of speaking well</u>." We would characterize it as *the <u>science of speaking skillfully and virtuously</u>*.

Today we need to take up this ancient art form and apply it to our lives. Take advantage of the practice from old days, and use it to advance God's kingdom. It is necessary to present the word—written or oral—in the best light and with the purest, most straightforward and logical structure.

What is Rhetoric?
Rhetoric is best defined as <u>the study of written and oral communications and the art of persuasion</u>. The study of Rhetoric contains the form of writing as well as the art. The following quotation from Hugh Blair says it quite well. The following was written long ago, when words and

sentences were more complex and flowery than that with which we are familiar today. Students will find it difficult to read at first, but once one's "ear" is accustomed to the language, the words will flow quite nicely. This is only the first of many such passages!

> All that regards the study of eloquence and composition, merits the higher attention upon this account, that it is intimately connected with the improvement of our intellectual powers. For I must be allowed to say, that when we are employed, after a proper manner, in the study of composition, we are cultivating reason itself. True rhetoric and sound logic are very nearly allied. The study of arranging and expressing our thoughts with propriety, teaches to think as well as to speak accurately. By putting our sentiments into words, we always conceive them more distinctly. Every one who has the slightest acquaintance with composition knows, that when he expresses himself ill on any subject, when his arrangement is loose, and his sentences become feeble, the defects of his style can, almost on every occasion, be traced back to his indistinct conception of the subject: so close is the connexion between thoughts and the words in which they are clothed. (Blair, in Corbett, *The Rhetoric of Blair, Campbell and Whately,* 33)

The use of Rhetoric

Rhetoric is used to beautify truth and justice (style). It must communicate complex matters to the ignorant or uninformed (persuasion). Rhetoric teaches how to discover poor arguments in others (reason), and avoid them oneself. Rhetoric may be used for self-defense (persuasion). Aristotle reasoned that the inability to defend oneself physically is disgraceful; how much more so is the inability to defend oneself verbally, since speech is more natural to man than a strong body. Quintillian's doctrine of virtue said that the most essential quality of an orator is that he be a good man. Ethics, he reasoned, are inseparable from Rhetoric. Thus according to him, an immoral man, no matter how eloquent, is not a Rhetorician.

St. Augustine, a student of Rhetoric, applauded its study. During his day, as well as today, critics of the study have questioned why a Christian would study an art devised by pagans. Heathens, Augustine reasoned, discovered much of what is true. They discovered truth, but they did not always recognize God as the author of truth. The pagans also invented many superstitions, Augustine noted. As Moses was schooled in Egypt, so may Christians profit from gaining wisdom from heathens. Christian students of Rhetoric must be grounded in the truth in order to discern superstition from truth. As the Israelites plundered the Egyptians in the Exodus, he concluded, so must Christians appropriate for themselves the truths learned from heathens.

Why Study Rhetoric?

> Discourse ought always to be obvious, even to the most careless and negligent hearer: so that the sense shall strike his mind, as the light of the sun does our eyes, though they are not directed upwards to it. We must study not only that every hearer may understand us, but that it shall be impossible for him not to understand us. (Ibid., Blair quoting Quintillian, 67)

Rhetoric is everywhere, used by everyone. This study will prepare us to respond critically to the rhetorical efforts of others in both the oral and written forms. By breaking down (analyzing) others' arguments and discourses, we can be better readers and discerners of truth.

The study of Rhetoric will help us to respond critically to advertisements, commercials, political messages, satires, irony and doublespeak of all varieties. It will, in the end, assist us in becoming more effective writers.

The purpose of studying speech

During the course of Rhetoric, we will study the techniques of speech. The purpose of speech is always to arouse your audience, to secure a reaction. Some speakers do not seem to want any defined response from their audiences. Some speakers fail to elicit the response they desire. But behind nearly every discourse, unless it is given purely for entertainment, one intends to have one's listener(s) follow a certain course of action.

Day One, Lesson One Assignment
What is the significance of the written word to the Christian? Talk about how God chose to communicate to us, and how He means for us to communicate as well. Use scripture. Three paragraphs.

Day Two, Lesson One Assignment
Knowing just a very little bit about Rhetoric, describe your goal for this school year in Rhetoric (one to two paragraphs). Add two more paragraphs about yourself, your interests and your educational background.

Day Three, Lesson One Assignment
What is acceptable today among contemporary audiences? Why/how can an immoral man or woman get a wide audience today? Consider as an example certain politicians, actors or singers/rappers who have engaged in immoral acts. Three paragraphs.

Day Four, Lesson One Assignment
Read at least three letters to the editor from a local paper or online. Then write your first persuasive writing assignment of the Rhetoric year. Write a letter to the editor, 150-200 words, about something of a timely nature in the news today. Turn in your letter to the editor, and post your own letter to the editor using the forum we have set up for this purpose.

WRITING TIPS LESSON I

Standards and Styles:
Every institute of higher learning uses a style manual. Every major employer requires its employees to adhere to certain styles when communicating with clients.

Every writer must adhere to a style when writing and communicating. Make sure you follow a style manual for every writing assignment. Some commonly used style manuals include the Modern Language Association (www.mla.org), Chicago Style Manual (www.chicagomanualofstyle.org), Gregg's Reference Guide (www.gregg.com), and more. Each of them will tell the writer how he needs to handle terms, common phrases and titles, bibliography, citations, etc.

If you study this independently and do not have a style manual, please find one right away. Use it. Get accustomed to its requirements.

The style manual for this course is based on MLA. Here are the very basic expectations I have for a written assignment that is handed in to me. I WILL NOT accept an assignment that does not adhere to these requirements.

Homework
- Typed in 12 pt. Times New Roman.
- Margins: 1 inch all around.
- Type: double space.
- Paragraphs: No extra space between paragraphs. Indent the first line of each paragraph ½ inch.
- Paragraphs: 5-12 sentences per paragraph.
- Header: Top left corner of the page: Name, date, and assignment title, each on a separate line. Double space these as well.
- Assignment titles: Each homework lesson is titled with a Lesson Number and Day Number, so title them accordingly. For example, the first assignment here is Lesson 1 Day 1. Give it that title.
- Use citations after a quotation. Refer to MLA for citation rules. This includes a "Works Cited" list at the end of your assignment.
- EXCEPTION to MLA citation rule: When quoting from a discourse we are all reading for an assignment, ALL you need to do is cite the PARAGRAPH NUMBER in parentheses after the quote, AND there is no need for a "Works Cited" list. Use full citation and "Works Cited" rules when you quote from a source

OTHER THAN an assigned discourse. For example, if you quote from paragraph four of Churchill's "Blood, Toil, Tears and Sweat" speech, your citation would look like this: (4).

- Discourse titles are in quotes. Book titles are italicized. Do not make this mistake.

* If you see that the minimum number of sentences per paragraph is five, and you ONLY write the minimum every time, your writing ability will not improve much. If you only give me five sentences, those five sentences should be the BEST you've ever written!

LESSON TWO

TYPES OF PERSUASIVE DISCOURSE (WEEK TWO)

(I)n order to be persuasive speakers in a popular assembly, it is, in my opinion, a capital rule, that we be ourselves persuaded of whatever we recommend to others. Never, when it can be avoided, ought we to espouse any side of the argument, but what we believe to be the true and the right one. Seldom or never will a man be eloquent, but when he is in earnest, and uttering his own sentiments. They are only the unassumed language of the heart or head, that carry the force of conviction.

I know, that young people, on purpose to train themselves to the art of speaking, imagine it useful to adopt that side of the question under debate, which, to themselves, appears the weakest, and to try what figure they can make upon it. But, I am afraid, this is not the most improving education for public speaking; and that it tends to form them to a habit of flimsy and trivial discourse. Such a liberty they should, at no time, allow themselves, unless in meetings where no real business is carried on, but where declamation and improvement of speech is the sole aim. Nor even in such meetings, would I recommend it as the most useful exercise. They will improve themselves to more advantage, and acquit themselves with more honour, by choosing always that side of the debate to which, in their own judgment, they are most inclined, and supporting it by what seems to themselves most solid and persuasive. (Ibid. 100)

Instructions for these lessons: When asked to read the material accompanying each lesson, read it more than once. The first time, read it just to become familiar with the language and tone. The second time, understand what is being said. In "Letter to a Noble Lord" the language is complicated. Give yourself time to become accustomed to the high style of the language. For each discourse, you will be given a small background of the author, the times and the circumstances, wherever possible. After reading a discourse, there will be a brief discussion of how it applies to the type of discourse you are studying.

One type of discourse: Deliberative oratory. In this type of discourse, a writer or speaker attempts to persuade someone to take action or believe what is said. The audience of a deliberative oratory is generally lawmakers; it will usually take place in front of a legislative body. It is political in nature. Its subject matter is exhortative, dissuasive, or advisory. Often one would seek to persuade a body of lawmakers—a Congress—to create a new law, proclaim war, or raise taxes.

Deliberative oratories seek to prove the expedient and the inexpedient. They want to concentrate on or emphasize whether something is worthwhile or whether it should be rejected as worthless. (Consider an argument in Congress about a certain tax. One side will argue it is worthwhile; the other will attack it as a waste of taxpayers' hard-earned money.) This type of discourse deals in the future, considering what will happen or should happen.

Read Edmund Burke's "Letter to a Noble Lord." This portion in the Appendix is only about one-third of the entire letter Edmund Burke wrote. Number the paragraphs by hand. Why is this deliberative?

Day One, Lesson Two Assignment:
Rewrite the above quote from Blair in your own words. Hugh Blair was an 18th century Scottish pastor and rhetorician. He taught at a university, commenting extensively on the study of Rhetoric. You will encounter his words often during the course of this study; it is appropriate that we start here with an assignment in which you must interpret his words regarding Rhetoric.

Day Two, Lesson Two Assignment:
View the letters to the editor written by your classmates (if you are in a class). Choose five and give constructive feedback on those letters. Tell the writer how he or she could improve the letter. Be specific. You are graded on your responses, so don't waste time (and space) with "Way to go!" or "Good job!" Two or more sentences, please. Sign your name.

Day Three, Lesson Two Assignment:
Read Winston Churchill's speech, "Blood, toil, tears and sweat." Since the copy of his speech in *Historic Speeches* is not complete, please use the one included in the Appendix.

Select three passages in which he uses emotional language. Discuss how it might have affected his audience. Remember to consider his audience *at that time*, at the beginning of World War Two.

Explain why this speech is considered deliberative, based on your understanding of deliberative discourses. To help your analysis, complete the worksheet and turn it in.

Do all of this in two to three paragraphs.

Day Four, Lesson Two Assignment:
Read Paul's delivery of testimony to synagogue in Antioch from Acts 13:16-41, and Paul's testimony to King Agrippa in Acts 26:1-31. Compare and contrast these two testimonies regarding a) Paul's techniques of argument, b) his understanding of his two different audiences, and c) how he persuaded. (This will take three to four paragraphs. Answer this one carefully.)

WRITING TIPS LESSON 2

Passive Versus Active

When writing, one must pay attention to the kinds of words used. Active verbs move the reader along. Passive verbs and phrases just sit still. A reader gets bored with passive word usage, so the writer must make his writing more interesting to his reader. That's his job.

We will first attack the dreaded "be-verb."
The "verb of being" consists of the following words: is, am, are, was, were, be, been, (and sometimes) being.

Limit yourself to just one be-verb per paragraph. If paragraphs contain 5-12 sentences each, then the writer is challenged to find a variety of words to say the same things. For example:

He was the first man to be elected president of the United States.
(contains two be-verbs)
BETTER:

He became the first president of the United States.
(no be-verbs, but "became" is still a passive verb)

BEST:
Americans elected him the first president of the United States.
(no be-verbs, more active verb)

This takes much more work and thought. When writing, a student may tend to get bogged down in avoiding be-verbs, and a writing project may take him a very long time. I advise a student to simply write, *then* go back over his work and rewrite or edit. The process of finally writing well will become part of his nature.

Pay attention to the words you use to replace be-verbs. Some students have decided that "exist" and "subsist" would make suitable replacements for verbs of being. In some cases I have forbidden these students to use those replacement words! Their writing became as boring as before when they thought they had the ideal replacements.

LESSON THREE

TYPES OF PERSUASIVE DISCOURSE, CONTINUED (WEEK THREE)

Forensic oratory: In this type of discourse, the speaker or writer seeks to persuade a judge and jury of the guilt or innocence of a certain person, or condemns or defends his own (or someone else's) actions. The audience of a forensic oratory is judges, juries, and others in a courtroom. It is legal or judicial in nature; its subject matter is accusation or defense.

A forensic oratory seeks to prove justice or injustice. It deals in the past—what has happened (court trials) and whether it is fact or fiction. In this Rhetoric course we will take very little time to cover this type of discourse.

It is interesting to find closing and opening remarks of trials. This will show us the kind of language and persuasive techniques attorneys utilize to win cases. For example, Johnnie Cochran's closing arguments in defense of OJ Simpson (1995) are long and rambling, use much emotion, and cast doubt on evidence brought up during the trial. In the end, Cochran's defense proved victorious.

Epideictic oratory: Ceremonial, pleasing and inspiring (pronounced eh-pee-dee-*ic*-tic). Its audience is broad-ranged and general. It is demonstrative and ceremonial in nature. Its subject matter is praise or blame of a topic or a person. It seeks to prove honor or dishonor of any subject or person.

Think of the occasions in which one would find a ceremonial discourse: presidential campaigns, graduation, marriage, funeral, dedication, inauguration, memorial, and other special events. Ronald Reagan's speech on the event of the space shuttle *Challenger's* explosion is epideictic. John F. Kennedy's inaugural address fits that category as well.

An epideictic oratory mostly takes place in the present time, although it will also deal with the past by referring to it in general terms and using it as example. It is by far the most popular and most-used type of persuasive discourse. Oftentimes a student will classify an uncertain discourse as epideictic simply because it does not work in the other categories. Simply by elimination, the classification of "epideictic" comes up and is an appropriate answer.

Day One, Lesson Three Assignment:

Read Socrates' *"Apology."* We will be reading this discourse again as a class. Answer the following questions in two to three paragraphs. Complete the worksheet and turn it in.

Against what is Socrates defending himself? Against whom?

What kind of defense is he using (describe his method of defending himself)?

How does this fit into the criterion of a forensic oratory?

Day Two, Lesson Three Assignment:

Read Lincoln's Gettysburg Address and answer the following questions. Complete the worksheet and turn it in.

What makes this speech epideictic?

What is the main point of his speech? What is most persuasive about his speech (in other words, what words does he use that are most persuasive?)

Day Three, Lesson Three Assignment:

Read Queen Elizabeth's speech, "I have the heart and stomach of a king," and Winston Churchill's "This was their finest hour" speech. Answer the following questions. Complete the worksheet and turn it in.

What makes these speeches epideictic?

What is the main point of these speeches? What is most persuasive about them?

Day Four, Lesson Three Assignment:

Read "They're Smiling in Heaven," by Don Lindman. Answer the following questions. Complete the worksheet and turn it in. Three paragraphs.

What makes this column epideictic?

What is persuasive about this essay? Point out words or phrases to support your answer.

WRITING TIPS LESSON 3

Literary Present Tense

For most of a student's elementary and junior high years, he practices writing reports and essays in the past tense. Sometimes the "tense" of his essay skips randomly from past to present and back again. The awkwardness of the tenses confuses the reader, but in the younger years a student remains uncertain how to fix the problem. Perhaps he does not even recognize the awkwardness.

Generally it is only until he reaches his high school years that he must begin to learn "literary present tense" writing. In this method he abandons all that he has thought sensible about writing about authors and their literary works!

Instead of saying, "Churchill gave his speech in front of Parliament," a student will now write, "Churchill gives his speech in front of Parliament." This enables the student to discuss in present terms the elements of the speech, as well as the author of that speech. See the example below. The student can fill in the blanks himself.

Winston Churchill gives his speech in front of Parliament at a time when all of England, and most of the rest of the world, anxiously awaits a message of strength and sanity. This follows a time in which the former Prime Minister, Neville Chamberlain, has adamantly insisted that war would not reach their country, and that Hitler is genuinely interested in peace with the rest of Europe. Churchill's thesis appears in paragraph __, in which he calls forth _____. Britain needs his strong leadership in this anxious period, and his speech shows his dedication to the job at hand.

While this may seem difficult, as with any new technique this one will become easier with frequent use. From this point forward, any analytical writing must utilize the literary present tense. Ask for assistance if this seems too difficult.

LESSON FOUR

TYPES OF PERSUASIVE DISCOURSE, CONTINUED (WEEK FOUR)

Propaganda is the negative side of rhetoric. It is not generally considered the fourth type of oratory by rhetoricians, but we include it here so that you can see its use. Propaganda is the expression of ideas in such a way that the speaker (or writer, etc.) gains power or influence. Advertising can be a form of propaganda, as it influences people's opinions so that the speaker can increase his wealth. Governments use propaganda to sway opinions about the country (in a positive way) or about its enemies (in a negative way). During wars, both sides use propaganda to influence the opinions of both enemies and allies.

In the 21st century worldwide war against terrorism, propaganda sees wide usage. Terrorist organizations use the Internet to play videos and make threats. In the aftermath of an attack, they bolster their claims by boasting proudly to the world about their actions. Similarly, countries warring against terrorism also engage in propaganda of another kind, informing its citizens of the need for safety and awareness. Thus one can see how propaganda can be used for good or evil.

Demagoguery is considered a part of propaganda. Demagogues are people who use lies, pointless or manipulative arguments, and emotional appeals to gain personal advantage while pretending to mean well. Propaganda can be considered speeches and other discourses as well as advertising.

Take time to look up some forms of propaganda by doing a search on the internet or checking out books in the library. Propaganda takes all forms.

Day One, Lesson Four Assignment:
Given the definition of propaganda above, is all advertising therefore bad? Why or why not? Can you give examples of advertising you would consider propaganda or demagoguery? Two to three paragraphs.

Day Two, Lesson Four Assignment:
Read Hitler's speech to Germany on February 20, 1938, and Hitler's speech on May 4, 1941. As with other assignments, number the paragraphs by hand. This is a long speech that requires your attention. Take notes on what you find to be persuasive language. You will be asked to write about it in tomorrow's assignment.

Day Three, Lesson Four Assignment:
It's hard to make a definite statement about someone or someone's work after having just read two discourses by him. But Hitler is one of those infamous people in history about whom we know or have heard much. From what you know, and from what you read, write 3 to 4 paragraphs describing how he used words to influence opinion and gain power. Use the worksheet to discuss both of Hitler's speeches. Remember to cite the speech by using the year of the speech (1938 or 1941). Complete the worksheet and hand it in.

Day Four, Lesson Four Assignment:
Take the quiz for this day.

WRITING TIPS LESSON 4

Sentence variety: sentence openers

Variety makes more interesting writing. The reader may not notice it, but he won't be as bored! From here on out, watch your paragraphs. Make sure that <u>no two sentences begin the same way within one paragraph, and that no two paragraphs begin the same way within an assignment</u>.

As a writer I am constantly watching out for sentence variety. Did I begin my sentences the same way twice? Did I use a variety of words and sentences? Are my sentences all long or do I have a variety of short and long, compound and simple?

The key to better writing exists in my ability to vary my words and sentences, making my writing more interesting to the reader.

In-class exercise: Take your homework and circle the first word of every sentence. Now look to see whether you have duplicated any of those words within the same paragraph as sentence beginners. Reword them if so. Do any of your paragraphs begin the same way? Reword. From this point forward you must avoid this error in your assignments.

LESSON FIVE

THE FIVE CANONS OF RHETORIC (WEEK FIVE)

But though the method be not laid down in form, no discourse, of any length, should be without method; that is, every thing should be found in its proper place. Every one who speaks, will find it of the greatest advantage to himself to have previously arranged his thoughts, and classed under proper heads, in his own mind, what he is to deliver. This will assist his memory, and carry him through his discourse without that confusion to which one is every moment subject who has fixed no distinct plan of what he is to say. And with respect to the hearers, order in discourse is absolutely necessary for making any proper impression. It adds both force and light to what is said. It makes them accompany the speaker easily and readily, as he goes along; and makes them feel the full effect of every argument which he employs. Few things, therefore, deserve more to be attended to, than distinct arrangement; for eloquence, however great, can never produce entire conviction without it. (Ibid. 102)

Before one delivers his speech (or writes his discourse), he undertakes many considerations. The two primary considerations are the **Objective and the Subjective.**

The Objective is the Audience. Analyze it; know how it should be approached. View the topic through the eyes of the audience you propose to address (practical psychology). Who is your audience? What is their general makeup? Are they believers, nonbelievers, men, women, old, young, affluent, poor, uneducated? Your discourse will obviously be aimed at your audience, so you must keep their needs and understandings in mind as you write.

The Subjective is the Ability within oneself to achieve the desired result of arousing a response. It is what God has planted inside you that enables you to speak or write.

Day One, Lesson Five Assignment:
Write the above quote by Blair in your own words.

Day Two, Lesson Five Assignment:
Try to describe what relevance Blair's quote, above, has on our own studies of Rhetoric. Could this old guy from Scotland just be saying a lot of empty words? Why or why not? Two to three paragraphs.

Day Three, Lesson Five Assignment:
Re-read Paul's two speeches in Acts (from Lesson Two). With "Objective is the Audience" in mind, comment on what he must have had in mind regarding each audience. Who were they? What did they need to hear from Paul? How did he meet their needs? Two to three paragraphs.

Day Four, Lesson Five Assignment:
Respond to a recent news event your teacher brings up to you, or you have discovered in the news with your parents. Write a 500-word (plus or minus 50 words) opinion piece in response. Be persuasive. Use examples to support your point. As always, be polite. Bring a copy to class, but also post it to the forum as your teacher directs.

WRITING TIPS LESSON 5

First/second person

Another writing challenge for the high school student includes avoiding first and second person. This means cutting out all references to **"I, me, my, mine, we, us, our, ours, you, and yours."** Some young writers have trouble moving to that new, more formal method. This IS more formal, and it aids the writer in attaining an expository tone.

From now on, <u>avoid</u> saying **"I believe the thesis is in paragraph three."** Just say "The thesis presents itself in paragraph three." Then go on to tell the reader why. You don't have to tell me this is what you think or believe. Since the essay has your name on it, you are already communicating that you think/believe these things.

Similarly, <u>avoid</u> addressing the reader as **"you."** Mature writers will steer clear of the **implied command**: **"Look at** paragraph three." **"Consider** the cross on which Christ died." **"Note that** Paul finds himself at the mercy of his jailers." Find other ways to write this. Consider it a challenge to expand your vocabulary and usage. Don't rely on the same way to do things; you'll fall into a writing rut! (<u>Notice that</u> the way this paragraph is written violates the very command to avoid second person! Instructional writing—as opposed to expository writing—will do that.)

Another rut that writers—especially Christian writers—fall into has to do with references to **groups** of people. **"We Christians** must…" **"As Americans, we…"** **"God tells us…"** All of these use the second person, and the writer must assiduously avoid this. The mature writer finds many different ways to get around this problem. He will notice that the first two examples are clichés anyway. Writers must diligently avoid cliché writing.

LESSON SIX

THE FIVE CANONS OF RHETORIC, CONTINUED (WEEK SIX)

Invention, Arrangement, Style, Memory, Delivery
In class, look up the meaning of Canon. Choose the one that is most pertinent to Rhetoric, given your understanding of the Five Canons of Rhetoric. Explain why.

The First Canon: Invention *(inventio)* - Discovery or invention, a method for finding arguments—The writer/speaker can talk about virtually anything, but he must first use research to find arguments to support his point of view. *Inventio* is defined as a method for finding topics or arguments. Two means of persuasion are available to the speaker: non-artistic and artistic. The artistic proofs will be covered more in-depth later in rhetoric. We will just touch on them for right now.

Non-artistic or *non-technical arguments* (Aristotle called them proofs)—discover material to back up your argument. These support your argument. They are primarily used in judicial arguments and presentations. They do not need to be invented; they already exist. They are:

*   Laws
*   Witnesses
*   Contracts
*   Tortures
*   Oaths

A word about Tortures: I have looked in several sources for a meaning of this word, almost hoping it would mean something other than the obvious. Cicero's *Ad Herennium* describes the use of tortures as if they were a normal part of gathering evidence. Perhaps during those days, an extraction of evidence by means of torture was commonplace and was considered irrefutable.

Artistic proofs persuade others by three means, which are covered by the category of rhetoric. We will cover these more in-depth. They are as follows:

Rational appeal (*logos*)—appeal to reason. We learned in Logic that we can draw conclusions from affirmative or negative statements (syllogism), or by observing several pieces of data.

Emotional appeal (*pathos*)—appeal to the audience's emotions to persuade.

Ethical appeal (*ethos*)—persuasion arises out of the speaker's character. The speaker or writer will communicate his virtue to the audience, thereby promoting good will toward himself. The speaker/writer could be the most skilled, but if he were not ethical (or did not appear to be ethical) his efforts to persuade would be fruitless.

The classical rhetoricians used the **Topics** to assist them in finding subjects for the three methods of appeal. Aristotle spent quite a lot of time discussing different ways one could search out a subject to discover ways of presenting and fleshing it out.

Two kinds of topics are 1) *the special topics*—those arguments used in certain types of discourse (such as closing arguments used exclusively in the law courts; certain types of ceremonial speeches such as funerals or weddings), and 2) *the common topics*—those used for any occasion or type of speech (such as graduation, political speeches, and so forth). For example, a politician or speaker who tours the country to speak to different audiences is not going to rewrite a new speech for each city he visits. He has a common topic—one we might call generic—that he pulls up on his computer screen, adjusts to fit a certain geographic area, perhaps, and then presents his speech. Common topics can take one of the following forms:

- More or less (topic of degree)
- The possible and the impossible
- Past fact and future fact
- Greatness and smallness (the topic of size as distinguished from the topic of degree)

The Second Canon: Arrangement—(*dispositio*), or organization is the systematical arrangement of the parts of a discourse. (Arrangement is covered in depth later in this course.) The arrangement of a classical discourse follows the same general format:

- Introduction (exordium)
- Statement of facts (narratio)

- Proof of the case (confirmatio)
- Refutation (confutatio)
- Conclusion (peroratio)

The Third Canon: Style *(elocutio)* is the adaptation of suitable words and sentences to the matter. Here we have mastered Invention and Arrangement, and now we are ready to make the words flow beautifully. This is where we examine a writer's use of language and ask ourselves, "Why did he choose the words he did?" "How did this communicate tone to the reader?" There are several types of style we can study:

- Low or plain style (attenuata, subtile), for instructing
- Middle or forcible style (mediocris) for moving the reader or listener
- High or florid style (gravis, florida) for charming

Style involves selecting the proper words. Here we study the *correct, pure, clear* words. We choose whether to be flowery or more simple. We make choices about the way we order our words, putting them together to sound the best and most evocative. We will take time to re-work sentences to see that the choices a writer makes truly do affect the way a sentence communicates. At this point we will also look at figures of speech and see how a writer or speaker employs them to effectively communicate and persuade.

The Fourth Canon: Memory *(memoria)* is memorizing speeches, the constant practice of a virtue well-rehearsed and lauded in ancient Greece. This was one of the most valued canons of Rhetoric during that time, and it has now fallen into disuse by most. We will concentrate on this during the second year of Rhetoric.

The Fifth Canon: Delivery *(pronuntiatio)* is the graceful regulation of voice, countenance, and gesture as one speaks. Here, in the second year of Rhetoric, we will study the practice of speech and present our own oratories, in verse and in prose. This is the point in the second year where we will also defend our Rhetoric 2 Thesis orally.

Day One, Lesson Six Assignment:
View your classmates' opinion pieces that have been posted and follow the same rules for critique as before. Be constructive, look for ways the writer can improve. You will be graded on this assignment. Critique at least five pieces. Minimum two sentences each.

Day Two, Lesson Six Assignment:
Looking at each of the discourses you have read up to this point, what style of writing (low/plain, middle/forcible, or high/florid) would you give to each of them? Why? One or two sentences per discourse would be sufficient. We read:

- "Hitler's speech to Germany on February 20, 1938"
- Winston Churchill's "This was their finest hour"
- Queen Elizabeth's "I have the heart and stomach of a king"
- "The Gettysburg Address"
- "They're Smiling in Heaven"
- Burke's "Letter to a Noble Lord"
- Churchill's "Blood Toil, Tears and Sweat"
- Paul's two speeches in Acts 13:16-41 and 26:1-31
- Socrates' "Apology"

Day Three, Lesson Six Assignment:
As Christians, what should be our attitude in addressing people? Why? Can you point out a verse or two that deals with your attitude toward others? Think in terms of you standing up to speak to a crowd about almost anything—it doesn't have to be your Christian witness. You might be instructing them in something or persuading them about something. Three paragraphs—avoid first/second person.

Day Four, Lesson Six Assignment:
Take the quiz for this day.

WRITING TIPS LESSON 6

Passive writing, continued.
As a writer becomes accustomed to eliminating be-verbs from his text, he then must look deeper and attack any other passive writing he encounters.

Look for: helper verbs, such as "will, had, have, would, could, should." For example:

"She has seen the river overflow its banks."
("has" as a passive helper)

"She watched the river overflow its banks."
("has seen" changed to "watched.")
OR:
"The evidence would seem to direct us to see the facts."
("would" helper verb is unnecessary)

"The evidence directs one to the facts."
(eliminate helper verb)

Find more active verb phrases that refuse to sit still. Use them. Change your sentences around to make your sentences more active and flow more smoothly.

LESSON SEVEN

FORMULATE A THESIS (WEEK SEVEN)

As we progress through Rhetoric, we will add skills to our repertoire for studying discourses. Already you are able to recognize types of discourses, from earlier lessons. Now you will be expected to find the thesis statement of any discourse. Some are easier to recognize than others, and there will always be room for discussion as to what the thesis statement actually is. We will spend time learning how to pick one out. It is also valuable to learn this, as the research paper you write in your first year must have a thesis statement.

Choosing the topic: Know your topic. Decide on the subject you want and what material to use in developing the topic. A good test for determining what is a good topic:

- The topic must fit your audience. Imagine giving a speech about the gift of tongues to a group of atheists. Not only would their frame of reference be zero, they would also be unwilling to sit and listen to your topic.
- The topic must fit the occasion. This is obvious. No one would expect to hear the dedication of a battleship at a funeral.
- The scope of the topic must be such that you may expect to discuss it reasonably well. Is the subject something you already know a little about? You would be better able to present a speech on that topic than, say, quantum physics (unless you are a physicist).

The beginning of all discourses is a topic, a question, a problem or issue. Once adequate research is done on a subject, one can convert it into a thesis. A topic with a broad subject range will need to be broken down into sub-topics. The unnecessary sub-topics can then be discarded as you narrow down your topic.

A thesis statement is stated in the form of a proposition: *a complete sentence or two that asserts or denies something about the subject.*

Aristotle said one must ask three questions to decide on a thesis:

- *an sit* (whether a thing is) - a question of fact
  For example: Did Brutus, as has been alleged, kill Caesar?
- *quid sit* (what is it?) - a question of definition
  If it is granted that Brutus did kill Caesar, was the act murder or self-defense?
- *quale sit* (what kind is it?) - a question of quality
  If it was in fact murder, was Brutus justified in murdering Caesar? (Corbett, *Classical Rhetoric*, 28).

Your thesis statement would then fall into one or more of the above categories. It would answer one or more of the above questions of fact, definition or quality.

It is important to *state the thesis in one or two declarative sentences*. (It might be best to limit yourself to one sentence.) Any more sentences may add too much, which eventually would muddle the argument. A thesis must assert or deny something about the subject. In other words, it must say something in the positive or negative about a topic. For example, "John F. Kennedy was the victim of a vast government plot." Or "William Shakespeare was not the author of numerous plays and sonnets; several men authored those works attributed to him." It can be something simple or something controversial. The more exact, the better.

Where can the thesis statement be found? It is usually in the first few paragraphs of the discourse. Rarely is there any exception to this rule.

If you are having a hard time coming up with the right thesis statement, just verbalizing the topic will suggest lines of development; it may define terms used later in the discourse. One sentence helps to clarify whether you can narrow your topic.

> For we may rest assured that whenever we express ourselves ill, there is, besides the mismanagement of language, for the most part, some mistake in our manner of conceiving the subject. Embarrassed, obscure, and feeble sentences are generally, if not always, the result of embarrassed, obscure, and feeble thought. Thought and language act and re-act upon each other mutually. (Blair, *Lectures on Rhetoric and Belles Lettres*, Lecture 12, from http://www.artsci.gmcc.ab.ca/people/einarssonb/blair.htm, accessed 6/22/00)

Failure to sharply define one's subject is the chief cause of fuzzy, disunified discourse. Vague beginnings invite chaotic endings. The audience for a discourse, whether written or spoken, can achieve no firmer grasp of the thesis than the writer or the speaker has. As a matter of fact, if we make allowance for what is inevitably lost in the process of transmission, the audience's grasp will always be less than the writer's or the speaker's. (Corbett, Classical Rhetoric, 31)

Sometimes the thesis does not occur to us until midway through the discovery and writing process. But the thesis statement must occur before the first rough draft is completed. The thesis sentence is a good starting-point in the composition process, because it forces the writer to determine at the outset just what it is that he or she wants to say about his topic. It is the basis for a discourse that makes a point and hangs together well. It also suggests some of the topics that can be used to develop the subject.

<u>When you read a discourse you will always (from here on out) be asked to arrive at a thesis statement and usually to explain why you arrived at your answer.</u> Later in this course you may find discourses that do not have a clear thesis. The purpose here is to begin to understand the necessity for a clear, sharply defined thesis statement, both in what you read and what you write. When reading discourses from here on out in this course, the natural process of analysis must include finding the thesis and explaining reasons for arriving at this thesis.

Day One, Lesson Seven Assignment:
List five topics on which you could realistically give a speech tomorrow, with minimal research and preparation. Only two can be how-to. The others must be persuasive. On those three, provide a thesis statement which you could reasonably support. This is a bulleted list, no more.

Day Two, Lesson Seven Assignment:
Read the following articles: "This House is Not for Sale" by Andy Rooney, and "She Did Good" by Paul Harvey. Decide on the thesis for each one. Explain why you chose that thesis. Use short answers. Some discourses, especially contemporary ones, may not have a clearly defined thesis, but you should find one or two sentences in these texts which you could identify as the thesis.

Day Three, Lesson Seven Assignment:
Take the quiz for this lesson.

Day Four, Lesson Seven Assignment:
Read "Planet of the Year" by Thomas Sancton. We will analyze that one later. Decide what is the thesis, and why. Discuss it in one well-worded paragraph. Complete the worksheet and turn it in.

WRITING TIPS LESSON 7

Agreement

When writing a formal essay, a writer must be aware of his words and the meanings he conveys. A writer should always make sure that his nouns, verbs, adjectives and pronouns agree in number. That is, if the noun is singular, the rest of the sentence must remain singular.

For example, the following sentence written by a student lacks agreement: "Many books that you will read within your lifetime will have a character change throughout it." The word "books" is plural, and the sentence works all the way through—until the very last word, "it." This makes no sense, due to the fact that "it" is singular. How would you reword this sentence?

Avoid mixing singular and plural words and phrases throughout your paragraphs.

Similarly, agreement deals with past and present tense. When writing in the past tense, stay in past tense. Do not begin a paragraph in the past and then move to the present. Keep each paragraph consistent. To be sure, some essays and research papers must transition from discussion of the past to relating to the present. Make certain those transitions are smooth, and keep them consistent.

For the purposes of Rhetoric, any analytical writing must remain in the literary present tense. Please refer to page 18 for more information about this technique.

LESSON EIGHT

THE PARTS OF A DISCOURSE (WEEKS EIGHT AND NINE)

Cicero, the great Roman speaker, said that the orator "ought first to find out what he should say; next to dispose and arrange his matter, not only in a certain order, but according to the weight of the matter and the judgment of the speaker" (Cicero, as quoted in Corbett, *Classical Rhetoric*, 257).

Arrangement

Hugh Blair advises us to use a method of organization in our discourse. Each part needs to build onto the previous one, so that from one section of a discourse to the next, there is a continuous, cohesive flow. Not every detail is necessary; only include points that will support your thesis as precisely as possible.

When arranging a discourse the writer must choose words carefully. Choose only the words necessary to make a point. Cut away (edit) those words that do not clearly communicate a point.

> On whatever subject any one intends to discourse, he will most commonly begin with some introduction, in order to prepare the minds of his hearers; he will then state his subject, and explain the facts connected with it; he will employ arguments for establishing his own opinion, and overthrowing that of his antagonist; he may, perhaps, if there be room for it, endeavour to touch the passions of his audience; and after having said all he thinks proper, he will bring his discourse to a close by some peroration or conclusion. (Blair, in Corbett, *Belles Lettres*, 106)

Having a logical approach to one's discourse is the most important element. It cannot persuade effectively if it is disorganized. When there is order, there is peace. By learning the order of historic discourses, you can grasp the importance of order in your own writing. Organization is vital when it comes time to write a thesis paper. Always take advantage of the opportunity to learn order and proper writing skills.

There is much reading in this section. On top of identifying the thesis in each piece (refer to the previous lesson), you will now begin to identify the different parts of the discourse.

The First Part of Arrangement: Introduction

The purpose of an introduction is to tell the audience what our discourse is about. Sometimes we do not have to generate interest in our subject; the subject itself will generate interest.

Often before writing an introduction, the following questions must be asked in order to clarify the introduction:

- What is our topic?
- Who is the audience?
- What is going on in the world/community that would affect the delivery or reception of this piece?
- What might be the audience's presuppositions?
- How much time or space may I take in delivering this? (It could be a 45-minute speech or a 500-word opinion piece.)

Following are the types of introductions found in formal Rhetoric. These were coined by Richard Whately in his *Elements of Rhetoric*.

- **Introduction inquisitive** – The topic asks a question to draw interest from the audience and cause them to want to read or hear more. It rouses interest.
- **Introduction paradoxical** – We recall from Logic that a paradox is something which appears one way, but actually is another. This type of introduction will show that although something may seem impossible it will actually be possible.
- **Introduction corrective** – In this type of introduction the speaker notes that there is a situation that has been neglected, or misunderstood, and goes about preparing the audience for a solution.
- **Introduction preparatory** – Here a speaker or writer will take a different method to introduce the topic. It may announce how a subject will be dealt with, or it may try to forestall some misunderstanding.
- **Introduction narrative** – Tells a story, which often works well to excite interest in the subject.

In the Introduction, one ingratiates himself with the audience. The writer seeking to establish himself as a credible source of information will do so subtly, not flaunting his credentials.

The writer may need to take time to counteract prejudices or misconceptions about himself or his topic. Corbett suggests **eight ways one would counteract prejudices or misconceptions,** as listed below (Corbett, *Classical Rhetoric*, 266). The **ninth item** was suggested by a former student who was concerned that not all of the possibilities were included for a Christian worldview. (Note: this list hits close to home when we recall some ways Bill Clinton answered some of the charges against him, ranging from taking drugs to perjury. Sometimes it becomes clear when we examine this list in light of such events.)

1. deny the charges that have created the prejudices against them
2. admit the charges but deny their alleged magnitude
3. cite a compensating virtue or action
4. attribute the discrediting action to an honest mistake on their part or to an accident or to an inescapable compulsion
5. cite others who were guilty of the same thing but were not so charged
6. substitute a different motive or cause for the one alleged
7. inveigh against calumny and malicious insinuation in general
8. cite the testimony of those who take a different view of the matter
9. repent and admit to error

In the introduction, if it is appropriate, a writer may also arouse hostility against his opponent. Recall reading Edmund Burke's "Letter to a Noble Lord," and recall how he roused hostility against his opponent (although that was not the introduction).

Corbett says: "The introduction seeks to render the audience *attentive*, *benevolent*—that is, well-disposed toward the writer and his or her cause, and *docile*—that is, ready to be instructed or persuaded" (Corbett, *Classical Rhetoric*, 267).

Functional Use of Introduction

Aristotle was careful to outline the important elements for writers of introduction. He emphasized that the length, style and content of the introduction were vital considerations. He instructed the rhetorician to eliminate excessive introduction—a lengthy one was unnecessary. Introductions that capture the reader's interest are "hooks" that draw a reader in to the rest of the discourse. The closing lines of an introduction should transition smoothly into the next section, not seeming to end abruptly.

From here on, you should be able to decide the type of introduction in any discourse you read. This builds on the previous sections, in which you discover the type of discourse and the thesis statement of the discourse.

Day One, Lesson Eight Assignment:

Read an example of Introduction Inquisitive, Cicero's speech from *Historic Speeches*, p 15. Number the paragraphs. What makes this an inquisitive introduction? What purpose does that kind of introduction serve for this particular discourse? Find the thesis, and explain (briefly) why you think this is the thesis. Two paragraphs.

Day Two, Lesson Eight Assignment:

Read Jean-Paul Sartre, "The Republic of Silence." What kind of introduction do you see here? Why? One paragraph.

Day Three, Lesson Eight Assignment:

Write and post an opinion piece on a chosen topic as provided by your teacher. Opinion pieces should be 500-750 words, use respectful language, provide examples, and have a solid thesis.

Day Four, Lesson Eight Assignment:

Read William Pitt, "I rejoice that America has resisted" from *Historic Speeches*. How is he *preparing* his audience here, and for what is he preparing them? How does he ingratiate himself? One paragraph.

Day Five, Lesson Eight Assignment:

Read Oliver Cromwell, "Let God be judge between me and you" from *Historic Speeches*. In two to three paragraphs, answer the following questions: What methods does he use to ingratiate himself or counteract prejudice with his audience in the introduction (refer to the list of nine ways one counteract prejudices)? What kind of introduction is this, and why? What kind of discourse is this, and why? What is the thesis, and why? Use (and turn in) the worksheet to help organize your thoughts.

Day Six, Lesson Eight Assignment:

Re-read Winston Churchill's "Blood, Toil, Tears and Sweat" and answer the following questions in two to three paragraphs. Be sure to give examples. Use the worksheet to help with the answers. Use the worksheet and turn it in.

- What kind of discourse is it? Why?
- What kind of introduction is it? Why?
- What is the thesis? Why?

Day Seven, Lesson Eight Assignment:
Read George W. Bush's "Freedom in Iraq and Middle East." In two to three pages answer the following questions. Use (and turn in) the worksheet to help organize your thoughts.

- Tell what kind of speech this is, and why.
- Tell what you believe the thesis is, and why. Where is it found?
- Tell what kind of introduction you find, and why. There could be more than one answer here. Tell me what paragraphs cover the introduction (paragraphs one through...?). Remember that since this is a longer speech, the intro may be more than just a couple of paragraphs. It must be, like a statement of facts, proportionate to the length of the discourse.
- Discuss the importance of this speech given the time (era) in which it is delivered. In other words, here is the time for you to do a little content analysis. Why is it important to discuss the topic at hand, at that time? Does it have relevance? Tell briefly the essence of what he says (perhaps by telling me how he supports his thesis).

Day Eight, Lesson Eight Assignment:
Read and comment on your classmates' opinion pieces, using the guidelines provided by your teacher.

Writing Tips Lesson 8

Integrating quotes

http://faculty.tamu-commerce.edu/scarter/integrating_quotes.ht
http://jerz.setonhill.edu/writing/academic/sources/integrating.ht

The web sites above provide excellent advice on smoothly integrating quotes into your writing. Writers must walk a fine line between plagiarism, quoting, and rewording. Decide what you will do and when. If you want to reword information into your own words, make sure you don't get anywhere close to plagiarism.

If you decide to integrate a quote into your text, make a smooth move from your words to the quote. Introduce the quote well. Finish it well, also. <u>Surround</u> a quote with your own words. <u>NEVER</u> begin or end a paragraph with a quote! We call that "bookending" a quote—surrounding it with your own words.

Remember that a quote, a reference to a source, or borrowing/rewording information from a source needs to be correctly and consistently cited. Refer to MLA for citation information.

Briefly, after the quote include the author's name, title of the work and page number in parentheses. If it is a web site, put the author and web address in parentheses. Follow the punctuation rules exactly. See the "Citations" writing tip in Lesson 9.

Please note that the above web sites are provided only to give you advice and general help. Follow citation rules from MLA.

LESSON NINE

ARRANGEMENT, CONTINUED PART II: STATEMENT OF FACT (WEEK TEN)

Statement of Fact (*narratio*) - Second division of a discourse (also called narration or explication by more ancient scholars)

Narration or Explication.
I put these two together, both because they fall nearly under the same rules, and because they commonly answer the same purpose; serving to illustrate the cause or the subject of which the orator treats, before he proceeds to argue either on one side or other; or to make any attempt for interesting the passions of the hearers... Quintillian very properly directs, 'In this part of a discourse, the speaker must be very careful to shun every appearance of art and cunning. For there is no time at which the judge is more upon his guard, than when the pleader is relating facts. Let nothing then seem feigned: nothing anxiously concealed. Let all that is said, appear to arise from the cause itself, and not to be the work of the orator. (Blair in Corbett, *Belles Lettres*, 115)

Statement of Facts must be connected to the Introduction with a transition. The final sentence or sentences must serve as a bridge from one to the next. In a court case, the prosecuting lawyer in Statement of Facts would set forth the essential facts of the case under consideration. The defending attorney might use this time to correct misstatements or add detail to the prosecutor's statements. Often in a ceremonial discourse which deals mostly in future events, a statement of facts will not be necessary.

Statement of Facts is an *expository* section. It describes the facts that have to do with the topic, or simply reminds an audience before going on. The writer in Statement of Facts must state all the facts that need to be known, in a clear, lucid manner. Keep in mind that the writer or speaker has a goal of transitioning from the introduction to the main points of the case. This is the transition, in which he lays out the points he will use or elaborate on later in his discourse.

This section is also orderly: Sometimes chronological order helps, or from general to particular or from the more familiar to the less familiar.

Palpability or vividness paints a word picture. If we paint a word picture instead of just telling what happened, the vividness will have an emotional impact which will forever impress the facts in the imagination of our readers. If we are on the losing side, our lucidity would not be advantageous.

Statement of Facts is characterized by *brevity*. A writer must be brief, only using as much time as it takes in proportion to the discourse. A short speech requires only a small statement of facts. Aristotle thought this was laughable, and asked, why can't the length be just right, instead of short or long? He believed that the length should be fitting to the subject at hand.

Start the recital of facts at a point where it begins to concern the readers. Exclude all irrelevancies: Take out anything which neither adds to nor detracts from your discourse. A writer or speaker is more plausible if he is ethical. If his authority and character is trusted, the discourse is bound to be more believable.

Confirmation: Proving a point
Hugh Blair notes that three things are required for persuasive discourses: Invention, arrangement, and persuasive style.

For invention, he teaches, two methods can be used: the analytic and synthetic. In the confirmation (proof of case) these two styles have two very different argumentative or persuasive value.

Analytic: the speaker or writer obscures the main points he wants to prove while he moves through his argument. Bit by bit he brings his audience to the point he tries to prove. As he progresses he moves his audience from one point to the next, until his audience sees the point he's been trying to prove all along. In other words, he has built his argument, like a building, brick by brick. Not until the last brick is in place does he finally see the construction.

This is the method C.S. Lewis uses in *Mere Christianity*, in which he begins with a basic agreement of a moral law existing in every person, and then he finally draws the reader to the conclusion that God, the author of the moral law, exists. The audience may not at first agree that God exists, but when one agrees with the first point, the existence of a universal moral law, one can then move on to the next point, and the next, until the conclusion is reached.

Synthetic: This method seems to be the reverse of the analytic. Here the writer or speaker will tell his audience the point he wants to prove (the thesis), and then he spends the rest of his argument proving it.

Day One, Lesson Nine Assignment
Take the quiz for this section.

Day Two, Lesson Nine Assignment:
Read Socrates' "Apology." Number the paragraphs, as always, and answer the following questions in two to three paragraphs. Use the worksheet and turn it in. What type of discourse is this? What type of introduction is this? Why? How does he ingratiate himself/counteract prejudice?

Day Three, Lesson Nine Assignment:
Read "Chronicle of an Undeception" by Michael Bauman. In 3-4 paragraphs, answer the following: Explain how paragraphs 4-9, as the statement of facts, lay out the facts that will be covered in this discourse. Why is it called the Statement of Facts? What is the thesis? Why/where found? What kind of discourse is this? Why? Use the worksheet and turn it in.

Day Four, Lesson Nine Assignment:
Another aspect of Progymnasmata is rewriting fables. Take the first fable, "The Goose that Laid the Golden Egg," and rewrite it in 50 words. Make sure your story retains all the main points of the fable. Then rewrite the fable to 500 words. Add character and dialogue whenever necessary. Retain the main sense of the fable.

Writing Tips Lesson 9

Correctly citing a quote

Each time you provide a quote from a source or use specific information from a source, you must also provide a citation. Include the source from your quote or specific information. MLA gives specific instructions on how this should look. A couple of examples are provided below.

When writing analyses for Rhetoric, from a discourse your teacher has assigned, you only need to cite the paragraph number of the discourse: "They did not fight openly like soldiers. In all circumstances they were alone" (2). The parentheses contain the paragraph number from where the quote came. If the assignment solely concerns one discourse, all you need to provide is the paragraph number.

Remember that the punctuation goes AFTER the citation.

When quoting from a source that is not the discourse assigned for homework, **cite it correctly by proving the author's last name and page number, if from a book (Smith 24). If a web site is your source, provide a shortened version of the web site (www. fastweb.com). Note that the period is AFTER the citation in each of these examples. THEN at the end of your assignment, include the full bibliographical notation of the source on a separate page called "Works Cited."**

Avoid dropping a citation into the middle of a sentence. To keep the sentence flowing smoothly, place the citation at the end of the sentence.

LESSON TEN

ARRANGEMENT, CONTINUED PARTS III AND IV: CONFIRMATION (PROOF OF THE CASE) AND REFUTATION (WEEK ELEVEN)

Confirmation (Proof of the Case), third division of the discourse. This is the meat of the discourse, where we do what we started out to do—to prove our point. This is the main body, where we explain or persuade. Once we have gone through the discovery process, we can arrange our material.

In this section, the largest of the discourse, we use the main bulk of information that was gathered during the process of invention. As we read and discover, we are mentally arranging the evidence. What points do we use, and in what order? A writer has many options of methods for presenting information:

- chronological, sometimes in an expository discourse
- from general to particular, for more complicated expository discourse
- from familiar to unknown, also for complicated expository
- or the nature of the topic will suggest the appropriate procedure

When organizing for argumentative discourse, one must decide whether to:

- begin with the weakest argument and build up to strongest argument,
- refute opposing arguments first and then present your arguments, or
- establish the case and then refute the opposition.

The first option is best, according to Aristotle. It leaves the strongest arguments as final thoughts in the audience's mind. Blair agreed that moving from weakest to strongest was best, "so that the speech might constantly grow and become stronger…when he can trust to his making a successful impression on the minds of the hearers" (Blair in Corbett, *Belles Lettres*, 120).

Refutation, fourth division of the discourse

Refutation means "rebuttal," or argument against the opposition. In this division one refutes opposing views in debate or in writing. In a debate where both views are presented, the debater must refute his opponent as his topics are being presented. In writing, the writer has the option of addressing all opposing views, or just some of them. However logical and reasonable our arguments may be, doubts will remain in the minds of our audience if we do not anticipate the objections to our thesis and answer those objections.

If the audience has received the opposing views favorably, refute first, then present your argument. If the opposing argument is weak, present your argument, then refute your opponent. The sequence is not set in stone! Use what works best.

Remember that classical refutation is a section or division of a discourse. Often in contemporary discourses refutation is scattered throughout the discourse.

There are **four methods** by which one can refute:

Refutation by appeal to reason. Here it is most helpful for students to remember their logic. In this method of refutation one will prove the contradictory (or the impossibility) of his opponent's argument. (Remember your Logic: a thing cannot *be* and *not be* at the same time.) Demolish the arguments by which the proposition is supported: One side argues the feasibility of one point, and the other side would argue that his opponent's point is not feasible, a classic argument.

One can deny the truth of one of the premises on which the argument rests and prove that the premise is false, through evidence or testimony, perhaps. One can object to the inferences drawn from the premises, by saying:

- "I admit the principle, but I deny that it leads to such a consequence."
- "I admit the principle but I deny that it applies in this case."
- "Your assertion is true, but it has no force as an argument to support your conclusion" (Corbett, *Classical Rhetoric*, 279).

Think of a current or recent event where some of this happens. Presidential politics, or examples of politicians' excuses for immoral behavior, are pretty good (irresistible) examples.

While there are ways to refute with logic, some arguments only use probabilities, which cannot be refuted by logic. While probabilities are more difficult to refute, one can use examples or look for the missing premise (enthymeme), if there is one, and refute that by exposing the unspoken, underlying premise.

Refutation by emotional appeals. Here one could appeal to the emotions of the audience, through pity or vivid descriptions, to sway their opinion and convince them that one's argument is more valid than another's. It is important to know the audience here; an emotional appeal could blow up in your face if the audience is not receptive to emotional appeal or if your refutation is disproportionate in relation to the argument.

One must gear his emotional refutation to appeal to the type of audience. Again, it is important to gauge the attitudes of the audience. Are they sympathetic to your case? In a largely mixed (heterogeneous) audience, you must decide which emotion will appeal to the largest majority of the audience as you refute your opponent.

Refutation by ethical appeal. Ethics must be present in every part of the discourse, but most importantly it must be maintained in the refutation. Aristotle said: "It is more fitting for a good man to display himself as an honest fellow than as a subtle reasoner" (Corbett, *Classical Rhetoric*, 280).

Sometimes when our argument is weak, we carry weight if we are more ethical than our opponent.

Refutation by wit. "It is the design of wit to excite in the mind an agreeable surprise, and that arising, not from any thing marvelous in the subject, but solely from the imagery she employs, or the strange assemblage of related ideas presented to the mind. This end is effected in one or other of these three ways: first in debasing things pompous or seemingly grave: I say seemingly grave, because to vilify what is truly grave has something shocking in it, which rarely fails to counteract the end: secondly, in aggrandizing things little and frivolous: thirdly, in setting ordinary objects, by means not only remote, but apparently contrary, in a particular and uncommon point of view" (Campbell, "The Philosophy of Rhetoric," *The Rhetoric of Blair, Whately and Campbell*, 150)

The Earl of Shaftesbury said, "Ridicule is the test of truth." If what is alleged to be the truth can survive the onslaught of ridicule, it must really be the truth. One warning about ridicule, or wit: even though it is truth, it can still be rendered absurd in the minds of the audience.

- Jokes can be effective but used with utmost discretion
- One can refute wit with a sober tone, or refute sobriety with wit
- You jeopardize an ethical appeal if your wit is just a cloak for weak or specious arguments
- Jokes as analogy allow the audience to take an objective view of the point being discussed
- Deprecating oneself can be effective; it harms no one and may make a point
- Irony can work with some audiences but might be taken seriously by some
- Sarcasm, "dirty jokes" are discouraged as offensive
- Satire is a most popular form of wit—most of the great English satirists were schooled in rhetoric

Day One, Lesson Ten Assignment:
Read Winston Churchill's "Be Ye Men of Valour" speech. Answer the following questions, and give reasons for your answers in two to three paragraphs. Use the worksheet and turn it in. What is the thesis? Where is the Proof of Case? (Use paragraph numbers.) How does he prove his case?

Day Two, Lesson Ten Assignment:
Read Nixon's "Checkers" speech, and number the paragraphs. Highlight all the refutations you find, using paragraph numbers as reference points.
Using the worksheet, define which type of refutation each one is, using just phrases instead of full sentences. (There are a lot!) Find at least 25, and identify all 4 types. Simply hand in the worksheet for this; no need to write up an essay.

Day Three, Lesson Ten Assignment:
Read Socrates' "Apology" again. List the refutations he employs, using paragraph numbers as reference points. (You should be very familiar with Socrates by now!) Use only the worksheet and turn it in.

Day Four, Lesson Ten Assignment:
Find a great political cartoon that employs satire. Turn it in.

WRITING TIPS LESSON 10

Use of numbers

Numbers must receive consistent treatment throughout your writing. The numbers from zero to ten must be spelled out, and any number above ten can be numerals. One exception to this is when numbers appear together in a sentence. In this case the writer must remain consistent. In one sentence when numbers below ten and above ten appear, treat the numbers similarly: either spell them out or use the numerals.

Never begin a sentence with a numeral. Spell out the number instead, or reword the sentence. Dates should be treated consistently: May 9, 1995. Do not write May the 9th, 1995 or May 9th, 1995. A variation that works would be the ninth of May, 1995, or the 25th of May.

LESSON ELEVEN

ARRANGEMENT, CONTINUED PART V: CONCLUSION (WEEK TWELVE)

Conclusion, fifth division of a discourse. *Epilogos* (to say in addition). Conclusion is the last impression we make on the audience. Without a conclusion, the discourse strikes us as merely stopping rather than ending with style. Our initial attempt might be to end with a flourish, with emotional intensity. Sometimes this is overdone and can detract from the solid achievements of the earlier parts of the discourse. Discretion is also important here.

> In all discourses, it is a matter of importance to hit the precise time of concluding, so as to bring our discourse just to a point; neither ending abruptly and unexpectedly; nor disappointing the expectation of the hearers, when they look for the close, and continuing to hover round and round the conclusion, till they become heartily tired of us. We should endeavour to go off with a good grace; not to end with a languishing and drawling sentence; but to close with dignity and spirit, that we may leave the minds of the hearers warm, and dismiss them with a favourable impression of the subject, and of the speaker. (Blair, quoted in *Blair, Campbell,* 128)

With conclusions, Aristotle suggests we might do one of the following:

- Inspire the audience with a favorable opinion of ourselves and an unfavorable opinion of our opponents,
- Amplify the force of the points we have made in the previous section and extenuate the force of the points made by the opposition,
- Rouse the appropriate emotions in the audience, or
- Restate in a summary way our facts and arguments (Corbett, *Classical Rhetoric*, 283-284).

Recapitulation (recap) occurs in the conclusion. Here we restate in capsule form the important points. It might be helpful to remind the audience what has been said. Sometimes facts which may have seemed buried in the middle of our discourse might sit nicely in capsule here.

Recapitulation is vital in a court trial. After much testimony the final argument, or recapitulation, is important to remind the jury of the major points of the trial, and his client's argument.

An emotional appeal can be best used here, and it is popular also, if used correctly and by a person of great ethical appeal. An emotional appeal can be overdone. "Bombastic" emotional appeals are used less now than they were fifty or more years ago. We rely more now on style and less on direct emotional appeals. People tend to be suspicious of a bombastic style.

An emotional conclusion can be a call to action: it can inspire patriotism, incite people to war, or encourage people to band together to solve problems.

A well-written conclusion can dispose the audience favorably toward the writer or speaker.

The ethical appeal in a conclusion is appropriate only if it has already been established earlier. Certain kinds of ethical appeal seem more appropriate in the conclusion:

- frank confession of our shortcomings
- honest acknowledgment of the strength of the opposing case
- magnanimous gestures toward vindictive opponents.

Day One, Lesson Eleven Assignment:
Read Neville Chamberlain's speech from 1939. Tell how he concludes, according to Aristotle's definition of conclusions. Also identify and discuss the thesis, type of discourse, type of introduction, and type(s) of refutation. One to two paragraphs. Use the worksheet provided to help organize your thoughts. Turn it in.

Day Two, Lesson Eleven Assignment:
Persuasive piece REWRITE. Take one of the opinion pieces you have written this year, review all comments on it, and rewrite it. Hand in the original piece (version 1) and the rewrite (version 2), using the version numbers at the top of each, together. Post version 2 for comment by your classmates.

Day Three, Lesson Eleven Assignment:
Review all of Arrangement. Take the quiz for this day.

Day Four, Lesson Eleven Assignment:
Read and rewrite the fable, "A Bundle of Sticks." First write it in 55-60 words, retaining the original sense of the fable. Then rewrite it to be 500-700 words, adding character and dialogue but retaining the sense of the original.

WRITING TIPS LESSON 11

Long quotes

To include a long quote (of forty words or four lines or more) in your text, you must set it apart visually. All text is double spaced (by requirement); the long quote must be indented. To include a long quote, hit Enter before typing the quote, as if you've made a new paragraph. Type or paste the quote. Then hit Enter again and continue the paragraph. Highlight the quote. Then put your cursor at the beginning of the paragraph and hit Tab, then Ctrl-T, to indent the quote ½" on the left (in Microsoft Word). The first line of the quote does not need to be indented more than the rest of the quote; all must be ½" on the left. Do not add extra space between the quote and the paragraph. See example, below. Make sure to cite the source.

See the example below, which includes the double-spacing and single-spacing you need to do correctly.

This text must go before the long quote. Remember that every quote must be "bookended," which means that you must surround your quote with your own words. Also note that this text, above the quote, is double-spaced. The space between this and the quote below must be only a double-space, no more.

> For we may rest assured that whenever we express ourselves ill, there is, besides the mismanagement of language, for the most part, some mistake in our manner of conceiving the subject. Embarrassed, obscure, and feeble sentences are generally, if not always, the result of embarrassed, obscure, and feeble thought. Thought and language act and re-act upon each other mutually. (Blair, www.artsci.gmcc.ab.ca/ people/einarssonb/blair.ht)

Following the long quote is a continuation of this paragraph, above. Do not indent this first line, since it's part of the above paragraph. Always bookend a quote. Also always provide good citation for a long quote.

LESSON TWELVE

THREE MODES OF PERSUASION: LOGIC/REASON (WEEKS THIRTEEN AND FOURTEEN)

According to Aristotle, we persuade others by three means: 1. by appealing to their reason (*logos*); 2. by appealing to their emotions (*pathos*); 3. by appealing with our personality or character (*ethos*). One, two, or all three of these methods can be used in one discourse. The following factors will determine which of these methods we use:

- Our topic,
- The events surrounding our topic, and
- The audience for the discourse.

Everyone develops some instincts for adapting methods of persuasion to fit the subject, occasion, and audience, but experience and education will enable some people to cultivate their ability to persuade. This is where persuasion becomes more of an art. When persuasion is an art, it becomes rhetoric.

Appeal to Reason (logos). Several different forms of persuasion fall under Appeal to Reason. The use of *definition*, *syllogism*, and *enthymeme* are just a few.

Definition is the foundation for the discussion of the rhetorical appeals to reason. A definition is a statement that gives the meaning of a term. The purposes for definitions are listed below.

1. *To show relationships:* How one thing relates to another. Here you might define one idea as it relates to another. For example, one might define marriage in the context of relationships, comparing it to other relationships, or to other marriages in the past.
2. *To remove ambiguity:* A *Lexical Definition* makes things clear, more specific. When a term has more than one meaning, a lexical definition removes verbal disagreement, which we will

see later when discussing fallacies. For example, someone might say, "That guy is mad!" Another might answer, "I don't know what you did to make him so angry." To which the other would reply, "No, I mean he is really mad. You know, insane." Here mad has two different meanings. The one who uses that word must make his meanings clear.

3. *To reduce vagueness* - a *Precising Definition* is focused as to its extent. This is used when a term is vague or unclear. A term may have one single meaning, but its use or application may be unclear. A person may say it is hot outside, and another will want to know how hot. A precising definition will make that more clear.

4. *To increase vocabulary*

5. *To explain theoretically* - a scientific or philosophical definition.

6. *To influence attitudes* - Often terms are defined, not necessarily for the purpose of clarifying their meaning, but in order to influence the attitudes and emotions of an audience. Some examples are abortion: murder or choice? marriage: union of man and woman or union of two people regardless of sex? These are called *persuasive definitions*. *(This information taken with permission from Doug* Wilson's *Intermediate Logic*, Mars Hill publication of Canon Press.)

Types of Definition
For this section we will be covering six types of definition: Exposition, Essential, Synonym, Etymology, Description, and Example.

A. An **Exposition** (expository work) is a form of definition, an explanatory work or speech. A dictionary is an explanatory work which defines words. A how-to book or manual explains or defines how something works or operates. And discourses that analyze or classify are also expository definitions.

B. An **Essential** definition is a term that designates what something is and distinguishes it from all other things; it spells out a thing's fundamental nature. "Man is a rational animal" cannot be true of any other being. That would be an essential definition; it distinguishes "man" from all other things.

Differentia distinguishes a term from every other thing. In the above definition, "a rational animal" is the differentia. If we were to define bird as "an animal with wings," the term "with wings" would be the differentia; it separates birds from all other animals. A **Genus** is the general class of the thing to be defined. (It can be remembered as the general term; differentia is the term that makes a difference.) Genus in the above definition would be "animal;" "with wings" would be the differentia. (The plural of differentia is differentiae.)

In the definition, "An airplane is a winged vehicle that flies in the sky," the genus is "vehicle" and the differentiae are "winged" and "flies in the sky." Does this differentiate it from a helicopter?

Differentiae in a definition often specify one or more of the four causes of a thing: the material, the formal, the efficient, and the final. The material cause is what makes up the thing. The formal cause is the physical description of the thing. The efficient cause is the producer or maker of the thing; what caused it to become that thing. And the final cause is the end use or purpose of the thing.

Here in the definition of "flute" we can see the use of the four causes and the genus.

A Flute is a musical instrument (genus) usually made of silver or nickel (material cause). It is long and hollow with keypads covering the holes (formal cause). A flute is made by an instrument maker or craftsman (efficient cause) and it is played by blowing across one end, which produces a high musical sound (final cause).

Keep in mind that the differentiae will change as we attempt to define various kinds of musical instruments. The causes will not always appear in that order, and in some definitions one will not always see every cause.

Look in a dictionary at a noun. You will find that most definitions use Aristotle's method of definition: the substantive is assigned to a general class and then differentiated in one or more ways.

C. Synonyms are words that mean the same. One will define using words that can be understood. Some words do not have synonyms, some synonyms may be hard to understand, and some synonyms do not have exact meanings.

Aristotle disliked this method of definition (synonyms), saying that a real definition could only be given within a phrase. This is correct; to understand the real meaning of a word, we must understand it within the context of its presentation.

D. Etymology is another way to define. Here one will describe the roots and history of a word. An etymological dictionary details the history of words. Students of Rhetoric who have taken Latin will recognize the Latin roots of many words we cover in this class. Here are some examples of etymology:

Essential: from Fr. Esse, to be. Latin ens, a thing.

Some meanings drift far from the etymology of the word. For example, the word *Read* is related to the Anglo-Saxon raedan, which means to counsel, consult, interpret. It is also related to the Latin, reri, to think. It is not always a close relationship to the origin.

E. Description is another method of definition. Types of Description include the following:

- Comparisons. One defines by comparison when relating one thing to another similar item. In comparing one could also contrast items.
- Analogy. One may also define by analogy much like Jesus did when speaking in parables. When he tells the parable of the Good Samaritan, he is drawing an analogy in order to define "neighbor."
- Metaphors. A metaphor defines in a more poetic way. A thing is described as being something else. For example, "Her teeth were pearls lined up in a row."
- Similes. Similar to a metaphor, this term compares one thing to another using the words *like* or *as*. For example, "The kingdom of heaven is like a pearl of great price."

F. Defining by Example (*exemplum*) will define by providing a similar, meaningful illustration. ("Faith" is leaning on someone because you trust him.)

Six rules should be our standard for defining terms:

1. *Defining terms should be clearer and more familiar than the term to be defined; do not be too broad or too narrow.* For example, one should define the word school as "an institution of higher learning," rather than something that is too unclear, such as "the place where students get tortured all day."
2. *A definition should not repeat the term to be defined* or use synonymous or derivative terms (an incorrect definition would be: "Abortion is the act of aborting a baby").
3. *A definition, whenever possible, should be stated positively, not negatively.* (It would not be: "Right to Life is against abortion." Instead it should be: "Right to Life advocates the choice of pregnancy over abortion").
4. *State the essential attributes of the term.* Adding to the definition with unnecessary words will not enhance the definition, but will take away from it. (A definition which does not just state the essential attributes of the term, but adds too many words, would be "To pause is to take one's time, to cease moving or acting, to rest in one's action or momentarily hesitate before going on.")

5. *A definition should not be figurative or unclear.* If, for example, the word "sun" is defined as "That great fiery orb that daily circles the globe," that definition is figurative; it is flowery. It is also unclear in that it does not adequately define the term.

6. *Nouns should define nouns; verbs should define verbs.* In other words, the definition should be of the same part of speech as the word to be defined. "Marrying is the state of a wedded union."

    These rules were found in two sources: Corbett, p. 37 and Douglas Wilson's *Intermediate Logic*, p. 24-25.

Day One, Lesson Twelve Assignment:
Read "Answers to Condemnation" by John Wycliffe (with the condemnation by Pope Gregory as an introduction) and answer the following questions in two to three paragraphs. Use the worksheet and hand it in. 1. What does Wycliffe define? 2. What is Wycliffe's purpose? 3. Who is his audience? 4. What are the circumstances?

Day Two, Lesson Twelve Assignment:
Find a newspaper or magazine article (not an advertisement!) in which there is a definition. Answer the following questions in short answer form.

- What is defined?
- What kind of definition is it (from "types of definition," above; i.e., synonym, essential, exposition, etc.)?
- How could the author of the article be trying to influence attitudes with his definition? (For example, an article about the galaxies and stars might include a definition about the beginning of the universe and therefore he is reinforcing evolutionary theory.)

Day Three, Lesson Twelve Assignment:
Read Chuck Colson's "Pretty Stones and Dead Babies" and answer the following questions in two paragraphs. Use the worksheet and hand it in. What does he define? What is his purpose? What is his thesis?

Day Four, Lesson Twelve Assignment:
Look up the following ten nouns in the dictionary. Write out the most complete definition you can find. (Use ONE definition, even if the dictionary gives you more than one.) Then identify and label the differentiae (efficient cause, formal cause, etc.). You might not find every cause! Nouns to define: **church, restaurant, carpet, desk, cross, hymnal, dictionary, piano, Bible, plate.** Use the worksheet for each of these steps (1-3) and hand it in.
Take four of the above nouns and write your own complete definitions, using the genus and every cause. Label/color the causes. Do this on a separate page.
Make up your own noun and define it **using genus and all four differentiae.**

Day Five, Lesson Twelve Assignment:
Below are words and verses that correspond. Each verse defines that word. For each verse, write the phrase in which the word is used, and define the word as it is used. You may use a dictionary, your Bible's notes, commentaries, etc. Use the worksheet only and turn it in.

For example:
    Word: **Seal**

1st Verse: Eph 1:13-14.

    Phrase that includes the word: "sealed with the Holy Spirit of promise."

    Means in this context: A sign or pledge of promise.

2nd Verse: 2 Cor 1:22

    Phrase that includes the word: "who also sealed us and gave us the Spirit in our hearts as a pledge."

    Means in this context: Joined us to Him. (Like sealing an envelope.)

3rd Verse: John 6:27

    Phrase that includes the word: "on Him the Father, even God, has set His seal"

    Means in this context: Mark of ownership.

Your words to define:

Glory
Ephesians 1:6, 12, 14 (one definition), Luke 2:32, 2 Corinthians 3:7

Wisdom
James 3:15, James 3:17

Holy
Exodus 3:5, Joel 3:17, 1 Peter 1:13-16

Grace
Acts 14:3, Romans 11:6, 2 Corinthians 8:7, Galatians 1:3

Day Six, Lesson Twelve Assignment:
Write an essay in which you define "life." You must give a full essay, including examples and discussing where, why, how, etc. Your essay must have a worldview reflecting your definition, or reflected in your definition. For example, if you take the pro-abortion point of view, your definition of life would be very different from the pro-life definition of life. 3-5 paragraphs.

Day Seven, Lesson Twelve Assignment:
Read and rewrite the story, "A Dissertation Upon Roast Pig," by Charles Lamb (found in the Appendix). This is a spoof about how cooked meat was discovered. Tell the story in 150 words, retaining the sense of the original story. Then write your own story (300-600 words) about how something that is now commonplace came about. Some ideas are (suggested; you may come up with your own): the napkin, waving a hand to say hello or goodbye; the use of forks, knives and spoons to eat; the invention of popcorn; and so forth.

Day Eight, Lesson Twelve Assignment:
Take the quiz for this lesson.

Day Nine, Lesson Twelve Assignment:
Comment on three of your classmates' opinion piece rewrites. Pay attention to the changes that were made. Be constructive, and watch for excellent writing!

WRITING TIPS LESSON 12

Use of titles and names
Names:

The first time a person is mentioned in your writing, refer to him using his full name. Thereafter you may use his last name or title. For example, "Winston Churchill" would be his full name, and then after the first mention you may refer to him as "Churchill." He also has a title, so you might refer to him as "Prime Minister Winston Churchill." Thereafter he could be called "Churchill" or "the Prime Minister." Never refer to him by his first name.

If someone has a readily identifiable other name, such as "Franklin Delano Roosevelt," you can (after referring to him properly the first time) call him "Roosevelt," "President Roosevelt," or "FDR."

Titles:

Book titles are ALWAYS italicized. Speech titles are in quotes.

Italicize these titles:
Books
Movies
Ships' names (including names of space ships)
Plays
Epic-length poems
Television series or radio show series
CD titles

These titles go in quotation marks:
Poems
Speeches
Songs (note: the CD title is italicized; the song is in quotes)
Short stories
Essays
Articles from newspapers or magazines
Episodes from television series or radio shows

LESSON THIRTEEN

LOGIC--THE FIRST MODE OF PERSUASION (WEEK FIFTEEN) ENTHYMEME, EXAMPLE, FALLACIES

Syllogism and enthymeme—Another Logical form of persuasion. Aristotle invented these to analyze and test deductive reasoning. Students should have had a good basic instruction in Logic before taking rhetoric. It might be helpful to review logic at this point. (See Doug Wilson's *Introductory Logic*, Mars Hill publication of Canon Press.)

An *Enthymeme* is a syllogism with a missing premise. Aristotle said, "The enthymeme must consist of few propositions, fewer often than those which make up a normal syllogism" (Corbett, *Classical Rhetoric*, 53). Essentially, the syllogism leads to a necessary conclusion from universally true premises, but the enthymeme leads to a tentative conclusion from probable premises (Corbett, *Classical Rhetoric*, 53). In other words, an enthymeme is persuasive but not conclusive. If he cannot *convince* his audience, the writer or speaker must *persuade* it. Rhetoric can persuade according to what is probable, what people believe *might* happen.

Deductive reasoning in the case of enthymemes is peculiar to rhetoric; here we must look at the implied premise. For example: "Susan will have to throw out those eggs since they've been left out this long."

Another example is "He must be a right-wing bigot because he says he is a Christian." The implied premise may be faulty: "All Christians are right-wing bigots." The argument may be logically true, but the implied premise is false. In rhetoric, then, our job is to refute this implied premise. That implied premise may be the vulnerable spot in the other person's argument.

Reasoning by Example

The example is another form of persuasion by reason. It uses inductive reasoning, going from the particular to the general. The example also uses verifiable phenomena. One can counteract an example by citing a valid example where the outcome is the opposite of the one given. An argument cannot solely rely on the example because it does not constitute real proof; it is mostly a probability. But it is, of itself, persuasive. But it is vital to remind one's reader that if someone has used example, one example does not prove the point.

The Fallacies

A fallacy is an error in reasoning; it is a false statement, an untruth which has to do with the *matter* or *form* of the argument. Here again it is important for the student of Rhetoric to have an understanding of Logic. This is a basic review of Fallacies from Logic, with more added on. Fallacies can be proven false.

Every statement can be analyzed and its veracity or fallacy detected only by one's knowledge of the facts. This, for the student of Rhetoric, is the reason for the need to know great amounts of information. How can you prove anything true or false if you know nothing about it, or even how to go about learning about it?

For an in-depth discussion of fallacies, read Corbett's section on that topic, pages 62-71. Many of the fallacies he supplies are included here. Other fallacies have been added from various sources.

Fallacies of reasoning in deduction

1. **Equivocation** uses the same term with two or more meanings. The argument may hinge on someone defining a word two different ways. For example, one person will say that Jane is mad (meaning angry), but the other may understand Jane to be mad (meaning insane).
2. **Accent** is a form of equivocation. One will change the meaning of a sentence not through definition, but by emphasizing different words. For example, "I don't always understand our Heavenly Father's commands" can be accented different ways. With the emphasis on the *I* one might think he is the only one who does not understand. Emphasizing *always* might mean that sometimes he does understand. And so forth.
3. **Undistributed Middle Term** does not supply a logical flow of the arguments. For example: "All Baptists are people. All Americans are people. Therefore all Americans are Baptists." In other words, one cannot draw a conclusion from the supplied premises. One who has had Logic will remember this as one of the tests of the validity of a syllogism.

4. **Conclusion from Two Negative Premises**. One cannot arrive at a negative conclusion with two negative premises. This does not establish a relationship among all three terms in a syllogistic chain of reasoning. For example: "No Protestants are Catholics, and no Catholics are Baptists, therefore no Protestants are Baptists." The premises do not lead to this conclusion and are faulty because they are negative.

5. **Affirmative Conclusion from a Negative Premise**. No affirmative conclusion can be drawn from negative premises. For example, "No believers are slaves, and no slaves are free men. Therefore, some believers are free men." Even though the conclusion may be true, one cannot logically draw that conclusion from the supplied premises.

6. **Either/or** fallacy oversimplifies the choices. "Either he believed in A or B." But what if there were a C? (This can also be called "False Dilemma.")

7. **Fallacy of Asserting the Consequent** uses a hypothetical proposition. This is also called a *non sequitur*. Here the premises don't support the conclusion. For example: "If I take driver's education I can drive the car. I drove the car, therefore I took driver's education." What if he took the car out for a ride without permission? It does not necessarily follow that he took driver's education.

8. **Fallacy of Denying the Antecedent** also reasons from hypothetical propositions. For example: "If I take driver's education I can drive the car. I didn't take driver's education, so I didn't drive the car." Again, it's not legal to get a license without taking driver's education, but a determined individual will not let that detail get in his way!

Fallacies of Reasoning in Induction

1. **Faulty generalization** jumps to a conclusion from inadequate evidence (gathered by observation or study). Some possibilities of faulty generalization arise when the particulars may be irrelevant, unrepresentative, or not enough to warrant the conclusion (this is also called *a priorism* – a sweeping generalization). Other examples of Faulty Generalization are:

2. **Faulty generalization based on evidence** derived from authority when the authority quoted is biased or prejudiced, incompetent, or outmoded. This can also be called the fallacy of *ipse dixit* (he said it himself).

3. **Faulty generalization when a competent authority is inaccurately quoted**, misinterpreted, or quoted out of context.

4. **Faulty casual generalizations are cause/effect generalizations** when we argue:--*from an effect to a cause* when we assign an inadequate cause to an effect or when we fail to take into account the fact that there could be more than

one cause for the same effect.--*from a cause to an effect* when we fail to establish that a potential cause of an effect could and did operate in a particular situation, or when we fail to take into account that the same cause can produce diverse effects. This last fallacy is also called *post hoc ergo propter hoc*—after this, therefore because of this. This is the fallacy that occurred when the rooster thought the sun rose because he crowed.

5. **Faulty Analogy**. An analogy never proves anything, but it may be persuasive if the audience does not recognize it as an error in reasoning.

Miscellaneous Fallacies

1. *Petitio principii* is also called Begging the Question. This is circular reasoning, where one assumes what must be proven. Look for words such as *obviously, of course, as everyone knows, really, unquestionably.*

2. *Ad hominem* (to the man) distracts from the main point of the argument or discussion and becomes an attack on the opponent. It may be reduced to name-calling or other insults.

3. *Ad populum* (to the people) appeals to *irrational* fears and prejudices to distract from the issues. It becomes an appeal to the emotions, or to the whole audience to do something because everyone else does it. Also called a "bandwagon" fallacy.

4. *Ad verecundiam* is similar to *ad populum* in that it appeals to emotions or prejudices. This appeals to the reverence for certain institutions (allegiance to the flag, country, school, political party, church).

5. *Ad invidiam* is also similar to *ad populum*. It appeals to hatred or dislike, prejudice, the stronger negative emotions.

6. *Ad captandum* occurs when a speaker has a captivating manner, and because of it, the audience believes him whether it's true or not.

7. **"Red Herring"** is a fallacy of distraction where an opponent dodges the issue by "changing the subject." Students like to call this one the "rabbit trail" fallacy, in which the speaker may divert attention from the main point by letting himself get sidetracked. One might say, "You say I have lied while in office. But look at how strong the economy is."

8. **The Complex Question** is a question framed in such a way as to exclude the only legitimate response. It sets someone up with a question: "When did you stop beating your wife?" It would be necessary to break it apart and answer each point.

9. *Ad Ignoratium* absence of proof, or assuming something that is, because the opposite cannot be proven. Because I can't see God, he does not exist.

10. *Ad baculum* (appeal to the stick) is committed when the speaker or writer uses a veiled threat to convince his audience

to do something or believe something. The audience members believe what they are told because they fear for their physical well-being. This appeals to people's personal anxiety.

11. **Bulverism** was a term coined by C.S. Lewis. Here one attacks the character of the individual and assumes his argument is incorrect because of his character. It says, "You're just saying that because you're a (fill in the blank)." The blank would be any characteristic of the person-Christian, woman, etc.

12. **Slippery Slope** occurs when someone lists events that occur from point A to point D, but one does not exactly lead to the other. In other words, one cannot get to D from A. Example: "Drinking can lead to the use of marijuana. Marijuana use can lead to harder drugs. Harder drugs can lead to heroin. Therefore, people should not drink because they will end up on heroin." Also called "*Reductio ad absurdam.*"

13. **Appeal to pity** is a tear-jerking story intended to provoke sympathy and a response. Photos of a poor starving child in Pakistan are not sufficient reason to support a mission in Pakistan. (What would be sufficient?)

14. **Appeal to vanity** causes envy, making one feel as if he is truly missing out on something someone else has. An ad making one want to be thin, athletic, sexy, etc. is an appeal to vanity.

15. **Straw man** oversimplifies an opponent's argument before refuting it. "We asked the senator to comment on the new spending bill. He said he was busy. He obviously considers his constituents too insignificant to waste his time on. Such an obnoxious attitude should be treated in kind. Don't vote for him this fall."

16. *Tu quoque* (also called *ad hominem tu quoque*): This fallacy is committed when it is concluded that a person's claim is false because 1) it is inconsistent with something else a person has said or 2) what a person says is inconsistent with her actions. The fact that a person makes inconsistent claims does not make any particular claim he makes false (although of any pair of inconsistent claims only one can be true—but both can be false). Also, the fact that a person's claims are not consistent with his actions might indicate that the person is a hypocrite, but this does not prove his claims are false. (From http://www.nizkor.org/features/fallacie)

17. **Amphiboly:** The fallacy here lies in the structure of the sentence. The sentence is structured in such a way as to confuse or mislead the listener. Often found in headlines. A famous amphiboly would be "Mary had a little lamb. I'll bet the doctor was surprised." Or "Iraqi head searches for arms."

18. **Composition:** This fallacy comes in when one believes that since the parts that make up the whole have one certain quality, the whole will also have that quality. For example,

"A DC-10 is made up of lightweight parts. That means a DC-10 is very lightweight." Or, "My sister is stupid and she voted for Bush. That means all Bush supporters are stupid."

19. **Division:** This is the opposite of Composition. In this fallacy, one makes the mistake of supposing that since the whole thing has a certain attribute, the parts that make up the whole also have the same attribute. For example, "Enron collapsed because it is an unstable, dishonest company. That means all those employees were dishonest and unstable as well."

20. **Chronological snobbery:** One commits this fallacy by assuming that because of the age of an individual or a thing, it is either good or bad. For example, "No one can rely on the Bible. It is outdated." Or, "My encyclopedia from 1942 is the best and most reliable because it was written so long ago." Or, "That kid must be doing something bad. He's a teenager, isn't he?"

From this point, you should be able to recognize persuasion by logic, as well as begin to identify fallacies in whatever you read for this class.

Day One, Lesson Thirteen Assignment

Work through the Enthymeme assignment (in this lesson), taken from Corbett's Rhetoric book. Find the implied premise. Some of these are much harder than others! Method: either rewrite as standard syllogisms to supply the missing premise, or just work through it by finding the conclusion. Only provide the missing premise.

Day Two, Lesson Thirteen Assignment

Find the implied premise(s) in the following verses. Explain your reasons. Use the same method as above. Give simple answers, supplying only the missing premise and one or two sentences as reasoning.

- Matthew 13:20-21 "The one who received the seed that fell on rocky places is the man who hears the word and at once receives it with joy. But since he has no root, he lasts only a short time. When trouble or persecution comes because of the word, he quickly falls away."
- Matthew 27:6 "The chief priests picked up the coins and said, 'It is against the law to put this into the treasury, since it is blood money.'"
- Matthew 6: 12 "Forgive us our debts, as we also have forgiven our debtors."

Day Three, Lesson Thirteen Assignment

Read Huss: "The Church—Not Man but Christ." Analyze his logical appeal. Discuss the logical techniques he uses to communicate his thesis (What does he define? How does this support his thesis?). What is his thesis? Discuss in two to three paragraphs. Use the worksheet and turn it in.

Day Four, Lesson Thirteen Assignment

Complete the fallacies worksheet, either together in class or on your own. On the next page.

Day Five, Lesson Thirteen Assignment

Read Chuck Colson's Breakpoint Article, "A History of God—Who's Got it Right?" Without naming the fallacy, Colson has pointed it out and corrected it. What is the fallacy (or are there more than one?)? How else would you counter this fallacy/fallacies? Discuss in 2-3 paragraphs.

Day Six, Lesson Thirteen Assignment

Comment on three of your peers' opinion pieces, using the criteria provided previously.

Logic Lesson Thirteen
Label the following fallacies

1. America: love it or leave it.

2. Since scientists cannot prove that global warming will occur, it probably won't.

3. Do you support freedom and the right to bear arms?

4. You had better agree that the new company policy is the best bet if you expect to keep your job.

5. Polls suggest that the Unity party will form a majority in government next year, so you may as well vote for them.

6. You are stupid to believe that God doesn't exist.

7. Why should I quit drinking? You were drunk all the time when you were my age.

8. Immigration from Germany to Chicago increased. Soon after, the welfare rolls increased. Therefore, the increased immigration caused the increased welfare rolls.

9. Since I'm not lying, it follows that I am telling the truth.

10. The sign said "fine for parking here," and since it was fine, I parked there.

11. Last night I shot a burglar in my pajamas.

12. It would be illegal to give away **FREE BEER!!!**

13. Germany is a militant country. Thus, each German is militant.

14. Each brick is three inches high, thus, the brick wall is three inches high.

15. It figures that a doctor would tell you that you are really sick. He just wants the money.

16. Fred said that he is smarter than Jill, but he didn't prove it, so it must be false.

17. Scientist grows artery from pig cells.

18. Have you stopped cheating on tests?

19. Dear Senator: Your vote on higher taxes will get you voted out of office.

20. Everyone knows that the Earth is flat, so why do you persist in your outlandish claims? (two fallacies)

21. Don't vote for the bill to fund the interstate highway, because the promoter of the bill, Senator Slugg, is a greedy pig.

22. Because the brain is capable of consciousness, each neural cell in the brain must be capable of consciousness.

23. Don't listen to your dad. He says you shouldn't go out to that movie, but I know he rented an R-rated movie the other night.

24. I asked six of my friends what they thought of the new spending restraints and they agreed it is a good idea. The new restraints are therefore generally popular.

25. We know that the Big Bang created the universe, because so many scientists say it did. (two fallacies)

26. A plane is a carpenter's tool, and the Boeing 747 is a plane, hence the Boeing 747 is a carpenter's tool.

27. The first mate, seeking revenge on the captain, wrote in his journal, "The Captain was sober today."

28. Conventional bombs did more damage in WWII than nuclear bombs. Thus, a conventional bomb is more dangerous than a nuclear bomb.

29. Confucianism has been around since the 500s BC. It must be a highly organized and respected religion.

Enthymeme Exercise For Day One Lesson Thirteen

(Reprinted with permission from Edward P.J. Corbett, *Classical Rhetoric for the Modern Student*, pp. 59-60.)

Reproducible page with the above permission line included.

Assignment: **Work on enthymeme exercise to convert enthymemes into full syllogisms by supplying the missing premise.**

1. He must be happy, because he's smiling all the time.

2. A nuclear war is inevitable, for our sworn enemy, Communist China, now has the hydrogen bomb.

3. He would not take the crown, Therefore 'tis certain he was not ambitious (Shakespeare, *Julius Caesar*, III, ii, 118)

4. Because 29.8 percent of Thurber's sentences are simple sentences, we can say that a good part of his essay is easy to understand. (Student theme) .

5. Since you didn't speak up in my defense at the meeting, you must be as much against me as the rest of them are.

6. John definitely didn't drive the car home last night. He never puts the car in the right hand side of the garage.

7. No, the fuse isn't blown. It's the light bulb that is bad. When you flip the wall-switch, all the other lights in the room go on, don't they?

8. In your statement you assert that our actions, even though peaceful, must be condemned because they precipitate violence. (Martin Luther King, Jr., "Letter from Birmingham Jail")

9. Since the bullet obviously entered through his back, we have to rule out suicide; quite certainly he was murdered.

10. Blessed are the poor in spirit, for they shall see God.

11. The most convincing evidence that cigarette-smoking causes lung cancer is that the number of nonsmokers who die from lung cancer is so minimal as to be negligible.

12. The Civilization of the Dialogue is the only civilization worth having and the only civilization in which the whole world can unite. It is, therefore, the only civilization we can hope for, because the world must unite or be blown to bits. (Robert M. Hutchins, "Morals, Religion, and Higher Education")

13. You deny that you took any of the chocolate candy from the cupboard. But just look at your hands.

14. My girl doesn't love me anymore. The last three times I called her for a date, she said she had to stay in and catch up on her schoolwork.

15. It is better to die, for death is gentler than tyranny. (Aeschylus, *Agamemnon*, lines 1450-51)

16. She must have lost her car keys somewhere between the checkout counter and the parking lot, because she remembers taking the keys out of her purse when she was paying her bill and laying them on the counter.

17. You say he's a great hitter. Hogwash! A great hitter doesn't strike out 113 times a season.

18. Since cultivation of mind is surely worth seeking for its own sake, there is a knowledge which is desirable, though nothing come of it. (John Henry Newman, *The Idea of a University*)

19. How do I know that the "silent majority" is indeed a majority? Well, they elected a conservative President, didn't they?

WRITING TIPS LESSON 13

Usage errors: The list below contains the most common problems with student writing.

Error	Correction
Prophecy/prophesy	Prophesy/prophesies is the <u>verb</u>.
Prophecies/prophesies	Prophecy/prophecies is the <u>noun</u>
Less/fewer	Fewer deals with the number of things: "Fewer mistakes." Less concerns the degree of things: "I am less concerned about your errors now."
Further/farther	"Farther" relates to distance. "Further" relates to ideas.
Towards/toward	"Towards" is not a proper word for writing
Lead/led	The past tense of "lead" is "led."
Based off of/based on	Somehow students tend to say things like "His ideas are based off of..." when instead they should say "His ideas are based on..."
Anyways	Not a word!
Irregardless	Not a word!
Orientated	Not a word!
Affect/Effect	<u>"Affect" is the verb; "Effect" is the noun</u>. The only exception is when Effect is used as a transitive verb: "The government was able to effect a change in taxation." The meaning here generally would be to bring about.
Accept/Except	Students know the difference; they just don't always proofread carefully. " ccept" means to receive or admit. "Except" means to exclude or leave out, or is a conditional term.

Many more usage errors exist. You may want to add more of your own.

Usage of he/she/they:
This common pronoun error causes more frustration with students than almost anything. To be sure your pronouns agree, make sure the tenses remain the same. If the subject is singular, the pronoun will be singular. For example, incorrect: "Each student must make sure their paper is stapled." The subject (student) is singular; therefore the pronoun must agree. "Each student must make sure his paper is stapled."

Note on political correctness: University professors and employers might insist that the generic pronoun "he" or "his" is sexist. They may require you to use "he/she" or "he or she." Historically the use of "he" referred to the generic, universal "human being."

Hyphenated words used as adjectives:
When describing a noun, sometimes words are grouped together and would be better treated with a hyphen. Example:

The often used term...

Might be better as: The often-used term...

Oil rich countries sell their product at a huge profit.

Might be better as: Oil-rich countries sell their product at a huge profit.

LESSON FOURTEEN

ETHICS--THE SECOND MODE OF PERSUASION (WEEK SIXTEEN) ETHICAL APPEAL

In the first place, what stands highest in the order of means, is personal character and disposition. In order to be a truly eloquent or persuasive speaker, nothing is more necessary than to be a virtuous man.

Bad as the world is, nothing has so great and universal a command over the minds of men as virtue. ...Nothing, therefore, is more necessary for those who would excel in any of the higher kinds of oratory, than to cultivate habits of the several virtues, and to refine and improve all their moral feelings. Whenever these become dead, or callous, they may be assured, that, on every occasion, they will speak with less power, and less success. The sentiments and dispositions particularly requisite for them to cultivate, are the following: The love of justice and order and indignation at insolence and oppression; the love of honesty and truth, and detestation of fraud, meanness, and corruption; magnanimity of spirit; the love of liberty, of their country, and the public; zeal for all great and noble designs, and reverence for all worthy and heroic characters. (Blair, quoted in *Blair, Campbell* 129-130)

Even the most ingenious and logical appeal could fall on deaf ears if the audience reacted unfavorably to the speaker's character. Quintillian said: "For he who would have all men trust his judgment as to what is expedient and honourable, should possess and be regarded as possessing genuine wisdom and excellence of character" (Corbett, *Classical Rhetoric*, 72).

In a discourse in which the speaker or writer is attempting to impress the audience of his ethics, his words alone should impress the audience that he is wise, that he is virtuous, and that he is benevolent—a man of good will. The discourse must exhibit the speaker's ethics and good sense. He must show that he knows how to reason, that he can be fairly objective in his argument, and that he knows a lot about this and other subjects.

The discourse must also reflect the writer's virtues or morals. He must also show that he abhors unscrupulous methods of reasoning or argumentation, that he respects "the commonly acknowledged virtues, and an adamant integrity" (Corbett, *Classical Rhetoric*, 72).

The discourse must manifest the writer's good will. It should "display his sincere interest in the welfare of the audience and a readiness to sacrifice any self-aggrandizement that conflicts with the benefit of others" (Corbett, *Classical Rhetoric*, 73). It must also exhibit his understanding of human psychology, being aware of the needs and emotions of people of different ages and in different stages of life (young/middle aged/old, wealthy/poor, educated/illiterate, well/sick, men/women). The writer should adapt his tone and sentiments to fit the audience, without compromising his ethical tone.

A writer or speaker's ethical appeal is jeopardized by a slip of behavior or words that might belie a false front. If one's integrity has come into question during the discourse, or he becomes irate or ill-tempered; if he has used false information or poor logic, his ethical appeal has been jeopardized.

Many consider ethical appeal to be the "hidden persuader."

Day One, Lesson Fourteen Assignment

Read Wilberforce's speech from 1789. What type of discourse is this? Find the thesis, the type of discourse, and tell what type of refutation you find. Use the worksheet and hand it in. Discuss and show examples of his ethical appeal. Three paragraphs.

Day Two, Lesson Fourteen Assignment

Read Joseph Stalin's speech from November, 1941. What type of discourse is this? Decide on the thesis and how he supports it. Would you call this an "ethical appeal"? Why or why not? What kinds of ethical appeal can you identify? Discuss in two to three paragraphs. Use the worksheet and hand it in.

Day Three, Lesson Fourteen Assignment

Read Joel Belz's "The Lie is Marching On" and analyze its use of ethical appeal. What kind of ethical appeal does he use, and where? Remember to consider what the thesis is and how he supports it, as well as what kind of introduction it is. Can you find any areas where he might actually jeopardize his own ethical appeal? Two to three paragraphs. Use the worksheet and hand it in.

Day Four, Lesson Fourteen Assignment

Look up "ethics in politics" OR "ethics in medicine" on a search engine on the Web. Find some articles that discuss this subject and write an essay discussing the world's definition of ethics today. You might compare what you find to what scripture says about moral and ethical behavior. You could also compare it to what Blair says in the passage above.

LESSON FIFTEEN

EMOTIONS--THE THIRD MODE OF PERSUASION (WEEK SEVENTEEN) THE EMOTIONAL APPEAL

Hugh Blair emphasized that the speaker must use an even tone in his emotions. He did not want the speaker to heat up his emotions too soon and wear out the audience. Highly intense emotions throughout the speech will also exhaust the topic. So one must intensify his emotional appeal gradually and organize his speech in order to build up to that intensity.

Let's consider the construction of emotions.

Many of our actions are prompted by the stimulus of our emotions or combination of reason and emotion. In other words, we will respond to emotions alone, or reason and emotion combined. This is important to consider as communicators; our argument should appeal to more than just reason alone.

An *argument* (appeal to the understanding) produces conviction about the practicality of the means to the desired end (use logic to persuade that going to war is reasonable). An *appeal to the emotions* makes the end seem desirable (use emotions to persuade that men are crying for freedom and therefore we need to go to war).

If someone like Churchill were to excite his people to war, he needed to do the following:

- remind them that the freedom and security of a nation is a desirable end (emotion)
- convince them that going to war is the best means of securing this end (reason).

A caution regarding emotional appeal: Some people exploit emotions for unscrupulous purposes. Some will ignore a logical or ethical appeal in exchange for an outright play on people's emotions. You may recall that Clinton told his audience once, "I feel your pain." He used their emotions to his advantage. Also, in the 2000 Democratic National Convention, Candidate Al Gore kissed his wife soundly after his speech, and immediately his popularity ratings went up several points.

Our will does not have direct control of our emotions. It is dangerous to announce to an audience that we are going to play on their emotions. We must get at the emotions in a roundabout manner, rather than outright stating that we will be twisting their emotions. We might arouse emotion by reflecting upon the thing that would arouse emotions (think of someone who wants to convince an audience of how pitiful it is to be homeless; one would describe the living conditions of a homeless person in order to evoke pity). Passionate emotions can be aroused even by unemotional descriptions (think of someone who wants his audience to be outraged at high taxes; he might describe how someone who scrapes to make ends meet, ends up in poverty because he can't pay his property taxes). One must appeal to the imagination, using a word-painting by use of sensory, specific detail. Think of how vivid descriptions can move someone to think a certain way, react in a certain manner, or arouse certain emotions.

Aristotle said we can analyze emotions from three angles: their <u>nature</u>, their <u>object</u> (the people or things toward whom we experience the emotion), and their <u>exciting causes</u> (what brings about the emotion?). We need to know <u>all three things</u> about an emotion if we hope to arouse it in others. (As restated by Corbett, *Classical Rhetoric*, 82).

Aristotle spent a great deal of his *Rhetoric* examining emotions and their opposites. No wonder, then, that he is considered a philosopher as well as a psychologist of sorts. Some examples of emotions (paired with their opposites) from Aristotle's viewpoint are as follows.

- Anger and meekness, love and hatred, fear and boldness, shame and shamelessness, courage and fear, despair and hope.
- Confused, exhausted, ecstatic, guilty, suspicious, angry, hysterical, frustrated, sad, confident, embarrassed, happy, mischievous, disgusted, frightened, enraged, ashamed, cautious, smug, depressed, overwhelmed, hopeful, lonely, lovestruck, jealous, bored, surprised, anxious, shocked, shy.

Sensing emotions and how to address them is instinctual for some. Others may have to work on concentrating on this concept. Intellectual appeal is often not enough to move people's will to act. As an audience member, be alert for emotional appeals from others. What is that commercial trying to get you to feel? (As Christians, we must always be aware of the underlying presuppositions which drive certain ideas and actions, and prompt certain emotions.)

Be natural; let the nature of the subject matter, the occasion, or the audience elicit the appropriate kind and the right amount of emotional appeal.

Read the text for the following ad, taken from the radio. Discuss with your class how well or how poorly emotion is used here. Think critically.

Somebody just died…while you're listening to me. And that somebody is somebody's sister, brother, mom, dad, daughter, son or friend. 450 people die a day. 19 an hour. From Lung Cancer. Six-hundred and fifty thousand people will die of the world's DEADLIEST cancer by the year 2010 if we don't do something now. Where's the outrage? Lung Cancer Matters Too. It's not what you think. It's not what you've heard. Don't believe that if you don't smoke you can NEVER get lung cancer. I'm Deborah Morosini and I lost my sister, Dana Reeve, to lung cancer. Please help us save lives at the Bonnie J. Addario Lung Cancer Foundation. Because we can.

Donate today at www lung cancer foundation dot org or call 866.926. LUNG. Lung Cancer Matters Too. And so does EVERYONE we love.

(Radio PSA from the Lung Cancer Foundation, 2007-08)

Day One, Lesson Fifteen Assignment

Earlier the text said that one's will does not have direct control of one's emotions. As a Christian communicator, how then does one speak to nonbelievers? Use scripture to answer this in 2-3 paragraphs.

Day Two, Lesson Fifteen Assignment

Read Thomas B. Macaulay's essay, "Lord Clive." Also read Pope Gregory XI's attack on John Wycliffe Write a paragraph for each article, using examples, as you analyze how each one used emotional appeal answering the following questions. Use the worksheet and turn it in. What are the emotions he arouses? How is he arousing the emotions? Analyze: For an audience member, how effective is the emotional appeal?

Day Three, Lesson Fifteen Assignment

Find four commercials or ads (radio, television, newspaper, billboard, or magazine) that use emotional appeal. You may scan the ads to show me or you may simply describe them in as much detail as possible. What kind of emotional appeal is used in each ad? What is the underlying message, if any?

Day Four, Lesson Fifteen Assignment

Read Cicero's "Cataline" speech. We will be analyzing this later. For now, describe the emotions you read in this speech. First, what emotions did Cicero express? What emotions did he try to arouse in his audience? From the editor's preface you have an idea how this affected his audience. Try to describe how this may have affected the outcome of Cataline's "trial." Two to three paragraphs.

LESSON SIXTEEN

ANALYSIS OF DISCOURSE (WEEK EIGHTEEN)

This next section of Rhetoric involves the analysis of discourses. So far we have analyzed discourses according to what we have learned with regard to the Five Canons. Now we will put it all together and analyze our first discourse. Refer to the list below for questions we answer when writing an analysis. We will answer in full sentences and paragraphs, answering the hows and whys of each question. Answers must include examples (quotes) from the work in question to support our answers.

Questions to Answer when Analyzing a discourse
1. What type of discourse is this?
2. What is the thesis?
3. Break into divisions by paragraph number.
4. Describe how each division supports the thesis.
5. What kind of introduction is it?
6. How does he persuade—ethically, emotionally, logically? Describe where each of these is used.
7. How does he conclude—what method does he employ?
8. What fallacies do you find, and what kind?
9. What figures of speech do you find, and what kind? (Rhetoric II only)

How each Question should be answered
1. **What type of discourse is this?** As we learned in the first few days of Rhetoric, a discourse is either epideictic (ceremonial), deliberative (in a legislative atmosphere), forensic (in a court of law), or propaganda (the use of a discourse in order to gain power by instilling fear). Give reasons.

2. **What is the thesis?** Most discourses contain the thesis in the first one or two sections. Sometimes it can be found farther down in the discourse. Remember that a thesis statement is one or two sentences that affirm or deny something about a particular subject. Tell why you chose that as the thesis.

3. **Break into divisions.** Using the divisions learned earlier in Rhetoric, divide the discourse into these divisions. Not every discourse will have every division, and not every discourse will have the divisions in the same order they were presented earlier (except for the introduction and conclusion, hopefully!). The point of this exercise is to take a careful look at how the discourse is constructed. If you don't find the divisions, say so.

4. **Describe how each division supports the thesis.** It is important to learn how a writer or speaker supports his thesis. Sometimes one might not support his thesis well, and it is important to see that a discourse falls apart when it is not supported. When describing how the thesis is supported in each division, you should be able to provide quotes and examples from the discourse. ("He supports the thesis in paragraph 19 where he says, ...") This is also the place where the student will explain how the writer moves his topic along, and what it might mean.

5. **What kind of introduction is it?** We learned about the different kinds of introductions—narrative, inquisitive, preparatory, corrective, and paradoxical. Here you will explain what kind of introduction the writer uses and why.

6. **How does he persuade—ethically, emotionally, logically?** Find examples throughout the discourse where he uses these three types of appeal. Again, it is important to quote examples of these types of appeal. ("An example of emotional appeal is evident in paragraph 14, and it says...")

7. **How does he conclude—what method does he employ?** Aristotle described four different methods for concluding. One can summarize his points, arouse emotions, make himself sound good and his opponent sound bad, and amplify his own points while extenuating his opponent's points.

8. **What fallacies do you find, and what kind?** Using your understanding of logic from the last section, students should find fallacies, if any. Some discourses will not contain any fallacies. It is still important for students to use their critical thinking skills in identifying the logical appeal (or lack thereof) of a writer or speaker. ("In paragraph 11 he commits the fallacy of *ad baculum* by saying, ...")

9. **What figures of speech do you find, and what kind?** This required section only pertains to students in Rhetoric II after they have learned Figures of Speech.

An analysis is written in paragraph form, in full sentences. Do not use the personal pronoun (I, me, my, mine) or the second person (you, your, we, our), so that you develop your analytical skills as a writer. **You must answer the questions WHY? HOW? and WHERE? as you write.**

Students usually choose one of two different methods for analyzing:

1. They might answer each question in order, or
2. They can answer the questions as they move through the discourse, from the introduction through the conclusion. That means that as they analyze the introduction they are also telling what kind of introduction it is, what kind of discourse it is, how this introduction supports the thesis (or if the thesis is in the introduction, say so here), how he persuades in the introduction, and so forth. Then the student moves on to discuss the rest of the discourse, in the order in which it is written. While this second method may seem more complicated, it actually uses higher-level thinking and organizational skills.

NOTES

Day One, Lesson Sixteen Assignment:
Read John F. Kennedy's Inaugural Address. Answer the analysis questions on the <u>worksheet</u>. Be sure to provide examples to prove your point.

Day Two, Lesson Sixteen Assignment:
Write the analysis of John F. Kennedy's Inaugural Address fully. Use complete paragraphs and provide examples.

Days Three and Four, Lesson Sixteen Assignment:
Read and analyze Thomas Jefferson's Inaugural Address.

LESSON SEVENTEEN

RESEARCH (WEEK NINETEEN)

At this point the teacher may be ready to assign a research paper project for the class. It could come at this time, or the teacher could wish to move it to an earlier time in the school year.

Resources

Since most students have done research projects in the past, this will mostly be review. However, students must all be up to speed on their research (and research paper-writing) skills so that not a lot of time much be spent teaching the "grammar" of writing a research paper.

Much research today is done on the Internet. While this is a handy source, two problems might arise if this is the only source used. First, not all Internet sites are reliable sources of information. You will not be able to rely on "Dave's World War Two Page" as readily as you could on a university or museum web site. Remember, too, that some unreliable sources will not contain the full text of a document, or it might be full of transcription errors, or just plain factually wrong.

Second, some very reliable, informative sources have not yet made it to the Internet. You may be missing out on some important facts or fascinating sources from books or old magazines if you rely solely on the Internet.

Note Cards

Every bit of information that is obtained for the research paper must be on note cards. Even the list of sources themselves must be listed on note cards. Use a separate card for each source. A source card must have the same information on it that you will use on your bibliography: Author or editor, title of article or book, publication title, publishing company, city, and year. The page numbers that you use may be placed here, but they most certainly must be placed on the card on which you write the information from that page! Give each source a code: A, B, C, etc.

Every card will contain the source code. On the top right corner, place the code you have assigned for that source. (For instance, if your first source is a book by John Smith, assign code A to that book and make sure that every card containing information from this book has the A on the top right hand corner.) This way you will never lose track of where you got the information.

Each card must also contain a topic word. If your paper is to discuss Civil War armaments, you will want to break down the paper into smaller subjects, such as canons, sidearms, bayonets, rapid-fire guns, etc. The card should have these topic words written at the top for easier organization.

Each card should also contain the page number(s) used. Try to write only on one side of the card. Number the card (A1, A2, A3, etc., for the source and the number of the cards from that source).

Outline
A topical outline is necessary for organizing all the information into a paper that progresses well, makes sense, and flows logically. Different teachers require different formats. I prefer to see topical outlines rather than full sentences, as this is a tool for the student. Items in Roman numerals should be major sections of the paper (Introduction, Body, Conclusion). Capital letters should indicate paragraphs. Think of the organization of this paper to follow the Arrangement we have learned in Rhetoric. What kind of introduction will you use? Where is the thesis? How are you supporting the thesis?

Thesis
Since this is something we have spent time learning in Rhetoric, a thesis statement must be included. Remember that a thesis statement is one or two sentences that affirm or deny something about a particular subject. Your research and the paper you write must support your thesis statement. This is a major portion of your grade.

Standard Format (MLA)
Every paper must adhere to a particular style format. Many schools use the MLA style, as this is what most colleges and universities require.

Bibliography/footnotes
Every paper must contain a bibliography (now called "Works Cited"). See a style book (MLA) for the format for a Works Cited page. Today most universities do not require footnotes. Endnotes (called in-text citations) are the most accepted way to refer to your sources. Refer to MLA for use of endnotes. I require citations. I will hand out a Style Manual as we begin this section of the class.

Days One-Four, Lesson Seventeen

Spend this week (and perhaps more) gathering research and organizing information for your research paper. A due date will be assigned.

THE TOPICS, AN AID TO INVENTION (WEEKS TWENTY AND TWENTY-ONE)

The writer or orator must have a body of knowledge from which to draw, before beginning to write on any certain topic. One draws from his extensive knowledge on a subject, or researches a certain topic, before beginning to write. *Topics* falls under the category of "what to write about." The subject of *Topics* is considered an aid to invention. There are three aids to invention: The common topics, the special topics, and external (research). We have looked at research and completed our research paper by now (one would hope!). Special topics involve certain discourses such as forensic or deliberative.

The Common Topics will provide students with a stock of general lines of argument that can be used in the development of any subject. These might be for any sort of occasion, as Aristotle described. His list of types of Common Topics is extensive, and a few of them have been outlined as follows.

Division
Division lists the parts that go to make something up, in an effort to define it. Here one lays out the organization of the exposition or argument that is to follow. An argument then might elaborate on the list as stated in the division. One could think of Division as a simple list that elaborates on the parts of the discourse. When arguing, this can be used to establish the grounds for an argument by elimination: one provides alternatives, then eliminates each one to arrive at the conclusion you want.

Corbett explained the use of division in the following manner: "A person in these circumstances might steal for any one of these reasons: (A)...; (B)...; (C)...; (D)... Now, we have firmly established that A and B could not possibly have been my client's motives. Furthermore, not even the prosecution has suggested in this trial that C or D could have been my client's motives. Since none of the possible motives are applicable in this case, it is clear that my client is innocent of the charge of stealing" (Corbett, *Classical Rhetoric*, 92). This is not only useful in a court trial (Forensic); it is useful in expository writing and in argumentative discourse.

Comparison

Comparison is a common method for teaching, defining, or reasoning—holding up two or more things to examine them for their relationships or differences.

Similarity, under the category of Comparison, is "the likeness of two or more things...the basic principle behind all inductive argument and all analogy. In induction: we note similarity among a number of instances and make an inference about a further unobserved or unconfirmed instance" (Corbett, *Classical Rhetoric*, 93). Analogy uses the similarities of similar topics (for example: If homosexuality is a sin, so is promiscuity). An analogy argues that if two things are alike in one or two characteristics, they are probably alike in another characteristic (argues from the similarities of dissimilar things). Analogy doesn't prove anything, but it has persuasive value.

The similarities between two things must concern valid, not trivial pieces of information. For an example of similarity, look in paragraph 25 from Martin Luther King Jr.'s "Letter from Birmingham Jail." For an example of analogy, look in paragraph 19 of Edmund Burke's "Letter to a Noble Lord."

Difference

Difference contrasts two or more things. It is used to gather arguments for confirmation or refutation. For examples of difference, read "Letter to a Noble Lord," paragraph 3; and "The Federalist No. 10," paragraph 15.

For more discussion of difference, read paragraph 16 of "Letter from Birmingham Jail." The discussion in "Letter from Birmingham Jail" progresses in the following manner:

- Just law: squares with the moral law of God. Unjust law: out of harmony with moral law.
- Just law: uplifts human personality. Unjust law: human law not rooted in eternal law.
- Just law becomes unjust: I/thou to I/it; relegates persons to the status of things.
- Segregation is separation (law on people): separation is sin; goes against the moral law of God.
- Integration is morally right--obey it. Segregation is morally wrong--disobey it.

Figure out the syllogism (one or more) you can find in here.

Day One, Lesson Eighteen Assignment:
To prepare for what's coming up, read Martin Luther King Jr.'s "I Have a Dream" speech. Find the emotional and ethical language he uses. You'll notice quite a few. List them and tell what kind of emotional or ethical appeal you have found, and where it's from. List at least five of each in a bulleted list.

Day Two, Lesson Eighteen Assignment:
Time to write another opinion piece of 500-700 words relating to a current topic of concern to you. This time use a quote from another source in your opinion piece to support your view, or use it by way of refutation (refute the quote with logic). Post it according to class standards.

Day Three, Lesson Eighteen Assignment:
Read and analyze Frederick Douglass' "I Hear the Mournful Wail of Millions" from the *Historic Speeches* book.

Day Four, Lesson Eighteen Assignment:
Analyze Martin Luther King Jr.'s "Letter From Birmingham Jail." Please note that this discourse does not follow the classic arrangement. Instead of pointing out the divisions, do the following: Find the three major questions the clergy asks him, and he answers. Then find the three grave disappointments he lists. The rest of your analysis should be the same (thesis, support, etc.).

ADDITIONAL NOTE: There were three main types of analogy. In the original Greek sense, analogy involved a comparison of two proportions or relations. Thus 'principle' was said to be an analogical term when said of a point and a spring of water because a point is related to a line as a spring is related to a river. This type of analogy came to be called the analogy of proportionality. In the second sense, analogy involved a relation between two things, of which one is primary and the other secondary. Thus 'healthy' was said to be an analogical term when said of a dog and its food because while the dog has health in the primary sense, its food is healthy only secondarily as contributing to or causing the health of the dog. This second type of analogy became known as the analogy of attribution, and its special mark was being said in a prior and a posterior sense (*per prius et posterius*). A third type of analogy, sometimes appealed to by theologians, appealed to a relation of likeness between God and creatures. Creatures are called good or just because their goodness or justice imitates or reflects the goodness or justice of God. This type of analogy was called the analogy of imitation or participation. (http://plato.stanford.edu/entries/analogy-medieval/ date accessed: 3-17-2003)

LESSON NINETEEN

TOPICS, CONTINUED (WEEK TWENTY-TWO)

Remember that Topics concerns subjects that we can come up with or ways to put together an argument (Invention). We are continuing to look at methods of invention here—ways to persuade an audience. While you read through this list, think of ways that these methods would supply material for an argument.

Degree
Differences in Degree deal with *more or less.* Aristotle provided a list of topics of degree in his Book I, Chapter 7 of The Rhetoric. Here are a few for discussion purposes.

1. "A greater number of things can be considered more desirable than a smaller number of the same things." This regards things of the same species. This is helpful only when all other things are equal.
2. "That which is an *end* is a greater good than that which is only a *means.*"
3. "What is scarce is greater than what is abundant."
4. "What men of practical wisdom would choose is a greater good than what ignorant men would choose."
5. "What the majority of men would choose is better than what the minority would choose."
6. "What men would really like to possess is a greater good than what men would merely like to give the impression of possessing."
7. "If a thing does not exist where it is more likely to exist, it will not exist where it is less likely to exist."

Regarding idea Six, above, Machiavelli said that if a man who sought power was not virtuous, he should at least *seem* virtuous in order to get what he wants. This implies that power is a greater good than morals, because power is what the ruler really wants, and in order to get it he must *pretend* to be virtuous. In other words, *The end justifies the means.*

Look at idea Seven, above. This is an *a fortiori* argument, meaning "from the stronger." It works from the greater to the lesser: "If a man lies to his wife, he will have no problem lying to his friends." This might also work from the lesser to the greater.

Day One, Lesson Nineteen Assignment:
Review and comment on at least three of your classmates' opinion pieces according to class standards.

Day Two, Lesson Nineteen Assignment:
Give at least two examples of Numbers Three and Four, above (each). Are these ideas true and valid? Why or why not? Discuss each one in turn. Use logic. Think in terms of how you would use these methods to persuade someone. Two to four paragraphs.

Day Three, Lesson Nineteen Assignment:
Read and analyze Cicero's "Among us you can dwell no longer" speech from *Historic Speeches*. Use the worksheet and hand it in.

Day Four, Lesson Nineteen Assignment:
Give at least two examples of Number Five, above. You can use examples from your own life or from things you have read. What kind of appeal does this topic of degree use? What is the fallacy here? Sometimes what the majority wants is not always the best. Under what conditions would this be true?

LESSON TWENTY

TOPICS CONTINUED (WEEK TWENTY-THREE)

Remember that a rhetorician's job is to persuade his audience of the possibility of something happening. Where in logic we arrived at absolutes by deduction and syllogistic reasoning, in rhetoric we want to <u>persuade</u>. So a cause might not be the absolute reason; what matters is whether we can <u>convince</u> our audience that this is <u>possible</u>.

Cause and effect

An effect can have a number of possible causes (a fallen tree could have fallen because it is old and rotten, or it fell in a wind, or was cut down). Find *the* cause that works. There is then a progression of thought that we follow to find the cause for a certain effect.

1. *The cause we assign for an effect must be capable of producing the effect.* (If there is a strange puddle on the kitchen floor, we wonder what caused that effect. The refrigerator may have leaked, or the toddler may have tried to pour herself a cup of juice. But then, there is that new puppy...)

2. *Once we think we have found sufficient cause for something, we must decide whether there might be other causes.* (Yes, there is the toddler who loves to drink juice, but the puppy hasn't been house-trained yet...)

3. *Consider whether the potential causes could exist* (if the toddler was at her grandmother's house, she is ruled out as a suspect).

4. *Consider whether the supposed cause would consistently produce an effect and whether it would without a doubt produce the same effect* (does the puppy always make messes on the floor, or is he getting better at waiting to go outside?).

5. *Post hoc ergo propter hoc.* This fallacy says, "after this, therefore because of this," or "every time I wash my car it rains." This supposes that *when two events occur near to each other in time, one has an effect on the other* (if the puppy walks through the room, there will always be a mess in that room).

In rhetoric we can argue from an effect back to a cause, or we can start with a cause and argue that it will produce a particular effect or effects.

Antecedent and Consequence

Antecedent and Consequence answers the following question: If A happens, does B follow? "Only if this man believes in Jesus Christ, he has eternal life in heaven." There is usually an implied premise with this argument. Here, it is "all believers in Jesus Christ will have eternal life." Often it is easy to refute an implied premise (see the section on enthymemes).

Regarding Antecedent and Consequence, read Martin Luther King Jr.'s "Letter from Birmingham Jail," paragraph 23.

Day One, Lesson Twenty Assignment:
Read Jonathan Swift's "A Modest Proposal." Use the worksheet for this lesson to answer questions about this discourse. Answer the questions only on the worksheet.

Day Two, Lesson Twenty Assignment:
After reading "A Modest Proposal," you can see how Swift used satire to draw attention to a problem. His "solution" is so gruesome that it is ridiculous. Here is an opportunity to brainstorm for which social ill of the day you would most like to propose a modest solution. This would have to be profitable to society (or a portion thereof) and almost so ludicrous that it might actually be considered by society. 1) Describe the problem, 2) Provide a solution, and 3) Describe the benefit to society.

Day Three, Lesson Twenty Assignment:
Read the first two sections of "The Communist Manifesto" found in the Appendix. Feel free to read the whole thing; it is very informative for today's Christians. In five paragraphs discuss its use of definition and historical analysis as he goes to prove his point (and what is his point? Discuss this also). We will write more about this in the future. Use whatever outside sources you would like to cite.

Day Four, Lesson Twenty Assignment:
Read and analyze Thomas Cranmer's "I shall declare unto you my very faith." Find examples of Antecedent and Consequence as well.

LESSON TWENTY-ONE

TOPICS, CONTINUED (WEEK TWENTY-FOUR)

The following arguments are used in many ways and on many occasions. Think of how these arguments are useful. Go beyond the obvious. Where can these arguments be useful in the biblical worldview?

Contradictions

A thing cannot at the same time and in the same respect be and not be. One cannot say "the light is shining" and "the light is not shining" at the same time. You either breathe or you don't breathe—you cannot do both at the same time. Remember Aristotle's Laws of Truth; they have their origin here.

Circumstance

The Possible and the Impossible - prove that something is either possible or impossible. An excellent way to do this is to convince them that others have succeeded in doing similar things, or that what is proposed is not at all possible.

Read an example of possible/impossible in Madison's "Federalist No. 10," paragraph 8. What is described as possible or impossible? How does he prove his point?

Days One and Two, Lesson Twenty-one Assignment:
Regarding Contradictions, this topic can be applied in many arguments. It's rather simple: You either breathe or you don't breathe—you cannot do both at the same time. God either exists or He doesn't. This type of argument agrees with the Laws of Thought from early Logic lessons. Which Law of Thought is this? Write an argument using this Law, proving either: God's existence, creation versus evolution, or life beginning upon conception. (5 paragraphs)

OR Write an essay on the Possible/Impossible (5 paragraphs).

Day Three, Lesson Twenty-one Assignment:
Read and analyze Franklin Delano Roosevelt's First Inaugural Address. Use the worksheet and turn it in.

Day Four, Lesson Twenty-one Assignment:
At this point in your education you have probably read some about government theory and philosophy. Now that you have read "The Communist Manifesto" and some presidential speeches, have a class discussion about the role of government. What is the biblical view of government? Your teacher could assign some writing as a follow-up.

LESSON TWENTY-TWO

TOPICS, CONTINUED (WEEK TWENTY-FIVE)

Aristotle supposed some possible/impossible topics to consider. These may seem strange, or even ridiculous and useless, but perhaps we can use some of these topics to develop our own. Think of as many examples as possible for each one. Get realistic with your topic ideas. Think according to a biblical worldview. For a start, work on a creation/ evolution argument.

1. "If one of a pair of contraries is possible, then the other is possible, too." For example, if you can get a kitchen (bathroom, bedroom, etc.) messy, you can also clean it up (an argument used by countless parents).

2. "If one of a pair of similar things is possible, the other thing is possible, too." If it's possible for a person to write with a pencil, it's also possible he can write with a pen.

3. "If the more difficult of two things is possible, then the easier is possible too." If you can ride a unicycle, you can certainly ride a tricycle.

4. "If something can have a beginning, it can have an end, and conversely, if something can have an end, it can have a beginning."

5. "If the parts of a thing are possible, then the whole is possible, and conversely, if the whole is possible, the parts are possible." The first leaders of the U.S. argued this, because they saw that separate confederations were possible, so a confederation of states was also possible.

6. "If a thing can be produced without art or preparation, it certainly can be done with the help of art or planning." In other words, if it can be done at midnight the night before, it can be done a few days in advance, with planning.

Day One, Lesson Twenty-two Assignment:
Read and analyze Ronald Reagan's "Brandenburg Gate" speech.

Day Two, Lesson Twenty-two Assignment:
Rewrite an opinion piece from earlier this year. Base it on comments from your peers and your teacher. Make sure it is posted with the original so that your teacher and classmates can see the rewrite.

Day Three, Lesson Twenty-two Assignment:
Regarding topic number 6, how does this argument apply to the creation/evolution theory? Is this a benefit or a detriment to the creationist's argument? Is there another possible/impossible topic on this list that also could apply to the creation/evolution argument (either way)? If so, which one, and why?

Day Four, Lesson Twenty-two Assignment:
Read the two articles titled "What the Press Saw at the Brandenburg Gate" and "Tear Down This Wall: President Reagan's Most Famous Line was almost Deleted," found in the Appendix. Discuss these two articles, and Reagan's speech, in class and/or an essay. What impact does the discussion of this speech and its impact have on you as a student of Rhetoric? You might speak about the meaning of words, the risk one takes to say what is right, or others. If your teacher assigns an essay, it should be 5+ paragraphs.

LESSON TWENTY-THREE

TOPICS, CONTINUED
(WEEK TWENTY-SIX)

Past Fact and Future Fact

This topic deals with whether or not something has happened, and whether or not something would happen. An example of this is seen in Martin Luther King Jr.'s "Letter from Birmingham Jail," paragraph 44. The reference to **Past Fact** is useful in court trials, dealing with whether or not something has occurred.

Past Fact:
1. "If the less probable of two events has occurred, the more probable event is likely to have occurred, too." For example, "If the early believers found two disciples in Acts guilty of lying to God, couldn't it have been possible that they were also lying to their friends?" (This argument is also applicable in the topic of *Degree.*)
2. "If someone had the power and the desire and the opportunity to do something, then he or she has done it."

Future Fact supposes:
1. "If the power and the desire to do something are present, then that something will be done." In other words, if one possesses a gun, it is likely that it will be used.
2. "If the antecedents of something are present, then the natural consequences will occur." For example, if a drunk person has started his car, there will be an accident. (This one deals with chance and circumstances; it may not happen every time, but the likelihood is higher.)
3. "If the means are available, the end will be accomplished."

Day One, Lesson Twenty-three Assignment:
Find a scriptural argument that contains Past Fact/Future Fact arguments and discuss it in three or more paragraphs.

Day Two, Lesson Twenty-three Assignment:
Comment on at least three of your classmates' opinion pieces, using the forum. Make sure to spread your comments around; don't allow anyone to go "un-commented-upon."

Day Three, Lesson Twenty-three Assignment:
Does item number Five, above, mean that human nature is such that if the opportunity exists to take revenge, one will do so? Does this negate the power of the Holy Spirit to resist temptation? Either take the "devil's advocate" role or take the biblical argument against Aristotle. Explain your answer in 5 paragraphs.

Day Four, Lesson Twenty-three Assignment:
Read Pericles' Funeral Oration, found in the Appendix. To better understand it, outline this discourse by summing the main points paragraph by paragraph. (This can be done in outline form or in sentence form.) Next, answer the following questions in 2-3 paragraphs: What is the main point of his oration (besides honoring the dead)? Discuss what he believes is the source of Athens' greatness.

LESSON TWENTY-FOUR

TOPICS, CONTINUED (WEEK TWENTY-SEVEN) TESTIMONY

Testimony, according to Aristotle, derives its material from outside. For an example of testimony, see Martin Luther King Jr.'s "Letter from Birmingham Jail," paragraphs 15 and 32. Following are different types of Testimony.

Authority is an informed opinion by someone in control. It carries less weight today than it once did. It is not infallible, but it has great persuasive force. A psychiatrist would have more authority when testifying about emotional side effects of abuse than an ordinary citizen. Sometimes experts offer conflicting testimony. Then we rely on other criteria to decide which opinion to accept. Good questions for discussion are:

1. "Is there anything inconsistent, contradictory, or illogical in the expression of the opinion itself?"
2. "Do the experts harbor any prejudices that might influence or color the proffered opinion?"
3. "Do any of the experts have an axe to more grind? An advantage to gain? A score to settle?"
4. "Is one expert's opinion based on more recent, reliable information than the other's is?"
5. "Is one expert's opinion accepted by more experts? By the more authoritative experts?"
6. "What are the basic assumptions behind the expressions of opinion? Are any of these assumptions vulnerable? Does the exposure of these assumptions reveal that the conflict between the experts is more apparent than real because they are viewing the same matter from different points of view?" (Corbett, *Classical Rhetoric*, 113-114).

Testimonials were persuasive during Aristotle's time and can be just as persuasive today. They can be remarkably persuasive in certain circumstances and with certain audiences, but they can also be vulnerable to refutation. An example can be found in Martin Luther

King Jr.'s "Letter from Birmingham Jail," paragraphs 31 and 46. Types of testimonials are as follows:

- personal recommendation
- advertising
- public announcement on the TV or radio
- someone attesting to the character of another
- opinion poll
- best-seller list
- audience-rating

Statistics are used to confirm statements, settle contrary and contradictory assertions, and discredit assertions.

Remember that when a poll is taken in order to gain statistics, the way a question is asked will likely affect the answer. Pollsters enter into their survey-taking after they have made assumptions. They have anticipated certain results, so their questions will be worded in such a way as to obtain those results. They assume the following: people always know their own mind on questions put to them, and people will give truthful answers to questions put to them. However, pollsters do not take into account other issues such as people who want to harm the results and give answers other than the ones they truly believe. Other factors which adversely affect results would be a polling of an inadequate cross-section of people, which would then make the results come out differently (for example, if pollsters wanted to get a statistic on the number of minorities in a city, but they wanted to inflate the numbers, they would do most of their surveying in parts of the city where more of those minorities reside).

Day One, Lesson Twenty-four:
Revisit Pericles' Funeral Oration from Lesson Twenty-three. Compare it to Lincoln's Gettysburg Address and discuss the comparison/contrast between the two. At this point you should be able to compare not only the content, but the construction of the two discourses. Two to three paragraphs.

Day Two, Lesson Twenty-four:
Analyze "Planet of the Year." Pay attention to authority/testimonials here.

Days Three and Four, Lesson Twenty-four:
Find four articles and opinion pieces (two news articles, two opinion pieces)* about environmentalism (i.e., global warming/climate change, etc.). Look for the use of statistics and other facts to support the point of the article or opinion. Compare with the way "Planet of the Year" treats data and facts. Write a 1-2 page essay that 1)compares/contrasts the use of data and facts, and 2) comments on the authors' use to support his or her thesis. For purposes of this essay, choose one that you have researched from which to quote specifically. Use the others in your Works Cited list.

> *Note: be careful of the source for your information. You will find evenly balanced articles, and you will find shockingly biased articles. Simply be aware of the bias of certain sources and authors. You may decide to quote from extremely biased sources on either side. It may turn out to be the point of your essay!

LESSON TWENTY-FIVE

TOPICS, CONTINUED (WEEK TWENTY-EIGHT)

Maxims are precepts, proverbs, or famous sayings. They could be clichés such as "The early bird catches the worm" or "It's always darkest before the dawn." They can also be general statements about human actions, or about things that are to be chosen or avoided in human action (you don't judge a book by its cover). One should avoid using maxims on which to base one's argument, because if it is challenged, one may be unprepared to defend its truth, and thus we have drawn attention from the focus of our discourse and onto the maxim.

Law - statutes, contracts, testaments, records, and documents that can be drawn on to substantiate or refute a claim. Documents are hard to refute. They provide excellent, convincing proof, unless one cannot prove that the author really wrote it, the document was not signed by witnesses, it was a photocopy, or appeared to have been tampered with.

The wording of documents is always open to interpretation. The U.S. Constitution is the document upon which our government is based, but the Supreme Court's main function is to interpret the wording of the Constitution.

Precedent - something that has happened before. Precedents bring to bear on a present case what has been done in a similar case in the past (this is done in court cases all the time). Often someone will refer to an incident or example that should serve to strengthen one's case or harm his opponent's case. For example, when arguing that a woman has the right to an abortion, a lawyer will always point to the Supreme Court case of Roe vs. Wade, which set a precedent on the rights of women to choose abortion.

Day One, Lesson Twenty-five
Choose a topic important today and write a 500-700-word opinion piece that reflects a biblical worldview. Post it in the normal fashion.

Day Two, Lesson Twenty-five
Read Dale Bumpers' closing remarks during the impeachment trial of President Bill Clinton, found in the Appendix. Take time to analyze the types of refutation he uses. We'll look at this more closely in Rhetoric 2. Discuss the discourse and its main points, his use of logic and the other methods he used in his closing remarks.

Day Three, Lesson Twenty-five
Refer to Edmund Burke's "Letter to a Noble Lord" paragraph 19 and Martin Luther King Jr.'s "Letter from Birmingham Jail" paragraphs 6, 7, 14, 21, 43 and 45. Describe the precedent that is described in each example.

Day Four, Lesson Twenty-five
If there's time, choose another opinion piece that you have written this year and rewrite it, taking your teacher's and classmates' comments into account.

LESSON TWENTY-SIX

OPINION PIECES (WEEKS TWENTY-NINE THROUGH THIRTY-ONE)

Another form of persuasive communication can be found on the Editorial page of the newspaper or news magazine. This is a place where the dialogue is usually current and always strongly opinionated. This is a place where the voice of reason is badly needed, and where the voice of truth is often absent. This is the place where the Christian voice must be introduced.

Begin reading the opinion pages of the local newspaper. If you do not get a local paper, find one over the internet from a major city.

Letters to the editor are shorter, generally from 100-200 words in length. Opinion pieces are the longer ones. Some are written by the newspaper's editorial staff, others are written by syndicated columnists, and still others may be written by members of the local community.

Day One, Lesson Twenty-six Assignment

Bring three sample letters to the editor, found in your local or online paper, to class. Using your three letters to the editor, comment on each one in the following manner. Answer each question, for each point, with two or more sentences.

- What is the main point of the letter?
- Does the writer make his point well?
- Does he resolve the subject (come up with a good conclusion or answer to the issues.
- What fallacies do you find, if any? Or does the writer point out a fallacy? What is it?

Day Two, Lesson Twenty-six Assignment

In light of what you have been reading, why should a Christian write letters to the editor? What could a Christian contribute? What does God promise about His Word being sent out into the world? Three paragraphs.

Day Three, Lesson Twenty-six Assignment

Comment on three of your classmates' opinion pieces using the class forum. Use the standards that have been required all along.

Day Four, Lesson Twenty-six Assignment

Write a second opinion piece. This time, apply scripture to the topic: inject a verse, or part of a verse, into your letter. This is how you skillfully weave God's truth into a current topic for readers to see. For examples of letters to the editor that have skillfully woven scripture, go to http://amyfound.org/penpower. html to see how one organization encourages letters to the editor that work to disciple readers of the secular press. Make this 500-700 words, and post it to the class forum.

APPENDIX: WORKS CITED

Aristotle. *The Rhetoric*

Blair, Hugh. *Lectures on Rhetoric*, Abridged. New York: Collins & Co., 1831.

Cherry, Richard L. and Robert J. Conley and Bernard A. Hirsch, eds. *The Essay: Structure and Purpose*. Boston: Houghton Mifflin Company, 1975.

Cicero. *Ad C. Herrenium*. Trans. Harry Caplan. Loeb Classical Library. Cambridge, Massachusetts: Harvard University Press, 1989.

Corbett, Edward P.J. Classical Rhetoric for the Modern Student. Oxford: Oxford University Press, 4th Edition, 1999.

Crowley, Sharon and Debra Hawhee. *Classical Rhetoric for the Contemporary Student*. Boston: Allyn & Bacon, 1999.

Golden, James and Edward P.J. Corbett, eds. *The Rhetoric of Blair, Campbell, and Whately* .New York: Holt, Rinehart and Winston, 1968.

Hill, David J. *The Elements of Rhetoric and Composition*. New York: Sheldon and Company, 1886.

Hogins, James Burl and Robert E. Yarber, eds. *Reading Writing and Rhetoric*. Chicago: Science Research Associates, Inc., 1976.

MacArthur, Brian, ed. *Historic Speeches*. London: Penguin Books, 1995.

Nance, James. Intermediate Logic. Moscow ID, First Edition, 2002.

Wilson, Douglas and James Nance. Introductory Logic. Moscow, ID, Third Edition, 2002.

Appendix

A: Worksheets

B: Discourses for reading and analyzing

Rhetoric 1
Worksheets for completion

Instructions:

Use the following worksheets to help you complete your work. If there is not enough space provided, use extra paper. <u>Photocopy pages from this section to hand in these pages. Do not tear them out of your book.</u>

(For Mrs. Howat's online students: Please submit worksheets in electronic form. You will find individual worksheets linked to the website in a location I will describe to you.)

Worksheet for Day 3, Lesson 2

Title of discourse: Blood, Toil, Tears, and Sweat

Type of discourse:

Reasons:

Quotes to support (with paragraph numbers):

Worksheet for Days 1 through 4, Lesson 3
Title of discourse: "Socrates' Apology"
Type of discourse:
Reasons:

Quotes to support:

Title of discourse: "Gettysburg Address"
Type of discourse:
Reasons:

Quotes to support:

Title of discourse: "Heart and stomach of a king"
Type of discourse:
Reasons:

Quotes to support:

Title of discourse: "This was their finest hour"
Type of discourse:
Reasons:

Quotes to support:

Title of discourse: "They're smiling in heaven"
Type of discourse:
Reasons:

Quotes to support:

Worksheet for Day 3, Lesson 4.
Discourse: Hitler, February 1938 Note: Citations should read (1938, 4), where "4" is the paragraph number.
Type of discourse:

Quotes/reasons to support

Examples of emotional language (give paragraph #s)

Discourse: Hitler, May 1941 Note: Citations should read (1941, 4), where "4" is the paragraph number.
Type of discourse:

Quotes/reasons to support

Examples of emotional language (give paragraph #s)

Worksheet for Day 4, Lesson 7
Discourse: Sancton's "Planet of the Year"
Type of discourse
Reasons (give paragraph # and/or quotes to support)

Thesis
Reasons (give paragraph # and/or quotes to support)

Worksheet for Day 5, Lesson 8
Discourse: Cromwell's "Let God judge between me and you"
Methods of ingratiation in intro
Reasons (give paragraph # and/or quotes to support)

Type of introduction
Reasons (give paragraph # and/or quotes to support)

Type of discourse
Reasons (give paragraph # and/or quotes to support)

Thesis
Reasons (give paragraph # and/or quotes to support)

Worksheet for Day 6, Lesson 8
Discourse: Churchill's "Blood, Toil, Tears and Sweat"
Type of introduction
Reasons (give paragraph # and/or quotes to support)

Type of discourse
Reasons (give paragraph # and/or quotes to support)

Thesis
Reasons (give paragraph # and/or quotes to support)

Worksheet for Day 2, Lesson 9
Discourse: Socrates' "Apology"
Type of discourse:
Reasons (give quotes and paragraph numbers for support):

Type of introduction:
Reasons (give quotes and paragraph numbers for support):

How does he counteract prejudice?
Reasons (give quotes and paragraph numbers for support):

Worksheet for Day 3, Lesson 9
Discourse: Bauman's "Chronicle of an Undeception"
Type of discourse:
Reasons (give quotes and paragraph numbers for support):

Why is that the statement of facts?
Reasons (give quotes and paragraph numbers for support):

Thesis
Reasons (give quotes and paragraph numbers for support):

Worksheet for Day 1, Lesson 10
Discourse: Churchill's "Be Ye Men of Valour"
Thesis:
Reasons (give quotes and paragraph numbers for support):

Where/ how does he prove his case?
Reasons (give quotes and paragraph numbers for support):

Worksheet for Day 2, Lesson 10
Discourse: Nixon's "Checkers Speech"
List <u>at least 25</u>, and find all 4 types of refutation.
Ethical refutation (list paragraph number plus a brief phrase from the quote)

1.

2.

3.

4.

5.

6.

7.

Emotional refutation (list paragraph number plus a brief phrase from the quote)

1.

2.

3.

4.

5.

6.

7.

Rational refutation (list paragraph number plus a brief phrase from the quote)

1.

2.

3.

4.

5.

6.

7.

Wit refutation (list paragraph number plus a brief phrase from the quote)

1.

2.

3.

4.

5.

6.

7.

Worksheet for Day 3, Lesson 10
Socrates' "Apology"
Type of Refutation
List where found, add brief quotes
Ethical

Emotional

Rational

Wit

Worksheet for Day 1, Lesson 11
Chamberlain's speech from 1938
Thesis:
Where found/brief quote/support:

Type of discourse:
Where found/brief quote/support:

How he concludes:
Where found/brief quote/support

Refutation:
Where found/brief quote/support

Introduction:
Where found/brief quote/support

Worksheet for Day 1, Lesson 12
Wycliffe's defense against the Pope
What does Wycliffe define?
Where found/brief quote/support

What is his purpose?
Where found/brief quote/support

Who is his audience?
Where found/brief quote/support

What are the circumstances?
Where found/brief quote/support

Worksheet for Day 3, Lesson 12
Colson's "Pretty Stones and Dead Babies"
What does Colson define?
Where found/brief quote/support

What is his purpose?
Where found/brief quote/support

What is his thesis?
Where found/brief quote/support

Definition worksheet (Day 4, Lesson 12: Parts 1-3)
Part 1
Church -- Definition:

Genus:
Material cause:
Efficient cause:
Formal cause:
Final cause:

Restaurant -- Definition:

Genus:
Material cause:
Efficient cause:
Formal cause:
Final cause:

Carpet -- Definition:

Genus:
Material cause:
Efficient cause:
Formal cause:
Final cause:

Desk -- Definition:

Genus:
Material cause:
Efficient cause:
Formal cause:
Final cause:

Cross -- Definition:

Genus:
Material cause:
Efficient cause:
Formal cause:
Final cause:
(Worksheet continued on next page)
Hymnal -- Definition:

Genus:
Material cause:
Efficient cause:
Formal cause:
Final cause:

Dictionary -- Definition:

Genus:
Material cause:
Efficient cause:
Formal cause:
Final cause:

Piano -- Definition:

Genus:
Material cause:
Efficient cause:
Formal cause:
Final cause:

Bible -- Definition:

Genus:
Material cause:
Efficient cause:
Formal cause:
Final cause:

Plate -- Definition:

Genus:
Material cause:
Efficient cause:
Formal cause:
Final cause:

(Worksheet continued on next page)

Part 2

Now choose four of the above nouns and write a full definition in your own words, using Genus and all four Differentiae. Color code or label the differentiae.

Noun 1:

Noun 2:

Noun 3:

Noun 4:

Part 3

Now make up your own new noun. It <u>must be a thing</u>, not an abstract concept. Write your own definition of it. Include Genus and all four Differentiae. Color code or label them.

Your own noun:

Definition, with Genus and Differentiae:

Worksheet for Day 5, Lesson 12
Bible verse/enthymeme study
Glory,Ephesians 1:6, 12, 14 (one definition for all)
    The phrase in which the word is found:
    Definition of word

Glory,Luke 2:32
    The phrase in which the word is found:
    Definition of word

Glory,2 Corinthians 3:7
    The phrase in which the word is found:
    Definition of word

Wisdom,James 3:15
    The phrase in which the word is found:
    Definition of word

Wisdom, James 3:17
    The phrase in which the word is found:
    Definition of word

(Worksheet continued on next page)

Holy, Exodus 3:5
    The phrase in which the word is found:
    Definition of word

Holy, Joel 3:17
    The phrase in which the word is found:
    Definition of word

Holy, 1 Peter 1:13-16
    The phrase in which the word is found:
    Definition of word

Grace, Acts 14:3
    The phrase in which the word is found:
    Definition of word

Grace, Romans 11:6
    The phrase in which the word is found:
    Definition of word

Grace, 2 Corinthians 8:7
    The phrase in which the word is found:
    Definition of word

Grace, Galatians 1:3
    The phrase in which the word is found:
    Definition of word

Worksheet for Day 3, Lesson 13
Huss, "The Church—Not Man but Christ"
Logic? Point out any logical techniques you can find.
Where found/cite examples:

What does he define?
Where found/cite examples:

Thesis
Where found:

How does he support thesis?
Where found/cite examples:

Worksheet for Day 1, Lesson 14
Wilberforce's speech
Type of discourse:
Where found/cite examples:

Thesis:
Where found:

How does he support thesis?
Where found/cite examples

Refutation method
Where found/cite examples

Types of ethical appeal
Where found/cite examples

Worksheet for Day 2, Lesson 14
Stalin's speech November, 1941
Type of discourse:
Where found/cite examples

Thesis:
Where found:

How does he support thesis?
Where found/cite examples:

Kinds of ethical appeal
Where found/cite examples

Worksheet for Day 3, Lesson 14
Joel Belz, "The Lie is Marching On"
Thesis
Where found:

How does he support thesis?
Where found/cite examples:

Type of Introduction
Where found/cite examples:

Kinds of ethical appeal
Where found/cite examples:

Jeopardize ethical appeal?
Where found/cite examples:

Worksheet for Day 2, Lesson 15
Macaulay, "Lord Clive"
and
Pope Gregory, "Attack on Wycliffe"
Emotions
How does Macaulay arouse emotions?
Where found/cite examples:

Emotions
How does Pope Gregory arouse emotions?
Where found/cite examples:

Full Analysis worksheet.
Use this for <u>any analysis you will do</u>, except for Martin Luther King Jr.'s "Letter from Birmingham Jail," found in the Lesson 18 sheets. This worksheet can be photocopied or electronically copied and pasted into a file.

Name of Discourse:

Type of discourse
Where found/cite examples:

What is the thesis?
Where found:

Divisions
Where found:

How does each division support the thesis? (Use the back of this paper—this is a long answer.)
Where found/cite examples:

What kind of intro is it?
Where found/cite examples:

(Worksheet continued on next page)
Page 2, analysis worksheet
How does he persuade? (Use the back of this paper—this is a long answer.)
Where found/cite examples:

How does he conclude, according to Aristotle's methods?
Where found/cite examples:

What fallacies do you find? Where found/cite examples:

Discourse: Martin Luther King Jr.'s "Letter from Birmingham Jail"
Type of discourse:
Where found/cite examples:

What is the thesis?
Where found:

What kind of intro is it?
Where found/cite examples:

Question 1, where, and how does it support the thesis?

Question 2, where, and how does it support the thesis?

Question 3, where, and how does it support the thesis?

(Worksheet continued on next page)

What is his first disappointment? Where? How does it support the thesis?

What is his second disappointment? Where? How does it support the thesis?

What is his third disappointment? Where? How does it support the thesis?

How does he persuade? (Use the back of this paper—this is a long answer.)
Where found/cite examples:

How does he conclude, according to Aristotle's methods?
Where found/cite examples:

What fallacies do you find?

Worksheet for Day 1, Lesson 20 Swift's Modest Proposal
Answer the following questions:

1. What point does he try to make with his satire?

2. Who are the papists and why does he use them as an example?

3. What does he comment on in the second point? (Para. 22)

4. The third point? (Para. 23)

5. What are his points in the last two paragraphs?

DISCOURSES FOR READING IN RHETORIC 1

Note: any other discourses mentioned may be found in Historic Speeches, edited by Brian MacArthur. Most of these and other discourses can be found on the internet as well. However, some will vary in style, and some may even mistakenly edit out some paragraphs or sentences. Read carefully.

Table of Contents
Discourses for Reading

THE CHRONICLE OF AN UNDECEPTION
BY MICHAEL BAUMAN

Michael Bauman is the Director of Christian Studies and a professor of Theology and Culture at Hillsdale College in Michigan. He is also a tutor in Renaissance Literature and Theology at the Centre for Medieval and Renaissance Studies in Oxford and a research fellow at the Kuyper Institute. Mr. Bauman has written or edited 14 books and published nearly 40 articles. This article won an Amy Foundation Journalism award in 1996.

I confess to believing at one time or another nearly all the pervasive and persistent fantasies of the '60s. In the words of Joni Mitchell's anthem for the Woodstock nation, I thought all I had to do was "get back to the land to set my soul free." I thought that flowers had power, that love could be free, and that the system was to blame. By 1968, I had the whole world figured out. I knew the cause of every evil—America—and I knew the solution to every problem—freedom and tolerance. If truth be told, of course, I knew nothing, at least nothing worth knowing. I knew how to posture, but not how to stand. I knew how to protest, but not how to protect. I knew how to work up an impressive case of moral outrage, but I didn't know morality. I knew about peace, but I didn't know enough to fight for it. I knew about self-indulgence, self esteem, self-preservation, and self-expression, but I didn't know about self-sacrifice and self-control.

Worse still, I didn't even know myself. I didn't know what Socrates knew about me—that I entered this world in a state of total and seamless ignorance, and that my ignorance could never be breached as long as I remained blissfully unaware of it. I didn't know what St. Augustine knew about me that the well of my soul was poisoned, and that whatever was down in the well would come up in the bucket. St. Augustine also knew this about my soul: No matter how hard it tried, no matter where it looked, it could never find its test anywhere but in God. I didn't know what Edmund Burke knew about me—that no government could fix what ailed me, either by the things it did or by the things it did not. The most any state could do was to help protect me from myself and from others. Most importantly, however, I didn't know that I was Everyman. When I learned that, I stopped being a liberal. My deepest problems, like those of all persons, are not susceptible to government solution—a rock-hard fact that explodes the pretensions of the left and its allegedly omni-competent state.

Like almost all dissidents of my generation, I was a protester without a plan and a visionary without a vision. I had not yet learned that you see only what you are able to see, and I was able to see only the egalitarian, relativistic, self-gratifying superstitions of the secular, wayward, Left. Please do not think that this was simply a case of prelapsarian innocence. It was not. It was ignorance and it was evil, although I would have denied it at the time.

Only slowly did I come to understand that my fellow dissidents and I had taken for ourselves the easiest and least productive of all tasks, that of denigrator. And only slowly did I come to understand that to destroy is easy, that to build is hard, and that to preserve is hardest of all.

But it was worse even than that, because my fellow dissidents and I were blind to the most obvious truths, especially to what Russell Kirk and others have called the tragic vision of life—the profound realization that evil is not something "out there," it is something "in here." The tragic vision of life arises from the fact that we are flawed—deeply, desperately, tragically flawed—and we cannot be trusted. We are broken at the soul; our defect is life wide and heart deep. Though we are capable of reason, because of our selfish passions and our moral weaknesses, we are rarely reasonable. We ourselves are what is chiefly wrong with the world. We are this planet's most malignant and enduring ailment. We have our dignity, to be sure, but we have our horror as well. I can tell you this: I did not wake up until I met the enemy face to face. I met him in the mirror. We all do.

I had to learn to stare squarely into that face in the mirror, into the face of hard, fallen reality, and not to flinch. I did not, in fact I could not, comprehend the tragic vision of life until I learned that the problem of the human heart is at the heart of the human problem. Once I examined with care and honesty the habits of my own heart and those of my dissident friends, I learned that C.S. Lewis was right: to be one of the sons of Adam or the daughters of Eve is both glory enough to raise the head of the lowest beggar and shame enough to lower the head of the highest king. I am a human being. That is my wealth; that is my poverty.

Before that undeception, I was like all other cultural and political liberals, I had fallen prey to what Jeane Kirkpatrick identified as the error of misplaced malleability. I thought that human institutions could be reshaped at will to fit the plans already existing inside my head. It cannot be done. Human institutions arise from human action; human action arises from human nature; and human nature is notoriously intractable. Apart from the grace of God, human nature cannot be fixed, no matter how badly it needs fixing. I finally learned that my deepest need was not more freedom, on the one hand, and not more government, on the other. I needed the grace and guidance of God. Until I understood that, I remained shamelessly superficial.

I had to put my insipid and airy romanticism where it belonged, on the burgeoning junk pile of the fatally flawed and conclusively overthrown fantasies to which the human mind seems continually to give rise. Not romanticism but religion, not Byron but the Bible, not poetry but Paul, not Voltaire but virtue, not trends but tradition, not idealism but ideas, not genius but grace, not freedom but faith could cure me. I had to exchange Wordsworth for the Word and revolution for repentance. Thus, while some of the things I valued were useful and good, they were not properly fundamental. I had to put first things first.

The tragic vision of life humbled me. From it I learned that it was not my prerogative to invent wisdom and virtue. That had already been done. My responsibility was to listen to the One who invented them and to those whom He taught. Wisdom and virtue, I had to learn, were not born with my generation or with Rousseau's, or Matthew Arnold's, or even Eugene McCarthy's. I had to learn in the last half of the twentieth century what was already old news even in the days of Jeremiah, the ancient prophet who wrote, "Stand at the crossroads, and look, and ask for the ancient paths, where the good way lies; and walk in it, and find rest for your souls" (Jer. 6:16).

Wisdom is found by walking the "ancient paths." Those "ancient paths" led through the wilderness, through the sea, even through the valley of the shadow of death, and not through Berkeley, Columbia the village, Height-Ashbury, Altamont, Watts, and not Woodstock.

The tragic vision of life also taught me that order is the most fundamental of all political and social needs. Because it is, I learned that the police are not pigs. They never were, and are not now, an occupying army intent upon destroying my freedom. Quite the opposite; imperfect as they sometimes are, the police are the guardians of freedom and the paid protectors of life and property. In the line of duty, some of them even died for me. The tragic vision of life taught me that you cannot reject authority—whether civil, familial, cultural or divine—and yet live in an orderly world. When you "off the pigs" (of whatever sort) you give birth to an outlaw culture, not to freedom. To live outside the rules, to live outside authority, to live without the wisdom of the ages and of God, is to court slavery and death. Enforceable law and law enforcement are requirements of the first rank. Because human nature is what it is, with our great volumes of enforceable law, freedom is impossible. As Dean Clarence Manion observed in the very last line he wrote before his death in 1979, "a society that is not held together by its teaching and observance of the laws of Almighty God is unfit for human habitation and doomed to destroy itself."

When is freedom not enough? Every time truth and righteousness are at stake. In a fallen world, that is almost always. Freedom must be exercised according to the dictates of truth and virtue, never the other way around. Freedom must be limited by the demands of justice, love and revelation. The most important consideration regarding any action is not "is it free?" but "is it good?" When I learned that, I stopped being a Libertarian. Freedom, furthermore, is an incomplete concept. Whenever someone insists upon freedom, you must ask, "freedom to do what?" You must ask that question because freedom, like tyranny, has its unintended and unforeseen consequences, some of which are colossally vile. In passing I name but one—abortion.

From the tragic vision of life I learned that you have to do what is right whether it suits you or not. In the '60s, we hardly did anything that did not suit us. I also learned that the enemy is not the CIA, not the FBI, and not the GOP; it is the NEA, NOW, NBC, ABC, CBS, DNC, WCC, and NPR, indeed the entire grab bag of alphabetized, leftist, subverters of culture, of tradition and of revelation. I learned that those who deprive themselves of the wisdom of western tradition are no more free than a baby abandoned by its parents to do as it pleases. I learned that politics is not about equality, but justice; that personal action is not about freedom, but righteousness; and that sex is not about pleasure, but love and privilege and posterity.

Those things and more I learned from the tragic vision of life. I commend them to you. They taught me that in many ways the '60s were twisted and misshapen.

The '60s are over, and it's a good thing. The '60s were a bad idea, if for no other reason than because the '60s had no ideas, only selfish desires hiding behind the shallow slogans and free-lance nihilism emblazoned on psychedelic bumper stickers, slogans like "I dissent, therefore I am." The only things about which we were intellectually modest in the '60s were the claims of objective truth. We seemed unable to wrap our minds around even the most obvious ideas. We seemed unable to realize, for example, that you cannot raise your consciousness until you have one. The '60s were perhaps the most unconscious decade in centuries. It was a time of suffocating intellectual mediocrity, from which our nation has not yet recovered.

I can imagine a student hearing these remarks and wondering, "This all might be well and good, but what does it have to do with me? I wasn't even alive in the '60s."

My answer is simply this: While the '60s are over, they are not dead, not by a long shot. They live, indeed they thrive, not only in the White House juvenocracy, but in the faculty lounges and endowed chairs of nearly every college and university in the United States. Tenured faculty members everywhere have traded their tie-dyed T-shirts and their bell bottom jeans for a cap and gown. Those faculty members are the entrenched purveyors of an unexamined and indefensible hand-me-down Marxism, and of what Allan Bloom called nihilism with a happy ending. They have become paid agents of the very colleges and universities they once tried to burn to the ground, and not because they gave up on the dreams of the '60s. What they failed to do as protestors they have succeeded in doing as professors. Quite possibly they have done it to you, because the entire teaching profession, from the pre-kindergarten level to the postgraduate, has become a political captive of the cultural Left. Like roving street gangs prowling the halls of academe, power hungry bands of leftist professors everywhere have instigated countless institutional turf wars, most of which they won. They succeeded in burying the accumulated wisdom of the ages in the name of learning; in overthrowing academic freedom in the name of tolerance; in stifling debate in the name of openness; in exalting egalitarianism above all other ideas in the name of equality; and in segregating and tribalizing the university, the nation, and the culture by gender, by age, by religion, by race, and by sexual preference, all in the name of unity. The schools and colleges that hire and then tenure them commit academic treason. I simply remind you that any intellectual community that is unwilling or unable to identify its enemies cannot defend itself. David Horowitz was exactly right: those who cherish free institutions, and the culture of wisdom and virtue that sustains them, must stand up boldly against the barbarians already inside the gates.

Because the '60s live, the '90s have become irrational, ignorant, and morally illiterate, as Mortimer Adler, William Bennett, and William Kirk Kilpatrick all recently demonstrated. If the '60s were majestically self-indulgent, the '90s are perhaps the most self-congratulatory decade our nation has ever seen, and not because we have succeeded where all other generations have failed, but in spite of the fact that we have failed where all other American generations have succeeded—in learning to worship. The '90s are a decade determined to ignore, if not belittle and malign, beauty, truth and goodness; three things most moderns foolishly believe are in the eye of the beholder. The '90s are the sworn enemy of revelation and of righteousness. If the threefold mantra of the '60s was "tune in, turn on and drop out," that of the '90s is comprised of that earlier mantra's four silly children, four sentences that no thinking man ever permits himself to utter in the face of a moral challenge, sentences like, "Everything is relative," "There is no right or wrong," "There are no absolutes," and "Who's to say?"

If you cannot figure out why belief in those four sentences is the death of learning and of virtue, then perhaps for that very reason you can understand why I spend nearly all my time and energy as a professor and as a writer defending the ancient liturgy of the enlightened mind—that right and wrong are matters of fact, not matters of feeling; that without God there is no good; that justice is not equality; that new is not necessarily better; and that relativism, secularism, and pragmatism are not the friends of truth and goodness. The denizens of modernity probably do not realize, and probably do not care, that they are the befuddled and bedeviled lackeys of designer truth, of made-to-order reality, and of ad hoc morals making. If you follow them, you walk into the night without a light, and into the woods without a compass. I want to tell you as plainly as I can that their vision of academic tolerance lacks intellectual virtue. It dilutes the high cultural inheritance of the past with the petty and insupportable leftisms of the present.

A moment ago, I imagined a student that might be wondering about the relevance of my semi-autobiographical musings. I can also imagine someone thinking that all I've done since the '60s is simply to change sides in the culture war that rages around us. To think so, however, is to assume that flower power and Christianity are morally equivalent and that hippies rank equally with saints; two false assumptions which, if you make them, show just how much a child of the '60s you really are. I have often wondered why the '90s feel like a '60s renaissance. I discovered the answer to that question in a college cafeteria and in conversations with some of my students' parents.

First, the parents. I have often noticed my students saying and thinking the same sorts of things their parents say and think when I speak with them. Such things happen because the acorn seldom falls far from the oak tree. That fact is significant because the parents of today's college students were probably the young men and women of the '60s. Many of the responses my students learned to give to life are responses they learned from their parents. More often than not, those responses are the stock responses of the '60s. In one way, of course, that's good; I want my students to learn all the truth they can from their parents. But insofar as my students' responses mimic the responses of the '60s, they too must learn the lessons that I had to learn. They too must come to understand, with all the clarity and courage they can muster, the truth of the tragic vision of life: We are, every one of us, morally defective, ethically twisted, and spiritually broken. If my students fail to come to that realization and to act upon it, both they and their world shall suffer.

Second the cafeteria. I often notice my students echoing some of the things they hear their teachers say. When talking with students in the cafeteria, for example, I sometimes have the eerie feeling that I'm not in the cafeteria at all; I'm in a faculty meeting. I say so because I frequently hear the clear and unmistakable intonations of my colleagues' voices, but coming from other people. Sometimes I even hear my own voice. Again, that's good; I want college students to learn all the truth they can from their professors. But here's the rub: Like me, many of their teachers were children of the '60s; and like me, many of those professors have made only an incomplete break with the mistakes of that era. From their other professors and from me, my students have gotten many of their ideas. Like my students themselves, their ideas have parents. World views and attitudes, just like the people who have them, show marked family resemblances. For that very reason, I often want to ask my students this question: From where do you imagine that your rampant relativism and your not very carefully hidden contempt for authority arise? In most cases, when I consider asking such a question, I already know the answer—from the '60s and from the people (like me) who reached their emotional and intellectual maturity at that time.

Here's my point: If you believe in the '60s, or if you believe in the '90s, you believe a lie. As I did, you need an undeception. In order to get it, you need to go back well beyond the '60s, back to a wisdom that is older than time. You need to go back to God and to the wisdom that spoke this universe into existence. You need to go back to the God who made you and redeemed you. Real answers are found nowhere else.

It should not surprise you when I tell you that, if you do what I suggest, you'll meet energetic and determined opposition, sometimes even from those who call themselves the friends of God and of tradition. As Socrates observed long centuries ago, most men do not take kindly to the preacher of moral reform, to the pursuer of the good. There's just no telling, he said in the *Gorgias*, what might happen to such a man. But don't let that stop you. Do it anyway. Do it because you need it; do it because it's right; and do it because it ought to be done. Your task will be difficult. It's always easy to be a modernist; it's always easy to go with the spirit of the age. But in the face of the world's downward slide you must be vigilant, strong, perceptive, and courageous. The world needs people like that, people unafraid to turn around and walk back into the light. Our world needs people like that now more than ever, because everywhere you look the adversary culture of the '60s has become the dominant culture of the '90s.

Our cultural patrimony is being embezzled from under our very noses. If you think of yourself as a Christian, or as a conservative, or as both, the view from here is haunting: We don't own the White House; we don't own the courts; we don't own the media; we don't own the arts; we don't own the sciences; we don't own the marketplace; we don't own the academy; we don't own anything. We don't even own the Church. It's all owned by the '60s.

Therefore if, as I did, you find yourself an unwilling or unwitting child of the '60s, I invite you, I exhort you, to turn with an open mind and an open heart to the prophets and apostles in Scripture and to the great poets and sages outside Scripture. They are your only liberation from modernist thralldom and from slavery to your own fallen desires. Put yourself on a quest for eternal truth, and never give up until you find Him.

While you're on this quest, you must always remember that most of the powers that be are of no help to you. Those who loved the '60s own the '90s. The Left still hates America, and it still hates what made America possible: faith in God, individual responsibility, local and limited government, also traditional morality, and the sacredness and inviolability of life and the family. The Leftists of the '90s are the enemies of heartland values. They want you to keep quiet. They want you to sit meekly in the corner of the room, hands folded and mouth shut. They want you to be nice. They want the friends of beauty, truth, and goodness to speak only when spoken to and, when they do speak, to speak only those things that offend no one. That they have offended you seems not to matter. They want you to stick to the script. They want you to keep your views to yourself and to act as if your views were not true, indeed as if there were not truth. That's what political correctness—or should I say political cleansing?—is all about.

Consider it for just a moment. What kind of man or woman would you be if you let yourself be controlled by the empty criticisms of the rootless Left, and what kind of world would you be creating for those who came after you if you neglected to restore realism to human though and turned your back on the only thing that can make you content even in dungeons, even in slums, even in the face of death?

My desire for you is that you throw off the vestiges of leftist cultural subversion, that you make yourself a devotee and guardian of the wisdom of the ages, that you become the sworn enemy of nonsense in all its forms, and most importantly, that you become the faithful and ardent friend of God. Then, and only then, can you be free.

What has been given to you as a heritage you must now accept as your quest. If you wish to be wise, you must learn to make peace with the wisdom of the ages and with those who gave it, regardless of their sex, their race, or their ethnic background. You must do so because wisdom and truth are not gender based, and thinking is very hard work. Knowledge is not parochial. It is not the private property of any race, any gender, any era, or any ethnic group. It belongs to those determined to get it, to those who seek it resolutely and who will not be denied, no matter how difficult the circumstances arrayed against them. Truth belongs to the diligent and the insightful, and to them only.

In that light, I invite you today to make one of the most important choices of your entire life: Which will you have? You cannot have both.

THE LIE IS MARCHING ON
BY JOEL BELZ

Four colossal errors--all of them profound shapers of contemporary society--keep marching blithely on, oblivious to their rootlessness in factual data and supporting evidence.

Lesbian Deb Price, for whom the Detroit News inexplicably syndicates a regular column, reminded me with one of her pieces two weeks ago how uncritically folks have come to accept the airiest of arguments. Ms. Price explained in detail how she and her full-time partner Joyce have concluded that they no longer have to feel a sense of obligation as a couple to "have children." "We are childless by choice," she says with a tone of moral superiority.

When you start out believing a lie, of course, you'd better get ready not just for that which is untrue but also for that which is preposterous. When people deliberately ignore God's explicit words and the plain evidence of the creation around them, as defenders of homosexual behavior clearly do, it's no wonder they end up thinking incoherently. "I suppose they're also announcing that they've chosen to quit walking on the ceiling," said a friend of mine on hearing about Ms. Price's announcement. But my friend was only 12 years old; you don't have to be terribly sophisticated to see the hollowness of what goes for argumentation these days.

Or take the perennial issue of origins. It would be one thing if there were a genuine hungering and thirsting for truth on the matter. Instead, we face an incredible propaganda machine that grinds genuine truth-seekers into the dust of embarrassment.

Just ask Michael Behe, the molecular biologist from Lehigh University in Bethlehem, Pa., who dared to be skeptical of the accepted wisdom about evolution. Instead, he reported what he actually saw through his microscope--something so incredibly complex that it simply didn't fit any of Darwin's theories or any modern updates of those theories. But Mr. Behe also had the nerve to report something else he saw: a total silence in the professional literature about how such complex organisms ever came to be.

So what has Mr. Behe earned for his efforts to ask the kinds of questions honest scientists are supposedly supposed to ask? Scorn from many of his colleagues. *The Real Issue*, a newsletter from Christian Leadership Ministries, reports on the response of the British popularizer of evolution, Richard Dawkins. Mr. Dawkins first refused to appear on TV with Mr. Behe. But in a solo interview, Mr. Dawkins was quick to jump all over Mr. Behe, who reports: "During the interview, which I had the opportunity to see recently, the show host asked him about my book. He seemed to grasp the idea of irreducible complexity pretty well. However, he said it was cowardly and lazy of me to come to a conclusion of intelligent design, and he said that if I thought for myself I would realize that there must be a Darwinian explanation out there somewhere, and I should get off my duff and go out and find it."

So much for the rigors of honest scholarship, academic fairness, and objective truth-seeking.

The parallel refusal of abortion advocates to engage the real question--does abortion involve the taking of a human life?--has long been the main obstacle to honest public discussion of this monumental issue. Only by constantly diverting discussion to matters like freedom to choose, birth deformities, the plight of poor mothers, teenage pregnancies, clinic violence, and other tangential issues can abortion backers avoid the main topic.

But such diversion--which characterizes the big TV networks, the major media, and nearly all entertainment forms--is precisely the point. Any even-handed moderator would suggest instead that no question in the debate should be ruled out of bounds. For pro-lifers, the only question that really matters has regularly been excluded from discussion.

Even in the environmental debate, an honest discussion using countable data and actual findings of the sort scientists, journalists, and historians are supposed to deal in has been eclipsed from the public view. Ask Julian Simon, featured in the February issue of *Wired* magazine--certainly no right-wing rag but an *avant garde* cheerleader for technology and a libertarian challenger of the status quo. *Wired* applauds Mr. Simon as a "doomsayer" for his fearless attacks on prevalent politically correct assertions about overpopulation, future food shortages, and the depletion of other natural resources. What drives Julian Simon crazy, says author Ed Regis in *Wired*, are "people who know in advance what the truth is, who don't need to avail themselves of any 'facts.'" But because Mr. Simon loves facts and figures, he is also regularly shunned by the media, the scientific community, and fellow academics.

All of which is a simple reminder that we do not live in a culture that seriously values truth. From the early days in the Garden, men and women have preferred the lie to the truth. Reason has its place, and Christians should always seek to be reasonable people. But it will always be God's Spirit--not the cleverness of our arguments--that turns around people's hearts and minds.

Reprinted with permission from World Magazine, February 15, 1997.

What the Press Saw at the Brandenburg Gate

By Stephen Bird

For reading in conjunction with Ronald Reagan's "Brandenburg Gate" address.

On this 20th anniversary of the day Ronald Reagan dared Mikhail Gorbachev to "Tear Down this Wall" while standing at the Brandenburg Gate, one needs only to read a few headlines from the week that followed to capture the angst of some in the Cold War press.

Much of that angst was directed at Reagan, who by June 12, 1987, had been written off as a cold warrior.

"A Potemkin President: Reagan is losing the air of authority," declared one column in The New York Times, before the writer went on to announce that the presidency was "ceasing to function" and predict, "19 months of a surreal Presidency to go. If it lasts." Perhaps one could call it a generation gap.

Reagan and his peers were the "Greatest Generation," one that confronted the enemy directly and won, one that rebuilt the world after winning a world war. Many emerged with an enduring optimism.

By contrast, some in the Cold War press reported the world through gloom-and-doom eyeshades. Mutually assured destruction was a constant threat. The best that could be hoped for was containment of the wrong powers that be rather than freedom for Europe.

"Keep Germany Divided: The Dirty Little Secret Is That It Means a Europe at Peace" headlined an opinion piece in The Washington Post two days after one of Reagan's finest moments.

"It's just that, considered as a unified nation, in a world parched for peace, the Germans are not quite ready for self-government," is how the Post writer ended his piece. Ronald Reagan didn't see it that way.

Six years before challenging Gorbachev to tear down the wall, Reagan revealed his strategy in a significant way. His first gesture was proposing to lift the grain embargo in a letter to Leonid Brezhnev.

While some may have seen this as caving to the Communists, Reagan was appealing to his roots: the common man. He met the immediate need of the masses.

So when the Great Communicator challenged Gorbachev to get rid of the Berlin Wall, only a few in the press saw the significance. Others painted a worst-case scenario, focusing on what they perceived as Reagan's legacy rather than on his appeal for freedom.

"After a lackluster European trip, Ronald Reagan turns his attention this week to arms control and deficit battling to revive his presidency," began a June 14 Chicago Tribune news story.

Echoing Walter Mondale, the reporter cited Reagan's age as a hint before suggesting that the president was in "political recuperation."

Others among the American press missed what happened at the Brandenburg Gate concentrating instead on what they thought went wrong.

The day-after story in The Washington Post described the atmosphere surrounding what was perhaps Reagan's greatest speech this way: "Even though Americans predominated in the front rows of the audience, many of Reagan's most provocative lines received only scattered applause."

And: "But the crowd, estimated by officials at 20,000, was about half the number that had been anticipated."

Even in TIME magazine's June 22 story, "Back to the wall; Reagan rallies with a strong speech," the president was portrayed as coming in second: "For all his eloquence, the aging President was repeatedly upstaged by the youthful and suavely dynamic image of the man who was not there: Mikhail Gorbachev."

And if that wasn't enough, a U.S. News & World Report writer piled on: "The overall impression was of a lame-duck President who knows all too well that his dream of carving out a shining place in history is eroding into bittersweet memories."

So while the press eyed presidential legacies, Reagan stuck to his lasting vision of freedom for the common man. And in the end, it was that vision that helped bring down a wall, freed a nation, and brought a legacy of freedom across Europe.

http://www.townhall.com/columnists/StephenBird/2007/06/12/what_the_press_saw_at_the_brandenburg_gate?page=full&comments=true

Closing Defense Arguments at the Impeachment Trial of William Jefferson Clinton

By Dale Bumpers, delivered 21 January 1999

Mr. Chief Justice, our distinguished House managers from the House of Representatives, colleagues:

I have seen the look of disappointment on many faces because I know a lot of people thought you were rid of me once and for all. And I've taken a lot of ribbing this afternoon, but I have seriously negotiated with some people, particularly on this side by an offer to walk out and not deliver this speech in exchange for a few votes. I understand three have it under active consideration.

It is a great joy to see you, and it is especially pleasant to see an audience which represents about the size of the cumulative audience I had over a period of 24 years.

I came here today for a lot of reasons. One was that I was promised a 40foot cord and I've been shorted 28 feet. Chris Dodd said that he didn't want me in his lap, and I assume that he arranged for the cord to be shortened.

I want to especially thank some of you for your kind comments in the press when it received some publicity that I would be here to close the debate on behalf of the White House Counsel and the President. I was a little dismayed by Senator Bennett's remark. He said, "Yes, Senator Bumpers is a great speaker, but I never he was never persuasive with me because I never agreed with him." I thought he could have done better than that.

You can take some comfort, colleagues, in the fact that I'm not being paid. And when I'm finished you will probably think the White House got their money's worth.

I have told audiences that over 24 years that I went home almost every weekend and returned usually about dusk on Sunday evening. And you know the plane ride into National Airport when you can see the magnificent Washington Monument and this building from the window of the airplane. And I've told these students at the university in a small, liberal arts school at home, Hendricks, after 24 years of that, literally hundreds of times, I never failed to get goose bumps.

Same thing is true about this chamber. I can still remember as though it were yesterday the awe I felt when I first stepped into this magnificent chamber so full of history. So beautiful. And last Tuesday, as I returned after only a short three-week absence, I still felt that same sense of awe that I did the first time I walked in this chamber.

Colleagues, I come here with some sense of reluctance.

The President and I have been close friends for 25 years. We've fought so many battles back home together in our beloved Arkansas, we tried mightily all of my years as Governor and his, and all of my years in the Senate when he was Governor, to raise the living standards in the Delta area of Mississippi, Arkansas, and Louisiana where poverty is unspeakable, with some measure of success not nearly enough. We tried to provide health care for the lesser among us, for those who are well-off enough they can't get on welfare, but not making enough to buy health insurance.

We have fought, above everything else, to improve the educational standards for a state that, for so many years, was at the bottom of the list or near the bottom of the list of income, and we have stood side-by-side to save beautiful, pristine areas in our state from environmental degradation.

We even crashed a twin-engine Beach Bonanza trying to get to the *Gillette Coon Supper*, a political event that one misses at his own risk. And we crashed this plane on a snowy evening on a rural airport, off the runway, sailing out across the snow, jumped out, jumped out and ran away unscathed, to the dismay of every budding politician in Arkansas.

The President and I have been together hundreds of times at parades, dedications, political events, social events. And in all of those years, and all those hundreds of times we've been together, both in public and in private, I have never one time seen the President conduct himself in a way that did not reflect the highest credit on him, his family, his state, and his beloved nation.

The reason I came here today with some reluctance please don't misconstrue that. It has nothing to do with my feelings about the President, as I've already said but it's because we are from the same state and we are long friends and I know that that necessarily diminishes to some extent the effectiveness of my words.

So if Bill Clinton the man, Bill Clinton the friend were the issue here, I'm quite sure I would not be doing this. But it is the weight of history on all of us and it is my reverence for that great document and you heard me rail about it for 24 years that we call our Constitution, the most sacred document to me next to the holy Bible. These proceedings go right to the heart of our Constitution where it deals with impeachment, the part that provides the gravest punishment for just about anybody, the President, even though the framers said we're putting this in to protect the public, not to punish the President.

Ah, colleagues, you have such an awesome responsibility. My good friend, the senior senator from New York, has said it well. He says, this a decision to convict holds the potential for destabilizing the office of [the] presidency. And those 400 historians and I know some have made light of that about those historians are they just friends of Bill? And last evening, I went over that list of historians, many of whom I know, among them.

In the South we love him. He is the preeminent southern historian in the nation. I promise you, he may be a Democrat, he may even be a he may be even a friend of the President. When you talk about integrity, he is the walking personification, exemplification of integrity. Well, colleagues, I have heard so many adjectives to describe this gathering and these proceedings. "Historic," "memorable," "unprecedented," "awesome" all of those words, all of those descriptions are apt. And to those I would add the word "dangerous" dangerous not only for the reasons I just stated, but because it's dangerous to the political process and it's dangerous to the unique mix of pure democracy and republican government Madison and his colleagues so brilliantly crafted, and which has sustained us for 210 years.

Mr. Chief Justice, this is what we lawyers call "dicta." This costs you nothing. It's extra. But the more I study that document and those four months at Philadelphia in 1787, the more awed I am. And you know what Madison did? The brilliance was in its simplicity. He simply said: Man's nature is to get other people to dance to their tune. Man's nature is to abuse his fellow man sometimes. And he said, the way to make sure that the majorities don't abuse the minorities, and the way to make sure that the bullies don't run over the weaklings is to provide the same rights for everybody.

And I had to think about that a long time before I delivered my first lecture at the University of Arkansas last week. And it made so much sense to me. But the danger, as I say, is to the political process. And dangerous for reasons feared by the framers about legislative control of the executive.

That single issue and how to deal with impeachment was debated off and on for the entire four months of the constitutional convention. But the word "dangerous" is not mine. It's Alexander Hamilton's brilliant, good-looking guy.

Mr. Ruff quoted extensively on Tuesday afternoon in his brilliant statement here. He quoted Alexander Hamilton precisely, and it's a little arcane; it isn't easy to understand. So if I may, at the expense of being slightly repetitious, let me paraphrase what Hamilton said. He said the Senate had a unique role in participating with the Executive branch in appointments.

And, two, it had a role in participating with the Executive in the character of a court for the trial of impeachments. But he said and I must say this, and you all know it he said it would be difficult to get a what he called well constituted court from wholly elected members. He said passions would agitate the whole community and divide it between those who were friendly and those who had inimical interest to the accused, namely the President. And then he said and this is his words the greatest danger was that the decision would be based on the comparative strength of the parties rather than the innocence or guilt of the President.

You have a solemn oath. You have taken a solemn oath to be fair and impartial. I know you all. I know you as friends, and I know you as honorable men, and I am perfectly satisfied to put that in your hands under your oath.

This is the only caustic thing I will say in these remarks this afternoon, but the question is, "How did we come to be here?" We're here because of a five-year, relentless, unending investigation of the President. Fifty billion dollars, hundreds of FBI agents fanning across the nation examining in detail the microscopic lives of people. Maybe the most intense investigation not only of a President but of anybody ever.

I feel strongly about this state just because of my state, and what we have endured. So you'll have to excuse me, but that investigation has also shown that the judicial system in this country can and does get out of kilter, unless it's controlled, because there are innocent people who have been financially and mentally bankrupt[ed].

One woman told me two years ago that her legal fees were 95,000 dollars. She said I don't have $95,000 and the only asset I have is the equity in my home, which just happens to correspond to my legal fees of 95,000 dollars. And she says the only thing I can think of to do is to deed my home.

This woman was innocent; never charged; testified before the grand jury a number of times. And since that time, she has accumulated an additional $200,000 in attorney fees. Javert's pursuit of Jean Valjean in *Les Miserables* pales by comparison.

I doubt that there are few people, maybe nobody in this body, who could withstand such scrutiny. And in this case those summoned were terrified not because of their guilt, but because they felt guilt or innocence was not really relevant.

But after all of those years and 50 million dollars of Whitewater, Travelgate, Filegate, you name it, nothing, nothing, the President was found guilty of nothing, official or personal.

We're here today because the President suffered a terrible moral lapse, a marital infidelity; not a breach of the public trust, not a crime against society, the two things Hamilton talked about in Federalist Paper number 65. I recommend it to you before you vote but it was a breach of his marriage vows. It was a breach of his family trust. It is a sex scandal. H.L. Mencken said one time, "When you hear somebody say, 'This is not about money' it's about money." And when you hear somebody say, "This is not about sex" it's about sex.

You pick your own adjective to describe the President's conduct. Here are some that I would use: "indefensible," "outrageous," "unforgivable," "shameless." I promise you the President would not contest any of those or any others.

But there's a human element in this case that has not even been mentioned, and that is the President and Hillary and Chelsea are human beings. This is intended only as a mild criticism of our distinguished friends in the House, but as I listened to the presenters to the managers make their opening statements, they were remarkably well prepared, and they spoke eloquently. More eloquent than I really had hoped.

But when I talk about the human element, I talk about what I thought was, on occasion, unnecessarily harsh and pejorative descriptions of the President. I thought that the language should have been tempered somewhat, to acknowledge that he is the President. To say constantly that the President lied about this and lied about that, as I say, I thought that was too much for a family that has already been about as decimated as a family can get.

The relationship between husband and wife, father and child has been incredibly strained, if not destroyed. There's been nothing but sleepless nights, mental agony for this family for almost five years day after day, from accusations of having assassinated, or had Vince Foster assassinated on down. It has been bizarre.

But I didn't sense any compassion, and perhaps none is deserved. The President has said for all to hear that he misled, he deceived, he did not want to be helpful to the prosecution. And he did all of those things to his family, to his friends, to his staff, to his cabinet and to the American people.

Why would he do that? Well, he knew this whole affair was about to bring unspeakable embarrassment and humiliation on himself, his wife whom he adored, and a child that he worshipped with every fiber in his body, and for whom he would happily have died to spare her this or to ameliorate her shame and her grief.

The House managers have said shame and embarrassment is no excuse for lying. Well, the question about lying, that's your decision. But I can tell you, you put yourself in his position, and you've already had this big moral lapse, as to what you would do. We are none of us perfect. Sure, you say, he should have thought of all that beforehand. And indeed he should. Just as Adam and Eve should have. Just as you and you and you and you, and millions of other people who have been caught in similar circumstances, should have thought of it before.

And I say none of us are perfect.

I remember, Chaplain, the chaplain's not here, is he? It's too bad. He ought to hear this story.

This evangelist was holding this great revival meeting, and at the close of one of his meetings he said, "Is there anybody in this audience who has ever known anybody who even comes close to the perfection of our Lord and Savior, Jesus Christ?" Nothing. He repeated the challenge, and finally a little bitty guy the in back of the audience kind of held up his hand.

And he said, "You are saying you've known such a person? Stand up." He stood up, and he said, "Tell us. Share it with us." Who was it?" He said, "My wife's first husband."

Make no mistake about it, removal from office is punishment; it is unbelievable punishment, even though the framers didn't quite see it that way. Again they said, and it bears repeating over and over again, they said they wanted to protect the people. But I can tell you this: the punishment of removing Bill Clinton from office would pale compared to the punishment he has already inflicted on himself.

There's a feeling in this country that somehow or other Bill Clinton's gotten away with something. Mr. Leader, I can tell you, he hasn't gotten away with anything. And the people are saying: Please don't protect us from this man; 76 percent of us think he's doing a fine job. Sixty-five to seventy percent of us don't want him removed from office.

And some have said, "We're not respected on the world scene." The truth of the matter is, this nation has never enjoyed greater prestige in the world than we do right now. You saw Carlos Menem, the President of Argentina, just here recently, say to the President, "Mr. President, the world needs you." The war in Bosnia is under control. The President has been as tenacious as anybody could be about Middle East peace. And in Ireland, actual peace, and maybe the Middle East will make it. And he has the Indians and the Pakistanis talking to each other as they've never talked to each other in recent times. Vaclav Havel said, "Mr. President, for the enlargement of the North Atlantic Treaty Organization there's no doubt in my mind that it was your personal leadership that made this historic development possible." King Hussein: Mr. President, I've had the privilege of being a friend of the United States and Presidents since the late President Eisenhower. And throughout all the years that have passed, I've kept in touch.

But on the subject of peace, the peace we're seeking, I have never with all due respect and all the affection I held for your predecessors, have known someone with your dedication, clear-headedness, focus and determination to help resolve this issue in the best way possible. Well, I'm not I've got Nelson Mandela and other world leaders who have said similar things in the last six months. Our prestige, I promise you, in the world is as high as it's ever been.

When it comes to the question of perjury, you know, there's perjury and then there's perjury.

Let me ask you if you think this is perjury. On November 23rd, 1997, President Clinton went to Vancouver, British Columbia. And when he returned, Monica Lewinsky was at the White House at some point, and he gave her a marble, carved marble bear. I don't know how big it was.

Question before the grand jury August 6th, 1998: "What was the Christmas present or presents that he got for you?"

Answer: "Everything was packaged in a big Black Dog or big canvass bag from the Black Dog store in Martha's Vineyard. And he got me a marble bear's head carving, sort of, you know, a little a little sculpture, I guess you'd call, maybe."

[Question]: "Was that the item from Vancouver?"

[Answer]: "Yes." Question on the same day of the same grand jury.

[Question]: "Okay, good. When the President gave you the Vancouver Bear on the 26th 28th, I guess it is no, 26th.

[Question]: When the President gave you the Vancouver Bear on the 28th, did he say anything about what it means?"

[Answer]: "Mmmm."

[Question]: "Well, what did he say?"

[Answer]: "I think he I believe he said that the bear is the, maybe, Indian symbol for strength, you know, and to be strong like a bear."

[Question]: "And did you interpret that to be 'strong in your decision to continue to conceal the relationship?'"

[Answer]: "No."

House Judiciary Committee report to the full House: On the other hand, knowing the subpoena requested gifts, his giving Ms. Lewinsky more gifts on December 28th seems odd, but Ms. Lewinsky's testimony reveals why he did so. She said that she, "Never questioned that we would ever do anything but keep this private and that meant to take whatever appropriate steps needed to be taken to keep it quiet." The only logical inference is that the gifts, including the bear symbolizing strength, were a tacit reminder to Ms. Lewinsky that they would deny the relationship even in the face of a federal subpoena.

She just got through saying "No," and yet this report says that's the only logical inference. And then the brief that came over here accompanying the articles of impeachment said, on the other hand: ...more gifts on December 28th. Ms. Lewinsky's testimony reveals the answer. She said she was never questioned she said that she, "Never questioned that we were ever going to do anything but keep this private, and that meant to take whatever appropriate steps needed to be taken to keep it quiet.

Again, they say in their brief, the only logical inference is that the gifts, including the bear symbolizing strength, were a tacit reminder to Ms. Lewinsky that they would deny the relationship even in the face of a federal subpoena.

Is it perjury to say the only logical inference is something when the only shred of testimony in the record is, "No," that was not my interpretation. I didn't imply I didn't infer that.[1] And yet here you have it in the committee report and you have it in the brief.

Now of course that's not perjury. First of all, it isn't under oath, but as a trial lawyer, I'll tell you what it is: It's wanting to win too badly. I tried three, four, maybe 500 divorce cases incidentally, you're being addressed by the entire South Franklin County, Arkansas Bar Association; I can't believe there were that many cases in that little town, but I had a practice in surrounding communities, too and in all those divorce cases, I would guess that in 80 percent of the contested cases, perjury was committed. And you know what it was about? Sex. Extramarital affairs.

But there's a very big difference in perjury about a marital infidelity in a divorce case and perjury about whether I bought the murder weapon or whether I concealed the murder weapon or not. And to charge somebody with the first and punish them as though it were the second stands justice, our sense of justice, on its head. There's a total lack of proportionality, a total lack of balance in this thing. The charge and the punishment are totally out of sync.

All of you have heard or read the testimony of the five prosecutors who testified before the House Judiciary Committee. Five seasoned prosecutors. And each one of them, veterans, said under the identical circumstances, the identical circumstances of this case, we would never charge anybody because we'd know we couldn't get a conviction. And in this case, the charges brought and the punishment sought are totally out of sync. There is no balance, there is no proportionality.

But even stranger, you think about it, even if this case had originated in the courthouse rather than the capitol, you would never have heard of it. How do you reconcile what the prosecutors said with what we're doing here?

Impeachment was debated off and on in Philadelphia for the entire four months, as I said. The key players were Governor [Lewis] Morris, Senator Specter, a brilliant Pennsylvanian, George Mason, the only man to reputedly to have been so brilliant that Thomas Jefferson actually deferred to him. And he refused to sign the Constitution, incidentally, even though he was a delegate, because they didn't deal with slavery and he was a strict abolitionist.

And then there was Charles Pinkney [ph]. Senator Hollings from South Carolina, just a youngster, 29 years old, I believe. Edmund Randolph from Virginia, who had a big role in the Constitution in the beginning; the Virginia Plan. And then there was, of course, James Madison, the craftsman.

They were all key players in drafting this impeachment provision. And uppermost in their mind during the entire time they were composing was they did not want any kings. They had lived under despots, they had lived under kings, they had lived under autocrats, and they didn't want any more of that. And they succeeded very admirably. We've had 46 presidents, and no kings.

But they kept talking about corruption. Maybe that ought to be the reason for impeachment, because they feared some President would corrupt the political process that's what the debate was about corrupt the political process and ensconce himself through a phony election, maybe as something close to a king.

They followed the British rule on impeachment, because the British said, the House of Commons may impeach, and the House of Lords must convict. And every one of the colonies had the same procedure: House, Senate. Though, in all fairness, House members, James or Alexander Hamilton was not very keen on the House participating.

But here was the sequence of events at Philadelphia that brought us here today. They started out with "maladministration," and Madison said that's too vague. What does that mean? So they dropped that. They went from that to "corruption" and they dropped that. Then they went to "malpractice." And they decided that was not definitive enough. And they went to "treason, bribery and corruption." And they decided that still didn't suit them. But bear in mind one thing, during this entire process, they are narrowing the things you can impeach the President for. They were making it tougher.

Madison said if we aren't careful, the President will serve at the pleasure of the legislature the Senate, he said. And then they went to "treason and bribery" and somebody said that's still not quite enough. And so they went to treason, bribery George Mason added "or other high crimes and misdemeanors against the United States." And they voted on it, and on September 10th they sent the entire Constitution to a committee.

They called a committee on style and arrangement, which was the committee that would draft the language in a way that everybody would understand; it would be well-crafted from a grammatical standpoint. But that committee, which was dominated by Madison and Hamilton, dropped "against the United States." And historians will tell you that the reason they did that was because of redundance, because that committee had no right to change the substance of anything. And they would not have dropped it if they hadn't felt that it was redundant.

And then, they put in for good measure and we can always be grateful the two-thirds majority.

Now this is one of the most important points of this entire presentation: the term first of all "treason and bribery," nobody quarrels with that, and we're not debating treason and bribery here in this chamber. We're talking about "other high crimes and misdemeanors."

And where did "high crimes and misdemeanors" come from? It came from the English law, and they found it in English law under a category which said, "distinctly political offenses against the state." Let me repeat that. They said, "high crimes and misdemeanors was to be," because they took it from English law, where they found it in the category that said, "offenses distinctly political against the state."

So colleagues, please, for just one moment, forget the complexities of the facts and the tortured legalisms. And we've heard them all brilliantly presented on both sides, and I'm not getting into that. But ponder this. If high crimes and misdemeanors was taken from English law by George Mason, which listed high crimes and misdemeanors as political offenses against the state, what are we doing here? If, as Hamilton said, it had to be a crime against society or a breach of the public trust, what are we doing here? Even perjury. Concealing or deceiving. An unfaithful relationship does not even come close to being an impeachable offense.

Nobody has suggested that Bill Clinton committed a political crime against the state. So, colleagues, if you honor the Constitution, you must look at the history of the Constitution and how we got to the impeachment clause. And if you do that and you do that honestly according to the oath you took, you cannot you can censure Bill Clinton; you can hand him over to the prosecutor for him to be prosecuted, but you cannot convict him. And you cannot indulge yourselves the luxury or the right to ignore this history.

There's been a suggestion that a vote to acquit would be something of a breach of faith with those who lie in Flanders Field and Anzio and Bunker Hill and Gettysburg and wherever. I didn't hear that; I read about it. But I want to say and, incidentally, I think it was Chairman Hyde who alluded to this and said: those men fought and died for the rule of law.

I can remember a cold November 3rd morning in my little home town of Charleston, Arkansas. I was 18 years old. I'd just gotten one semester in at the university when I went into the Marine Corps. And so, I was to report to Little Rock to be inducted. My, it was cold. The drug store was the bus stop. I had to be there by eight o'clock to be sworn in, and I had to catch the bus down at the drug store at three o'clock in the morning so my mother and father and I got up at two o'clock and got dressed and went down there.

I'm not sure I can tell you this story. [*Overcome somewhat with emotion*]

And the bus came over the hill I was rather frightened anyway about going in. I was quite sure I was going to be killed, only slightly less frightened that Betty would find somebody else while I was gone. And the bus came over Schoolhouse Hill, and my parents started crying. I had never seen my father cry. I knew I was in some difficulty. Now, as a parent at my age, I know he thought he was giving not his only begotten son, but one of his forgotten begotten sons. Can you imagine? You know that scene. It was repeated across this nation millions of times.

And then happily, I survived that war; saw no combat; was on my way to Japan when it all ended. I'd never had a terrible problem with dropping the bomb, though that's been a terrible moral dilemma for me, because that the estimates were that we would lose as many as a million men in that invasion.

But I came home into a generous government who provided me, under the GI Bill, an education in a fairly prestigious law school which my father could never have afforded. And I practiced law in this little town for 18 years; loved every minute of it.

But I didn't practice constitutional law, and I knew very little about the Constitution. But when I went into law school, I did study constitutional law, though Mr. Chief Justice, it was fairly arcane to me. And trying read The Federalist Papers and Tocqueville all of those things law students are expected to do, that was tough for me, I confess.

So after 18 years in law practice I jumped up and ran for governor and I served for governor as governor for four years, and I still I guess I knew what the rule of law was but I still didn't really have much reverence for the Constitution. I just did not understand any of the things I just got through telling you. No. My love for that document came day after day and debate after debate right here in this chamber.

Some of you perhaps read an op-ed piece I did a couple of weeks ago when I said I was perfectly happy for my legacy of a 24-year senator-to-be I never voted for a constitutional amendment. And it isn't that I wouldn't. I think they made a mistake in not giving you fellows four years. You're about to cause me to rethink that one.

And the reason I developed this love of it is because I saw Madison's magic working time and time again, keeping bullies from running over weak people, keeping majorities from running over minorities. And I thought about all the unfettered freedoms we had. The oldest organic law in existence made us the envy of the world.

Mr. Chairman, we've also learned that the rule of law includes presidential elections. That's a part of the rule of law in this country. We have an event, a quadrennial event in this country which we call "Presidential Elections." And that's the day when we reach across this aisle and hold hands, Democrats and Republicans. And we say, "Win or lose, we will abide by the decision." It is a solemn event, presidential elections, and they should not be undone lightly; or just because one side has the clout and the other one doesn't.

And if you want to know what men fought for in World War II, for example, or in Vietnam, ask Senator Inouye. He left an arm in Italy. He and I were in the presence at Normandy on the 50th anniversary. But we started off on Anzil [ph].

Senator Domenici, were you with us?

It was one of the most awesome experiences I've ever had in my life certified war hero. I think his relatives were in an internment camp, so ask him what he was fighting for? Or ask Bob Kerrey, certified Medal of Honor winner what was he fighting for? Probably get a quite different answer. Or Senator Chafee, one of the finest men ever to grace this body and certified marine hero of Guadalcanal ask him. And Senator McCain, a genuine hero ask him.

You don't have to guess. They're with us, and they're living. And they can tell you. And one who is not with us here in the Senate anymore, Robert Dole. Ask Senator Dole what he was fighting for. Senator Dole had what I thought was a very reasonable solution to this whole thing that would handle it fairly and expeditiously.

The American people are now and for some time have been asking to be allowed a good night's sleep. They're asking for an end to this nightmare. It is a legitimate request. I'm not suggesting that you vote for or against the polls. I understand that. Nobody should vote against the polls just to show their mettle and their courage. I have cast plenty of votes against the polls and it's cost me politically a lot of times. This has been going on for a year, though.

And in that same op-ed piece I talked about meeting Harry Truman my first year as governor of Arkansas. Spent an hour with him. An indelible experience. People at home kid me about this, because I very seldom make a speech that I don't mention this meeting. But I will never forget what he said, "Put your faith in the people. Trust the people. They can handle it." They have shown conclusively time and time again that they can handle it.

Colleagues, this is easily the most important vote you will ever cast. If you have difficulty because of an intense dislike of the president and that's understandable rise above it. He is not the issue. He will be gone. You won't. So don't leave a precedent from which we may never recover and almost surely will regret.

If you vote to acquit, Mr. Leader, you know exactly what's going to happen. You're going to back to your committees. You're going to get on this legislative agenda. You're going to start dealing with Medicare and Social Security and tax cuts and all those things which the people of the country have a nonnegotiable demand that you do. If you vote to acquit, you go immediately to the people's agenda.

But if you vote to convict, you can't be sure what's going to happen. James G. Blaine was a member of the Senate when Andrew Johnson was tried in 1868, and 20 years later he recanted. And he said: "I made a bad mistake." And he says "as I reflect back on it, all I can think about is having convicted Andrew Johnson would have caused much more chaos and confusion in this country than Andrew Johnson could ever conceivably have tried."

And so it is with William Jefferson Clinton. If you vote to convict, in my opinion you're going to be creating more havoc than he could ever possibly create. After all, he's only got two years left. So don't, for God's sakes heighten people's alienation that is at an all time high toward their government.

The people have a right and they are calling on you to rise above politics, rise above partisanship. They're calling on you to do your solemn duty. And I pray you will. Thank you, Mr. Chief Justice.

1The sender or source of a message may "imply." The receivers of a message may "infer." Senders do NOT infer and receivers do NOT imply.

http://www.americanrhetoric.com/speeches/dalebumpersdefenseofclinton.htm

Letter to a Noble Lord

By Edmund Burke

In 1794, after the trial of Warren Hastings, in which he had been one of the relentless prosecutors, Edmund Burke (1729-97) retired from the House of Commons, where he had served for almost thirty years, and his son Richard was nominated to take his place. As a reward for his long service in the government, Burke was proposed for the peerage, with the title of Lord Beaconsfield, but upon the death of his son Richard in August of 1794, Burke lost all interest in any titular honors. King George III then bestowed a pension on Burke but failed to go through the formality of submitting the award to Parliament for approval. Francis Russell (1762-1802), the fifth Duke of Bedford, raised an objection to the pension in the House of Lords. Burke attempted to vindicate himself in the form of an "open letter," which John Morley, the nineteenth-century critic, called "the most splendid repartee in the English language." Only about a third of the 1796 Letter is reproduced here; about twenty paragraphs have been omitted from the beginning of the Letter and about the same number of paragraphs from the end. In the paragraph immediately preceding the first paragraph printed here, Burke said, "The awful state of the time, and not myself or my own justification, is my true object in what I now write, or in what I shall ever write or say."

The Duke of Bedford conceives that he is obliged to call the attention of the House of Peers to his Majesty's grant to me, which he considers excessive and out of all bounds.

I know not how it has happened, but it really seems that, whilst his Grace was meditating his well-considered censure upon me, he fell into a sort of sleep. Homer nods; and the Duke of Bedford may dream; and as dreams (even his golden dreams) are apt to be ill-pieced and incongruously put together, his Grace preserved his idea of reproach to *me,* but took the subject-matter from the Crown grants *to his own family.* This is "the stuff of which his dreams are made." In that way of putting things together his Grace is perfectly in the right. The grants to the house of Russell were so enormous, as not only to outrage economy, but even to stagger credulity. The Duke of Bedford is the leviathan among all the creatures of the Crown. He tumbles about his unwieldy bulk; he plays and frolics in the ocean of the royal bounty. Huge as he is, and whilst "he lies floating many a rood," he is still a creature. His ribs, his fins, his whalebone, his blubber, the very spiracles through which he spouts a torrent of brine against his origin and covers me all over with the spray—everything of him and about him is from the throne. Is it for *him* to question the dispensation of the royal favour?

I really am at a loss to draw any sort of parallel between the public merits of his Grace, by which he justifies the grants he holds, and these services of mine, on the favourable construction of which I have obtained what his Grace so much disapproves. In private life, I have not at all the honour of acquaintance with the noble Duke. But I ought to presume, and it costs me nothing to do so, that he abundantly deserves the esteem and love of all who live with him. But as to public service, why truly it would not be more ridiculous for me to compare myself in rank, in fortune, in splendid descent, in youth, strength, or figure, with the Duke of Bedford, than to make a parallel between his services and my attempts to be useful to my country. It would not be gross adulation, but uncivil irony, to say that he has any public merit of his own to keep alive the idea of the services by which his vast landed pensions were obtained. My merits, whatever they are, are original and personal; his are derivative. It is his ancestor, the original pensioner, that has laid up this inexhaustible fund of merit, which makes his Grace so very delicate and exceptious about the merit of all other grantees of the Crown. Had he permitted me to remain in quiet, I should have said, 'tis his estate; that's enough. It is his by law; what have I to do with it or its history? He would naturally have said on his side, 'tis this man's fortune.—He is as good now as my ancestor was two hundred and fifty years ago. I am a young man with very old pensions; he is an old man with very young pensions,—that's all.

Why will his Grace, by attacking me, force me reluctantly to compare my little merit with that which obtained from the Crown those prodigies of profuse donation, by which he tramples on the mediocrity of humble and laborious individuals? I would willingly leave him to the herald's college, which the philosophy of the *sans culottes* (prouder by far than all the Garters, and Norroys, and Clarencieux, and Rouge Dragons, that ever pranced in a procession of what his friends call aristocrats and despots) will abolish with contumely and scorn. These historians, recorders, and blazoners of virtues and arms, differ wholly from that other description of historians, who never assign any act of politicians to a good motive. These gentle historians, on the contrary, dip their pens in nothing but the milk of human kindness. They seek no further for merit than the preamble of a patent or the inscription on a tomb. With them every man created a peer is first a hero ready made. They judge of every man's capacity for office by the offices he has filled; and the more offices the more ability. Every general officer with them is a Marlborough; every statesman a Burleigh; every judge a Murray or a Yorke. They who, alive, were laughed at or pitied by all their acquaintance make as good a figure as the best of them in the pages of Guillim, Edmondson, and Collins.

To these recorders, so full of good nature to the great and prosperous, I would willingly leave the first Baron Russell, and Earl of Bedford, and the merits of his grants. But the aulnager, the weigher, the meter of grants, will not suffer us to acquiesce in the judgment of the prince reigning at the time when they were made. They are never good to those who earn them. Well then; since the new grantees have war made on them by the old, and that the word of the sovereign is not to be taken, let us turn our eyes to history, in which great men have always a pleasure in contemplating the heroic origin of their house.

The first peer of the name, the first purchaser of the grants, was a Mr. Russell, a person of an ancient gentleman's family raised by being a minion of Henry the Eighth. As there generally is some resemblance of character to create these relations, the favourite was in all likelihood much such another as his master. The first of those immoderate grants was not taken from the ancient demesne of the Crown, but from the recent confiscation of the ancient nobility of the land. The lion having sucked the blood of his prey threw the offal carcass to the jackal in waiting. Having tasted once the food of confiscation, the favourites became fierce and ravenous. This worthy favourite's first grant was from the lay nobility. The second, infinitely improving on the enormity of the first, was from the plunder of the church. In truth his Grace is somewhat excusable for his dislike to a grant like mine, not only in its quantity, but in its kind so different from his own.

Mine was from a mild and benevolent sovereign; his from Henry the Eighth.

Mine had not its fund in the murder of any innocent person of illustrious rank or in the pillage of any body of unoffending men. His grants were from the aggregate and consolidated funds of judgments iniquitously legal and from possessions voluntarily surrendered by the lawful proprietors, with the gibbet at their door.

The merit of the grantee whom he derives from was that of being a prompt and greedy instrument of a *levelling* tyrant, who oppressed all descriptions of his people, but who fell with particular fury on everything that was *great and noble.* Mine has been, in endeavouring to screen every man, in every class, from oppression, and particularly in defending the high and eminent, who in the bad times of confiscating princes, confiscating chief governors, or confiscating demagogues, are the most exposed to jealousy, avarice, and envy.

The merit of the original grantee of his Grace's pensions was in giving his hand to the work and partaking the spoil with a prince, who plundered a part of the national church of his time and country. Mine was in defending the whole of the national church of my own time and my own country, and the whole of the national churches of all countries, from the principles and the examples which lead to ecclesiastical pillage, thence to a contempt of all prescriptive titles, thence to the pillage of *all* property, and thence to universal desolation.

The merit of the origin of his Grace's fortune was in being a favourite and chief adviser to a prince, who left no liberty to their native country. My endeavour was to obtain liberty for the municipal country in which I was born and for all descriptions and denominations in it. Mine was to support with unrelaxing vigilance every right, every privilege, every franchise, in this my adopted, my dearer, and more comprehensive country; and not only to preserve those rights in this chief seat of empire, but in every nation, in every land, in every climate, language, and religion, in the vast domain that is still under the protection, and the larger that was once under the protection, of the British Crown.

His founder's merits were, by arts in which he served his master and made his fortune, to bring poverty, wretchedness, and depopulation on his country. Mine were, under a benevolent prince, in promoting the commerce, manufacture, and agriculture of his kingdom; in which his Majesty shows in eminent example, who even in his amusements is a patriot, and in hours of leisure an improver of his native soil.

His founder's merit was the merit of a gentleman raised by the arts of a court, and the protection of a Wolsey, to the eminence of a great and potent lord. His merit in that eminence was, by instigating a tyrant to injustice, to provoke a people to rebellion. My merit was, to awaken the sober part of the country, that they might put themselves on their guard against any one potent lord, or any greater number of potent lords, or any combination of great leading men of any sort, if ever they should attempt to proceed in the same courses, but in the reverse order; that is, by instigating a corrupted populace to rebellion and, through that rebellion, introducing a tyranny yet worse than the tyranny which his Grace's ancestor supported and of which he profited in the manner we behold in the despotism of Henry the Eighth.

The political merit of the first pensioner of his Grace's house was that of being concerned as a counsellor of state in advising, and in his person executing, the conditions of a dishonourable peace with France; the surrendering the fortress of Boulogne, then our out-guard on the Continent. By that surrender, Calais, the key of France and the bridle in the mouth of that power, was, not many years afterwards, finally lost. My merit has been in resisting the power and pride of France, under any form of its rule; but in opposing it with the greatest zeal and earnestness, when that rule appeared in the worst form it could assume; the worst indeed which the prime cause and principle of all evil could possibly give it. It was my endeavour by every means to excite a spirit in the House where I had the honour of a seat, for carrying on, with early vigour and decision, the most clearly just and necessary war, that this or any nation ever carried on; in order to save my country from the iron yoke of its power and from the more dreadful contagion of its principles; to preserve, while they can be preserved, pure and untainted, the ancient, inbred integrity, piety, good nature, and good humour of the people of England, from the dreadful pestilence, which, beginning in France, threatens to lay waste the whole moral, and in a great degree the whole physical, world, having done both in the focus of its most intense malignity.

The labours of his Grace's founder merited the curses, not loud but deep, of the Commons of England, on whom *he* and his master had effected a *complete parliamentary reform,* by making them, in their slavery and humiliation, the true and adequate representatives of a debased, degraded, and undone people. My merits were, in having had an active, though not always an ostentatious, share, in every one act, without exception, of undisputed constitutional utility in my time, and in having supported, on all occasions, the authority, the efficiency, and the privileges of the Commons of Great Britain. I ended my services by a recorded and fully reasoned assertion on their own journals of their constitutional rights and a vindication of their constitutional conduct. I laboured in all things to merit their inward approbation; and (along with the assistance of the largest, the greatest, and best of my endeavours) I received their free, unbiased, public, and solemn thanks.

Thus stands the account of the comparative merits of the Crown grants which compose the Duke of Bedford's fortune as balanced against mine. In the name of common sense, why should the Duke of Bedford think that none but of the House of Russell are entitled to the favour of the Crown? Why should he imagine that no king of England has been capable of judging of merit but King Henry the Eighth? Indeed, he will pardon me; he is a little mistaken; all virtue did not end in the first Earl of Bedford. All discernment did not lose its vision when his Creator closed his eyes. Let him remit his rigour on the disproportion between merit and reward in others, and they will make no inquiry into the origin of his fortune. They will regard with much more satisfaction, as he will contemplate with infinitely more advantage, whatever in his pedigree has been dulcified by an exposure to the influence of heaven in a long flow of generations, from the hard, acidulous, metallic tincture of the spring. It is little to be doubted that several of his forefathers in that long series have degenerated into honour and virtue. Let the Duke of Bedford (I am sure he will) reject with scorn and horror the counsels of the lecturers, those wicked panders to avarice and ambition, who would tempt him, in the troubles of his country, to seek another enormous fortune from the forfeitures of another nobility and the plunder of another church. Let him (and I trust that yet he will) employ all the energy of his youth and all the resources of his wealth to crush rebellious principles which have no foundation in morals and rebellious movements that have no provocation in tyranny.

Then will be forgot the rebellions, which, by a doubtful priority in crime, his ancestor had provoked and extinguished. On such a conduct in the noble Duke, many of his countrymen might, and with some excuse might, give way to the enthusiasm of their gratitude and, in the dashing style of some of the old declaimers, cry out that if the fates had found no other way in which they could give a Duke of Bedford and his opulence as props to a tottering world, then the butchery of the Duke of Buckingham might be tolerated; it might be regarded even with complacency, whilst in the heir of confiscation they saw the sympathizing comforter of the martyrs who suffered under the cruel confiscation of this day; whilst they behold with admiration his zealous protection of the virtuous and loyal nobility of France and his manly support to his brethren, the yet standing nobility and gentry of his native land. Then his Grace's merit would be pure, and new, and sharp, as fresh from the mint of honour. As he pleased he might reflect honour on his predecessors or throw it forward on those who were to succeed him. He might be the propagator of the stock of honour, or the root of it, as he thought proper.

Had it pleased God to continue to me the hopes of succession, I should have been, according to my mediocrity and the mediocrity of the age I live in, a sort of founder of a family; I should have left a son, who, in all the points in which personal merit can be viewed, in science, in erudition, in genius, in taste, in honour, in generosity, in humanity, in every liberal sentiment and every liberal accomplishment, would not have shown himself inferior to the Duke of Bedford or to any of those whom he traces in his line. His Grace very soon would have wanted all plausibility in his attack upon that provision which belonged more to mine than to me. He would soon have supplied every deficiency and symmetrized every disproportion. It would not have been for that successor to resort to any stagnant wasting reservoir of merit in me or in any ancestry. He had in himself a salient, living spring of generous and manly action. Every day he lived he would have re-purchased the bounty of the Crown and ten times more, if ten times more he had received. He was made a public creature; and had no enjoyment what ever but in the performance of some duty. At this exigent moment, the loss of a finished man is not easily supplied.

But a Disposer whose power we are little able to resist and whose wisdom it behooves us not at all to dispute, has ordained it in another manner and (whatever my querulous weakness might suggest) a far better. The storm has gone over me; and I lie like one of those old oaks which the late hurricane has scattered about me. I am stripped of all my honours, I am torn up by the roots and lie prostrate on the earth! There, and prostrate there, I most unfeignedly recognize the Divine justice and in some degree submit to it. But whilst I humble myself before God, I do not know that it is forbidden to repel the attacks of unjust and inconsiderate men. The patience of Job is proverbial. After some of the convulsive struggles of our irritable nature, he submitted himself and repented in dust and ashes. But even so, I do not find him blamed for reprehending, and with a considerable degree of verbal asperity, those ill-natured neighbours of his, who visited his dunghill to read moral, political, and economical lectures on his misery. I am alone. I have none to meet my enemies in the gate. Indeed, my Lord, I greatly deceive myself, if in this hard season I would give a peck of refuse wheat for all that is called fame and honour in the world. This is the appetite but of a few. It is a luxury, it is a privilege, it is an indulgence for those who are at their ease. But we are all of us made to shun disgrace, as we are made to shrink from pain and poverty and disease. It is an instinct; and under the direction of reason, instinct is always in the right. I live in an inverted order. They who ought to have succeeded me are gone before me. They who should have been to me as posterity are in the place of ancestors. I owe to the dearest relation (which ever must subsist in memory) that act of piety which he would have performed to me; I owe it to him to show that he was not descended, as the Duke of Bedford would have it, from an unworthy parent.

The Crown has considered me after long service; the Crown has paid the Duke of Bedford by advance. He has had a long credit for any service which he may perform hereafter. He is secure, and long may he be secure in his advance, whether he performs any services or not. But let him take care how he endangers the safety of that constitution which secures his own utility or his own insignificance; or how he discourages those who take up, even puny arms, to defend an order of things which, like the sun of heaven, shines alike on the useful and the worthless. His grants are ingrafted on the public law of Europe, covered with the awful hoar of innumerable ages. They are guarded by the sacred rules of prescription, found in that full treasury of jurisprudence from which the jejuneness and penury of our municipal law has, by degrees, been enriched and strengthened. This prescription I had my share (a very full share) in bringing to its perfection. The Duke of Bedford will stand as long as prescriptive law endures; as long as the great stable laws of property, common to us with all civilized nations, are kept in their integrity and without the smallest intermixture of laws, maxims, principles, or precedents of the grand Revolution. They are secure against all changes but one. The whole revolutionary system, institutes, digest, code, novels, text, gloss, comment, are not only the same but they are the very reverse, and the reverse fundamentals, of all the laws on which civil life has hitherto been upheld in all the governments of the world. The learned professors of the rights of man regard prescription, not as a title to bar all claim, set up against all possession—but they look on prescription as itself a bar against the possessor and proprietor. They hold an immemorial possession to be no more than a long-continued and therefore an aggravated injustice.

Such are *their* ideas; such *their* religion, and such *their* law. But as to *our* country and *our* race, as long as the well-compacted structure of our church and state, the sanctuary, the holy of holies of that ancient law, defended by reverence, defended by power, a fortress at once and a temple, shall stand inviolate on the brow of the British Sion—as long as the British monarchy, not more limited than fenced by the orders of the state, shall, like the proud Keep of Windsor, rising in the majesty of proportion and girt with the double belt of its kindred and coeval towers, as long as this awful structure shall oversee and guard the subjected land—so long the mounds and dykes of the low, fat Bedford level will have nothing to fear from all the pickaxes of all the levellers of France. As long as our sovereign lord the king and his faithful subjects, the Lords and Commons of this realm—the triple cord which no man can break; the solemn, sworn, constitutional frank-pledge of this nation; the firm guarantees of each other's beings and each other's rights; tie joint and several securities, each in its place and order, for every kind and every quality of property and of dignity; as long as these endure, so long the Duke of Bedford is safe: and we are all safe together—the high from the blights of envy and the spoliations of rapacity; the low from the hand of oppression and the insolent spurn of contempt....

Freedom in Iraq and Middle East

By President George W. Bush, 20th Anniversary of the National Endowment for Democracy, United States Chamber of Commerce, Washington, D.C. 11/06/03

Thank you all very much. Please be seated. Thanks for the warm welcome, and thanks for inviting me to join you in this 20th anniversary of the National Endowment for Democracy. The staff and directors of this organization have seen a lot of history over the last two decades, you've been a part of that history. By speaking for and standing for freedom, you've lifted the hopes of people around the world, and you've brought great credit to America.

I appreciate Vin for the short introduction. I'm a man who likes short introductions. And he didn't let me down. But more importantly, I appreciate the invitation. I appreciate the members of Congress who are here, senators from both political parties, members of the House of Representatives from both political parties. I appreciate the ambassadors who are here. I appreciate the guests who have come. I appreciate the bipartisan spirit, the nonpartisan spirit of the National Endowment for Democracy. I'm glad that Republicans and Democrats and independents are working together to advance human liberty.

The roots of our democracy can be traced to England, and to its Parliament -- and so can the roots of this organization. In June of 1982, President Ronald Reagan spoke at Westminster Palace and declared, the turning point had arrived in history. He argued that Soviet communism had failed, precisely because it did not respect its own people -- their creativity, their genius and their rights.

President Reagan said that the day of Soviet tyranny was passing, that freedom had a momentum which would not be halted. He gave this organization its mandate: to add to the momentum of freedom across the world. Your mandate was important 20 years ago; it is equally important today. (Applause.)

A number of critics were dismissive of that speech by the President. According to one editorial of the time, "It seems hard to be a sophisticated European and also an admirer of Ronald Reagan." (Laughter.) Some observers on both sides of the Atlantic pronounced the speech simplistic and naive, and even dangerous. In fact, Ronald Reagan's words were courageous and optimistic and entirely correct. (Applause.)

The great democratic movement President Reagan described was already well underway. In the early 1970s, there were about 40 democracies in the world. By the middle of that decade, Portugal and Spain and Greece held free elections. Soon there were new democracies in Latin America, and free institutions were spreading in Korea, in Taiwan, and in East Asia. This very week in 1989, there were protests in East Berlin and in Leipzig. By the end of that year, every communist dictatorship in Central America had collapsed. Within another year, the South African government released Nelson Mandela. Four years later, he was elected president of his country -- ascending, like Walesa and Havel, from prisoner of state to head of state.

As the 20th century ended, there were around 120 democracies in the world -- and I can assure you more are on the way. (Applause.) Ronald Reagan would be pleased, and he would not be surprised.

We've witnessed, in little over a generation, the swiftest advance of freedom in the 2,500 year story of democracy. Historians in the future will offer their own explanations for why this happened. Yet we already know some of the reasons they will cite. It is no accident that the rise of so many democracies took place in a time when the world's most influential nation was itself a democracy.

The United States made military and moral commitments in Europe and Asia, which protected free nations from aggression, and created the conditions in which new democracies could flourish. As we provided security for whole nations, we also provided inspiration for oppressed peoples. In prison camps, in banned union meetings, in clandestine churches, men and women knew that the whole world was not sharing their own nightmare. They knew of at least one place -- a bright and hopeful land -- where freedom was valued and secure. And they prayed that America would not forget them, or forget the mission to promote liberty around the world.

Historians will note that in many nations, the advance of markets and free enterprise helped to create a middle class that was confident enough to demand their own rights. They will point to the role of technology in frustrating censorship and central control -- and marvel at the power of instant communications to spread the truth, the news, and courage across borders.

Historians in the future will reflect on an extraordinary, undeniable fact: Over time, free nations grow stronger and dictatorships grow weaker. In the middle of the 20th century, some imagined that the central planning and social regimentation were a shortcut to national strength. In fact, the prosperity, and social vitality and technological progress of a people are directly determined by extent of their liberty. Freedom honors and unleashes human creativity -- and creativity determines the strength and wealth of nations. Liberty is both the plan of Heaven for humanity, and the best hope for progress here on Earth.

The progress of liberty is a powerful trend. Yet, we also know that liberty, if not defended, can be lost. The success of freedom is not determined by some dialectic of history. By definition, the success of freedom rests upon the choices and the courage of free peoples, and upon their willingness to sacrifice. In the trenches of World War I, through a two-front war in the 1940s, the difficult battles of Korea and Vietnam, and in missions of rescue and liberation on nearly every continent, Americans have amply displayed our willingness to sacrifice for liberty.

The sacrifices of Americans have not always been recognized or appreciated, yet they have been worthwhile. Because we and our allies were steadfast, Germany and Japan are democratic nations that no longer threaten the world. A global nuclear standoff with the Soviet Union ended peacefully -- as did the Soviet Union. The nations of Europe are moving towards unity, not dividing into armed camps and descending into genocide. Every nation has learned, or should have learned, an important lesson: Freedom is worth fighting for, dying for, and standing for -- and the advance of freedom leads to peace. (Applause.)

And now we must apply that lesson in our own time. We've reached another great turning point -- and the resolve we show will shape the next stage of the world democratic movement.

Our commitment to democracy is tested in countries like Cuba and Burma and North Korea and Zimbabwe -- outposts of oppression in our world. The people in these nations live in captivity, and fear and silence. Yet, these regimes cannot hold back freedom forever -- and, one day, from prison camps and prison cells, and from exile, the leaders of new democracies will arrive. (Applause.) Communism, and militarism and rule by the capricious and corrupt are the relics of a passing era. And we will stand with these oppressed peoples until the day of their freedom finally arrives. (Applause.)

Our commitment to democracy is tested in China. That nation now has a sliver, a fragment of liberty. Yet, China's people will eventually want their liberty pure and whole. China has discovered that economic freedom leads to national wealth. China's leaders will also discover that freedom is indivisible -- that social and religious freedom is also essential to national greatness and national dignity. Eventually, men and women who are allowed to control their own wealth will insist on controlling their own lives and their own country.

Our commitment to democracy is also tested in the Middle East, which is my focus today, and must be a focus of American policy for decades to come. In many nations of the Middle East -- countries of great strategic importance -- democracy has not yet taken root. And the questions arise: Are the peoples of the Middle East somehow beyond the reach of liberty? Are millions of men and women and children condemned by history or culture to live in despotism? Are they alone never to know freedom, and never even to have a choice in the matter? I, for one, do not believe it. I believe every person has the ability and the right to be free. (Applause.)

Some skeptics of democracy assert that the traditions of Islam are inhospitable to the representative government. This "cultural condescension," as Ronald Reagan termed it, has a long history. After the Japanese surrender in 1945, a so-called Japan expert asserted that democracy in that former empire would "never work." Another observer declared the prospects for democracy in post-Hitler Germany are, and I quote, "most uncertain at best" -- he made that claim in 1957. Seventy-four years ago, The Sunday London Times declared nine-tenths of the population of India to be "illiterates not caring a fig for politics." Yet when Indian democracy was imperiled in the 1970s, the Indian people showed their commitment to liberty in a national referendum that saved their form of government.

Time after time, observers have questioned whether this country, or that people, or this group, are "ready" for democracy -- as if freedom were a prize you win for meeting our own Western standards of progress. In fact, the daily work of democracy itself is the path of progress. It teaches cooperation, the free exchange of ideas, and the peaceful resolution of differences. As men and women are showing, from Bangladesh to Botswana, to Mongolia, it is the practice of democracy that makes a nation ready for democracy, and every nation can start on this path.

It should be clear to all that Islam -- the faith of one-fifth of humanity -- is consistent with democratic rule. Democratic progress is found in many predominantly Muslim countries -- in Turkey and Indonesia, and Senegal and Albania, Niger and Sierra Leone. Muslim men and women are good citizens of India and South Africa, of the nations of Western Europe, and of the United States of America.

More than half of all the Muslims in the world live in freedom under democratically constituted governments. They succeed in democratic societies, not in spite of their faith, but because of it. A religion that demands individual moral accountability, and encourages the encounter of the individual with God, is fully compatible with the rights and responsibilities of self-government.

Yet there's a great challenge today in the Middle East. In the words of a recent report by Arab scholars, the global wave of democracy has -- and I quote -- "barely reached the Arab states." They continue: "This freedom deficit undermines human development and is one of the most painful manifestations of lagging political development." The freedom deficit they describe has terrible consequences, of the people of the Middle East and for the world. In many Middle Eastern countries, poverty is deep and it is spreading, women lack rights and are denied schooling. Whole societies remain stagnant while the world moves ahead. These are not the failures of a culture or a religion. These are the failures of political and economic doctrines.

As the colonial era passed away, the Middle East saw the establishment of many military dictatorships. Some rulers adopted the dogmas of socialism, seized total control of political parties and the media and universities. They allied themselves with the Soviet bloc and with international terrorism. Dictators in Iraq and Syria promised the restoration of national honor, a return to ancient glories. They've left instead a legacy of torture, oppression, misery, and ruin.

Other men, and groups of men, have gained influence in the Middle East and beyond through an ideology of theocratic terror. Behind their language of religion is the ambition for absolute political power. Ruling cabals like the Taliban show their version of religious piety in public whippings of women, ruthless suppression of any difference or dissent, and support for terrorists who arm and train to murder the innocent. The Taliban promised religious purity and national pride. Instead, by systematically destroying a proud and working society, they left behind suffering and starvation.

Many Middle Eastern governments now understand that military dictatorship and theocratic rule are a straight, smooth highway to nowhere. But some governments still cling to the old habits of central control. There are governments that still fear and repress independent thought and creativity, and private enterprise -- the human qualities that make for a -- strong and successful societies. Even when these nations have vast natural resources, they do not respect or develop their greatest resources -- the talent and energy of men and women working and living in freedom.

Instead of dwelling on past wrongs and blaming others, governments in the Middle East need to confront real problems, and serve the true interests of their nations. The good and capable people of the Middle East all deserve responsible leadership. For too long, many people in that region have been victims and subjects -- they deserve to be active citizens.

Governments across the Middle East and North Africa are beginning to see the need for change. Morocco has a diverse new parliament; King Mohammed has urged it to extend the rights to women. Here is how His Majesty explained his reforms to parliament: "How can society achieve progress while women, who represent half the nation, see their rights violated and suffer as a result of injustice, violence, and marginalization, notwithstanding the dignity and justice granted to them by our glorious religion?" The King of Morocco is correct: The future of Muslim nations will be better for all with the full participation of women. (Applause.)

In Bahrain last year, citizens elected their own parliament for the first time in nearly three decades. Oman has extended the vote to all adult citizens; Qatar has a new constitution; Yemen has a multiparty political system; Kuwait has a directly elected national assembly; and Jordan held historic elections this summer. Recent surveys in Arab nations reveal broad support for political pluralism, the rule of law, and free speech. These are the stirrings of Middle Eastern democracy, and they carry the promise of greater change to come.

As changes come to the Middle Eastern region, those with power should ask themselves: Will they be remembered for resisting reform, or for leading it? In Iran, the demand for democracy is strong and broad, as we saw last month when thousands gathered to welcome home Shirin Ebadi, the winner of the Nobel Peace Prize. The regime in Teheran must heed the democratic demands of the Iranian people, or lose its last claim to legitimacy. (Applause.)

For the Palestinian people, the only path to independence and dignity and progress is the path of democracy. (Applause.) And the Palestinian leaders who block and undermine democratic reform, and feed hatred and encourage violence are not leaders at all. They're the main obstacles to peace, and to the success of the Palestinian people.

The Saudi government is taking first steps toward reform, including a plan for gradual introduction of elections. By giving the Saudi people a greater role in their own society, the Saudi government can demonstrate true leadership in the region.

The great and proud nation of Egypt has shown the way toward peace in the Middle East, and now should show the way toward democracy in the Middle East. (Applause.) Champions of democracy in the region understand that democracy is not perfect, it is not the path to utopia, but it's the only path to national success and dignity.

As we watch and encourage reforms in the region, we are mindful that modernization is not the same as Westernization. Representative governments in the Middle East will reflect their own cultures. They will not, and should not, look like us. Democratic nations may be constitutional monarchies, federal republics, or parliamentary systems. And working democracies always need time to develop -- as did our own. We've taken a 200-year journey toward inclusion and justice -- and this makes us patient and understanding as other nations are at different stages of this journey.

There are, however, essential principles common to every successful society, in every culture. Successful societies limit the power of the state and the power of the military -- so that governments respond to the will of the people, and not the will of an elite. Successful societies protect freedom with the consistent and impartial rule of law, instead of selecting applying -- selectively applying the law to punish political opponents. Successful societies allow room for healthy civic institutions -- for political parties and labor unions and independent newspapers and broadcast media. Successful societies guarantee religious liberty -- the right to serve and honor God without fear of persecution. Successful societies privatize their economies, and secure the rights of property. They prohibit and punish official corruption, and invest in the health and education of their people. They recognize the rights of women. And instead of directing hatred and resentment against others, successful societies appeal to the hopes of their own people. (Applause.)

These vital principles are being applied in the nations of Afghanistan and Iraq. With the steady leadership of President Karzai, the people of Afghanistan are building a modern and peaceful government. Next month, 500 delegates will convene a national assembly in Kabul to approve a new Afghan constitution. The proposed draft would establish a bicameral parliament, set national elections next year, and recognize Afghanistan's Muslim identity, while protecting the rights of all citizens. Afghanistan faces continuing economic and security challenges -- it will face those challenges as a free and stable democracy. (Applause.)

In Iraq, the Coalition Provisional Authority and the Iraqi Governing Council are also working together to build a democracy -- and after three decades of tyranny, this work is not easy. The former dictator ruled by terror and treachery, and left deeply ingrained habits of fear and distrust. Remnants of his regime, joined by foreign terrorists, continue their battle against order and against civilization. Our coalition is responding to recent attacks with precision raids, guided by intelligence provided by the Iraqis, themselves. And we're working closely with Iraqi citizens as they prepare a constitution, as they move toward free elections and take increasing responsibility for their own affairs. As in the defense of Greece in 1947, and later in the Berlin Airlift, the strength and will of free peoples are now being tested before a watching world. And we will meet this test. (Applause.)

Securing democracy in Iraq is the work of many hands. American and coalition forces are sacrificing for the peace of Iraq and for the security of free nations. Aid workers from many countries are facing danger to help the Iraqi people. The National Endowment for Democracy is promoting women's rights, and training Iraqi journalists, and teaching the skills of political participation. Iraqis, themselves -- police and borders guards and local officials -- are joining in the work and they are sharing in the sacrifice.

This is a massive and difficult undertaking -- it is worth our effort, it is worth our sacrifice, because we know the stakes. The failure of Iraqi democracy would embolden terrorists around the world, increase dangers to the American people, and extinguish the hopes of millions in the region. Iraqi democracy will succeed -- and that success will send forth the news, from Damascus to Teheran -- that freedom can be the future of every nation. (Applause.) The establishment of a free Iraq at the heart of the Middle East will be a watershed event in the global democratic revolution. (Applause.)

Sixty years of Western nations excusing and accommodating the lack of freedom in the Middle East did nothing to make us safe -- because in the long run, stability cannot be purchased at the expense of liberty. As long as the Middle East remains a place where freedom does not flourish, it will remain a place of stagnation, resentment, and violence ready for export. And with the spread of weapons that can bring catastrophic harm to our country and to our friends, it would be reckless to accept the status quo. (Applause.)

Therefore, the United States has adopted a new policy, a forward strategy of freedom in the Middle East. This strategy requires the same persistence and energy and idealism we have shown before. And it will yield the same results. As in Europe, as in Asia, as in every region of the world, the advance of freedom leads to peace. (Applause.)

The advance of freedom is the calling of our time; it is the calling of our country. From the Fourteen Points to the Four Freedoms, to the Speech at Westminster, America has put our power at the service of principle. We believe that liberty is the design of nature; we believe that liberty is the direction of history. We believe that human fulfillment and excellence come in the responsible exercise of liberty. And we believe that freedom -- the freedom we prize -- is not for us alone, it is the right and the capacity of all mankind. (Applause.)

Working for the spread of freedom can be hard. Yet, America has accomplished hard tasks before. Our nation is strong; we're strong of heart. And we're not alone. Freedom is finding allies in every country; freedom finds allies in every culture. And as we meet the terror and violence of the world, we can be certain the author of freedom is not indifferent to the fate of freedom.

With all the tests and all the challenges of our age, this is, above all, the age of liberty. Each of you at this Endowment is fully engaged in the great cause of liberty. And I thank you. May God bless your work. And may God continue to bless America.

ADDRESS

BY PRIME MINISTER NEVILLE CHAMBERLAIN IN THE HOUSE OF COMMONS - SEPTEMBER 1, 1939

I do not propose to say many words to-night. The time has come when action rather than speech is required. Eighteen months ago in this House I prayed that the responsibility might not fall upon me to ask this country to accept the awful arbitrament of war. I fear that I may not be able to avoid that responsibility. But, at any rate, I cannot wish for conditions in which such a burden should fall upon me in which I should feel clearer than I do to-day as to where my duty lies. No man can say that the Government could have done more to try to keep open the way for an honorable and equitable settlement of the dispute between Germany and Poland. Nor have we neglected any means of making it crystal clear to the German Government that if they insisted on using force again in the manner in which they had used it in the past we were resolved to oppose them by force. Now that all the relevant documents are being made public we shall stand at the bar of history knowing that the responsibility for this terrible catastrophe lies on the shoulders of one man - the German Chancellor, who has not hesitated to plunge the world into misery in order to serve his own senseless ambitions.

I would like to thank the House for the forbearance which they have shown on two recent occasions for not demanding from me information which they recognized I could not give while these negotiations were still in progress. I have now had all the correspondence with the German Government put into the form of a White Paper. On account of mechanical difficulties I am afraid there are still but a few copies available, but I understand that they will be coming in in relays while the House is sitting. I do not think it necessary for me to refer in detail now to these documents, which are already past history. They make it perfectly clear that our object has been to try and bring about discussions of the Polish-German dispute between the two countries themselves on terms of equality, the settlement to be one which safeguards the independence of Poland and of which the due observance would be secured by international guarantees. There is just one passage from a recent communication, which is dated the 30th August, which I should like to quote, because it shows how easily the final clash might have been avoided had there been the least desire on the part of the German Government to arrive at a peaceful settlement. In this document we said:

> *His Majesty's Government fully recognizes the need for speed in the initiation of discussions and they share the apprehensions of the Chancellor arising from the proximity of two mobilized armies standing face to face. They would accordingly most strongly urge that both parties should undertake that during the negotiations no aggressive military movements should take place. His Majesty's Government feel confident that they could obtain such an undertaking from the Polish Government if the German Government would give similar assurances.*

That telegram, which was repeated in Poland, brought an instantaneous reply from the Polish Government, dated the 31st August, in which they said:

> *The Polish Government are also prepared on a reciprocal basis to give a formal guarantee in the event of negotiations taking place that Polish troops will not violate the frontiers of the German Reich provided a*

corresponding guarantee is given regarding the non-violation of the frontiers of Poland by troops of the German Reich.

We never had a reply from the German Government to that suggestion, one which, if it had been followed, might have saved the catastrophe which took place this morning. In the German broadcast last night, which recited the 16 points of the proposals which they have put forward, there occurred this sentence: "In these circumstances the Reich Government considers its proposals rejected."

I must examine that statement. I must tell the House what are the circumstances. To begin with let me say that the text of these proposals has never been communicated by Germany to Poland at all. The history of the matter is this. On Tuesday, the 29th August, in replying to a Note which we had sent to them, the German Government said, among other things, that they would immediately draw up proposals for a solution acceptable to themselves and "...will, if possible, place these at the disposal of the British Government before the arrival of the Polish negotiator."

It will be seen by examination of the White Paper that the German Government had stated that they counted upon the arrival of a plenipotentiary from Poland in Berlin on the 30th that is to say, on the following day. In the meantime, of course, we were awaiting these proposals. The next evening, when our Ambassador saw Herr von Ribbentrop, the German Foreign Secretary, he urged upon the latter that when these proposals were ready - for we had heard no more about them - he should invite the Polish Ambassador to call and should hand him the proposals for transmission to his Government. Thereupon, reports our Ambassador, in the most violent terms Herr von Ribbentrop said he would never ask the Ambassador to visit him. He hinted that if the Polish Ambassador asked him for an interview it might be different.

The House will see that this was on Wednesday night, which according to the German Statement of last night, is now claimed to be the final date after which no negotiation with Poland was acceptable. It is plain, therefore, that Germany claims to treat Poland as in the wrong because she had not by Wednesday night entered upon discussions with Germany about a set of proposals of which she had never heard.

Now what of ourselves? On that Wednesday night, at the interview to which I have just referred, Herr von Ribbentrop produced a lengthy document which he read out in German aloud, at top speed. Naturally, after this reading our Ambassador asked for a copy of the document, but the reply was that it was now too late, as the Polish representative had not arrived in Berlin by midnight. And so, Sir, we never got a copy of those proposals, and the first time we heard them - WE heard them - was on the broadcast last night. Well, Sir, those are the circumstances in which the German Government said that they would consider that their negotiations were rejected. Is it not clear that their conception of a negotiation was that on almost instantaneous demand a Polish plenipotentiary should go to Berlin - where others had been before him - and should there receive a statement of demands to be accepted in their entirety or refused? I am not pronouncing any opinion upon the terms themselves, for I do not feel called upon to do so. The proper course, in our view - in the view of all of us - was that these proposals should have been put before the Poles, who should have been given time to consider them and to say whether, in their opinion, they did or did not infringe those vital interests of Poland which Germany had assured us on a previous occasion she intended to respect. Only last night the Polish Ambassador did see the German Foreign Secretary, Herr von

Ribbentrop. Once again he expressed to him what, indeed, the Polish Government had already said publicly, that they were willing to negotiate with Germany about their disputes on an equal basis. What was the reply of the German Government? The reply was that without another word the German troops crossed the Polish frontier this morning at dawn and are since reported to be bombing open towns. In these circumstances there is only one course open to us. His Majesty's Ambassador in Berlin and the French Ambassador have been instructed to hand to the German Government the following document:

> *Early this morning the German Chancellor issued a proclamation to the German Army which indicated that he was about to attack Poland. Information which has reached His Majesty's Government in the United Kingdom and the French Government indicates that attacks upon Polish towns are proceeding. In these circumstances it appears to the Governments of the United Kingdom and France that by their action the German Government have created conditions, namely, an aggressive act of force against Poland threatening the independence of Poland, which call for the implementation by the Government of the United Kingdom and France of the undertaking to Poland to come to her assistance. I am accordingly to inform your Excellency that unless the German Government are prepared to give His Majesty's Government satisfactory assurances that the German Government have suspended all aggressive action against Poland and are prepared promptly to withdraw their forces from Polish territory, His Majesty's Government in the United Kingdom will without hesitation fulfill their obligations to Poland.*

If a reply to this last warning is unfavorable, and I do not suggest that it is likely to be otherwise, His Majesty's Ambassador is instructed to ask for his passports. In that case we are ready. Yesterday, we took further steps towards the completion of our defensive preparation. This morning we ordered complete mobilization of the whole of the Royal Navy, Army and Royal Air Force. We have also taken a number of other measures, both at home and abroad, which the House will not perhaps expect me to specify in detail. Briefly, they represent the final steps in accordance with pre-arranged plans. These last can be put into force rapidly, and are of such a nature that they can be deferred until war seems inevitable. Steps have also been taken under the powers conferred by the House last week to safeguard the position in regard to stocks of commodities of various kinds.

The thoughts of many of us must at this moment inevitably be turning back to 1914, and to a comparison of our position now with that which existed then. How do we stand this time? The answer is that all three Services are ready, and that the situation in all directions is far more favorable and reassuring than in 1914, while behind the fighting Services we have built up a vast organization of Civil Defense under our scheme of Air Raid Precautions. As regards the immediate man-power requirements, the Royal Navy, the Army and the Air Force are in the fortunate position of having almost as many men as they can conveniently handle at this moment. There are, however, certain categories of service in which men are immediately required, both for Military and Civil Defense. These will be announced in detail through the Press and the B.B.C. The main and most satisfactory point to observe is that there is today no need to make an appeal in a general way for recruits such as was issued by Lord Kitchener 25 years ago. That appeal has been anticipated by many months, and the men are already available.

So much for the immediate present. Now we must look to the future. It is essential in the face of the tremendous task which confronts us, more especially in view of our past experiences in this matter, to organize our man-power this time upon as methodical, equitable and economical a basis as possible. We, therefore, propose immediately to introduce legislation directed to that end. A Bill will be laid before you which for all practical purposes will amount to an expansion of the Military Training Act. Under its operation all fit men between the ages of 18 and 41 will be rendered liable to military service if and when called upon. It is not intended at the outset that any considerable number of men other than those already liable shall be called up, and steps will be taken to ensure that the man-power essentially required by industry shall not be taken away.

There is one other allusion which I should like to make before I end my speech, and that is to record my satisfaction of His Majesty's Government, that throughout these last days of crisis Signor Mussolini also has been doing his best to reach a solution.

It now only remains for us to set our teeth and to enter upon this struggle, which we ourselves earnestly endeavored to avoid, with determination to see it through to the end. We shall enter it with a clear conscience, with the support of the Dominions and the British Empire, and the moral approval of the greater part of the world. We have no quarrel with the German people, except that they allow themselves to be governed by a Nazi Government. As long as that Government exists and pursues the methods it has so persistently followed during the last two years, there will be no peace in Europe. We shall merely pass from one crisis to another, and see one country after another attacked by methods which have now become familiar to us in their sickening technique. We are resolved that these methods must come to an end. If out of the struggle we again re-establish in the world the rules of good faith and the renunciation of force, why, then even the sacrifices that will be entailed upon us will find their fullest justification.

© 1997 The Avalon Project. http://www.yale.edu/lawweb/avalon/wwii/gb1.htm (7/2/07)

BE YE MEN OF VALOUR

BY WINSTON CHURCHILL, BBC, MAY 19, 1940, FIRST BROADCAST AS PRIME MINISTER TO THE BRITISH PEOPLE

By May 14, the news from the front was uniformly bad. The Germans had broken through the French defenses at Sedan, and everywhere the French forces were reeling under a devastating barrage from land and air. "At almost all points where the armies had come in contact," Churchill later wrote, "the weight and fury of the German attack was overwhelming." Holland fell on May 15, and Churchill flew to Paris on the same day to confer with the French leaders. It was evident that the military situation was near to catastrophic, and that the military commanders and political leaders were resigned to overwhelming defeat. Churchill agreed to send ten fighter squadrons to France, thereby imperilling the situation in England, as a desperate attempt to restore the spirits of his Ally. On May 19, the Cabinet was informed that Lord Gort was "examining a possible withdrawal towards Dunkirk." In these sombre circumstances, Churchill made this, his first broadcast as Prime Minister to the British people.

I speak to you for the first time as Prime Minister in a solemn hour for the life of our country, of our empire, of our allies, and, above all, of the cause of Freedom. A tremendous battle is raging in France and Flanders. The Germans, by a remarkable combination of air bombing and heavily armored tanks, have broken through the French defenses north of the Maginot Line, and strong columns of their armored vehicles are ravaging the open country, which for the first day or two was without defenders. They have penetrated deeply and spread alarm and confusion in their track. Behind them there are now appearing infantry in lorries, and behind them, again, the large masses are moving forward. The re-groupment of the French armies to make head against, and also to strike at, this intruding wedge has been proceeding for several days, largely assisted by the magnificent efforts of the Royal Air Force.

We must not allow ourselves to be intimidated by the presence of these armored vehicles in unexpected places behind our lines. If they are behind our Front, the French are also at many points fighting actively behind theirs. Both sides are therefore in an extremely dangerous position. And if the French Army, and our own Army, are well handled, as I believe they will be; if the French retain that genius for recovery and counter-attack for which they have so long been famous; and if the British Army shows the dogged endurance and solid fighting power of which there have been so many examples in the past -- then a sudden transformation of the scene might spring into being.

It would be foolish, however, to disguise the gravity of the hour. It would be still more foolish to lose heart and courage or to suppose that well-trained, well-equipped armies numbering three or four millions of men can be overcome in the space of a few weeks, or even months, by a scoop, or raid of mechanized vehicles, however formidable. We may look with confidence to the stabilization of the Front in France, and to the general engagement of the masses, which will enable the qualities of the French and British soldiers to be matched squarely against those of their adversaries. For myself, I have invincible confidence in the French Army and its leaders. Only a very small part of that splendid Army has yet been heavily engaged; and only a very small part of France has yet been invaded. There is a good evidence to show that practically the whole of the specialized and mechanized forces of the enemy have been already thrown into the battle; and we know that very heavy losses have been inflicted upon them. No officer or man, no brigade or division, which grapples at close quarters with the enemy, wherever encountered, can fail to make a worthy contribution to the general result. The Armies must cast away the idea of resisting behind concrete lines or natural obstacles, and must realize that mastery can only be regained by furious and unrelenting assault. And this spirit must not only animate the High Command, but must inspire every fighting man.

In the air -- often at serious odds, often at odds hitherto thought overwhelming -- we have been clawing down three or four to one of our enemies; and the relative balance of the British and German Air Forces is now considerably more favorable to us than at the beginning of the battle. In cutting down the German bombers, we are fighting our own battle as well as that of France. My confidence in our ability to fight it out to the finish with the German Air Force has been strengthened by the fierce encounters which have taken place and are taking place. At the same time, our heavy bombers are striking nightly at the tap-root of German mechanized power, and have already inflicted serious damage upon the oil refineries on which the Nazi effort to dominate the world directly depends.

We must expect that as soon as stability is reached on the Western Front, the bulk of that hideous apparatus of aggression which gashed Holland into ruin and slavery in a few days will be turned upon us. I am sure I speak for all when I say we are ready to face it; to endure it; and to retaliate against it -- to any extent that the unwritten laws of war permit. There will be many men and many women in the Island who when the ordeal comes upon them, as come it will, will feel comfort, and even a pride, that they are sharing the perils of our lads at the Front -- soldiers, sailors and airmen, God bless them -- and are drawing away from them a part at least of the onslaught they have to bear. Is not this the appointed time for all to make the utmost exertions in their power? If the battle is to be won, we must provide our men with ever-increasing quantities of the weapons and ammunition they need. We must have, and have quickly, more aeroplanes, more tanks, more shells, more guns. there is imperious need for these vital munitions. They increase our strength against the powerfully armed enemy. They replace the wastage of the obstinate struggle; and the knowledge that wastage will speedily be replaced enables us to draw more readily upon our reserves and throw them in now that everything counts so much.

Our task is not only to win the battle - but to win the war. After this battle in France abates its force, there will come the battle for our Island -- for all that Britain is, and all that Britain means. That will be the struggle. In that supreme emergency we shall not hesitate to take every step, even the most drastic, to call forth from our people the last ounce and the last inch of effort of which they are capable. The interests of property, the hours of labor, are nothing compared with the struggle of life and honor, for right and freedom, to which we have vowed ourselves.

I have received from the Chiefs of the French Republic, and in particular from its indomitable Prime Minister, M. Reynaud, the most sacred pledges that whatever happens they will fight to the end, be it bitter or be it glorious. Nay, if we fight to the end, it can only be glorious.

Having received His Majesty's commission, I have formed an Administration of men and women of every Party and of almost every point of view. We have differed and quarreled in the past; but now one bond unites us all -- to wage war until victory is won, and never to surrender ourselves to servitude and shame, whatever the cost and the agony may be. This is one of the most awe-striking periods in the long history of France and Britain. It is also beyond doubt the most sublime. Side by side, unaided except by their kith and kin in the great Dominions and by the wide empires which rest beneath their shield - side by side, the British and French peoples have advanced to rescue not only Europe but mankind from the foulest and most soul-destroying tyranny which has ever darkened and stained the pages of history. Behind them - behind us- behind the Armies and Fleets of Britain and France - gather a group of shattered States and bludgeoned races: the Czechs, the Poles, the Norwegians, the Danes, the Dutch, the Belgians - upon all of whom the long night of barbarism will descend, unbroken even by a star of hope, unless we conquer, as conquer we must; as conquer we shall.

Today is Trinity Sunday. Centuries ago words were written to be a call and a spur to the faithful servants of Truth and Justice: "Arm yourselves, and be ye men of valour, and be in readiness for the conflict; for it is better for us to perish in battle than to look upon the outrage of our nation and our altar. As the Will of God is in Heaven, even so let it be."

Blood, Toil, Tears and Sweat, May 13, 1940, to House of Commons

By Winston Churchill

On May 10, 1940, Winston Churchill became Prime Minister. When he met his Cabinet on May 13 he told them that "I have nothing to offer but blood, toil, tears and sweat." He repeated that phrase later in the day when he asked the House of Commons for a vote of confidence in his new all-party government. The response of Labour was heart-warming; the Conservative reaction was luke-warm. They still really wanted Neville Chamberlain. Churchill commented to General Ismay: "Poor people, poor people. They trust me, and I can give them nothing but disaster for quite a long time."

I beg to move, that this House welcomes the formation of a Government representing the united and inflexible resolve of the nation to prosecute the war with Germany to a victorious conclusion.

On Friday evening last I received His Majesty's commission to form a new Administration. It was the evident wish and will of Parliament and the nation that this should be conceived on the broadest possible basis and that it should include all parties, both those who supported the late Government and also the parties of the Opposition. I have completed the most important part of this task. A War Cabinet has been formed of five Members, representing, with the Opposition Liberals, the unity of the nation. The three party Leaders have agreed to serve, either in the War Cabinet or in high executive office. The three Fighting Services have been filled. It was necessary that this should be done in one single day, on account of the extreme urgency and rigour of events. A number of other positions, key positions, were filled yesterday, and I am submitting a further list to His Majesty to-night. I hope to complete the appointment of the principal Ministers during to-morrow. The appointment of the other Ministers usually takes a little longer, but I trust that, when Parliament meets again, this part of my task will be completed, and that the administration will be complete in all respects.

I considered it in the public interest to suggest that the House should be summoned to meet today. Mr. Speaker agreed, and took the necessary steps, in accordance with the powers conferred upon him by the Resolution of the House. At the end of the proceedings today, the Adjournment of the House will be proposed until Tuesday, 21st May, with, of course, provision for earlier meeting, if need be. The business to be considered during that week will be notified to Members at the earliest opportunity. I now invite the House, by the Motion which stands in my name, to record its approval of the steps taken and to declare its confidence in the new Government.

To form an Administration of this scale and complexity is a serious undertaking in itself, but it must be remembered that we are in the preliminary stage of one of the greatest battles in history, that we are in action at many other points in Norway and in Holland, that we have to be prepared in the Mediterranean, that the air battle is continuous and that many preparations, such as have been indicated by my honorable friends below the Gangway, have to be made here at home. In this crisis I hope I may be pardoned if I do not address the House at any length today. I hope that any of my friends and colleagues, or former colleagues, who are affected by the political reconstruction, will make allowance, all allowance, for any lack of ceremony with which it has been necessary to act. I would say to the House, as I said to those who have joined this government: "I have nothing to offer but blood, toil, tears and sweat."

We have before us an ordeal of the most grievous kind. We have before us many, many long months of struggle and of suffering. You ask, what is our policy? I can say: It is to wage war, by sea, land and air, with all our might and with all the strength that God can give us; to wage war against a monstrous tyranny, never surpassed in the dark, lamentable catalogue of human crime. That is our policy. You ask, what is our aim? I can answer in one word: It is victory, victory at all costs, victory in spite of all terror, victory, however long and hard the road may be; for without victory, there is no survival. Let that be realised; no survival for the British Empire, no survival for all that the British Empire has stood for, no survival for the urge and impulse of the ages, that mankind will move forward toward its goal. But I take up my task with buoyancy and hope. I feel sure that our cause will not be suffered to fail among men. At this time I feel entitled to claim the aid of all, and I say, "come then, let us go forward together with our united strength."

A History of God: Who's Got It Right? By Charles Colson, BreakPoint Commentary #010626 - 06/26/2001

Eight years ago, a former nun named Karen Armstrong wrote an unlikely bestseller called A History of God. The book purported to tell readers how Judaism, Christianity, and Islam have "shaped and altered the conception of God." Now that book has been turned into a television show—one that, like the book, manages to get some very important questions very wrong.

The Arts & Entertainment network's presentation of "A History of God" didn't feature a single evangelical or conservative Catholic scholar. Instead, viewers got the story of Christianity from people famous for their rejection of Christian orthodoxy—people like Princeton's Elaine Pagels.

Viewers were told that the Christian belief in the divinity of Christ was something essentially invented by the fourth-century church. Viewers were assured that "Jesus never claimed to be God." Nor, for that matter, did St. Paul believe in Jesus' divinity.

This is not only contrary to traditional Christian teaching, it also runs contrary to a lot of contemporary scholarship—especially the kind that approaches the subject matter with an open mind.

Take the statement "Jesus never claimed to be God." Even liberal scholars agree that Jesus called himself the "Son of Man." The phrase comes from Daniel 7 in which the prophet describes one come down from heaven, and who is given "authority, glory and sovereign power." His is an "everlasting dominion that will not pass away . . . " [7:14].

As scholars note, by the first century, the phrase had messianic, divine connotations—overtones that Jesus would have been aware of when he used that expression. But Armstrong disregards this usage, and turns Jesus' use of the phrase into an expression of his own mortality.

This kind of disregard for the straightforward and the obvious is also at work in her claim that St. Paul didn't teach Jesus' divinity. In at least three of his epistles, Paul refers to what scholars call the "cosmic Christ." Scholars agree that the most famous of these passages, found in Philippians 2, is based on an ancient hymn—one that predates the letter to the Philippians.

In other words, less than two decades after Jesus' resurrection, Christians all over the known world were already singing hymns about his divinity—contrary to what the A&E TV viewers were told.

The exact definition of Jesus' relationship to the Father wasn't finalized until the fourth and fifth centuries. But this was simply a refinement of –and not a departure from—what the first-century Church believed about Jesus.

What programs like "A History of God" don't acknowledge is that the Scriptures remain the very best source for information about Jesus and the early church. Archeology and other scholarship haven't discredited this essential text; on the contrary, each new discovery has helped confirm its trustworthiness.

It's those who posit a Christianity other than what we read in the New Testament who are ignoring the evidence, and not the believers.

From BreakPoint, June 26, 2001, reprinted with permission of Prison Fellowship www.breakpoint.org.

Pretty Stones and Dead Babies: Abortion's New Language

By Charles Colson, BreakPoint Commentary
October 1, 2003

There's an abortion clinic in Pittsburghdefies all the stereotypes. The walls are lined with pink paper hearts containing heartfelt messages from parents to their aborted children. Family members are encouraged to write in a journal in the waiting room. And at the end of every pre-abortion counseling session, the patient is given a pretty, colorful stone to take with her.

What does a pretty, colorful stone have to do with abortion? The answer proves to be as bizarre as the question.

This novel approach to abortion is the trademark of a group of abortion clinics called the November Gang. A story in the September *Glamour* magazine explains that at these clinics, "intensive counseling is offered to patients . . . Despite being staunchly pro-choice, counselors venture more willingly into areas like grief and regret than at most abortion clinics." They talk with the women about religious and psychological issues and let the women talk about their feelings toward their unborn babies.

Though the story doesn't say so, I wouldn't be surprised if the members of the November Gang are simply copying the counseling-centered approach pioneered by pro-life crisis pregnancy centers. But what the abortion clinic counselors are counseling is very different.

The *Glamour* article reports, "One of the questions November Gang clinics sometimes ask patients is, Can you see abortion as a 'loving act' toward your children and yourself?" Faced with that query, "a lot of them are totally taken aback," says [clinic director Debi] Jackson. "Then they actually think about it, and they're like, 'Yeah, that's what I'm doing. I do love this child, but I can't [have] it right now.'" If a woman asks if God will forgive her, a counselor will turn the question back to her: "'Do you think there are any things that God considers completely unforgivable?'"

What these abortion counselors are doing is coaching patients to twist their own words, emotions, and moral understanding so that they can feel justified doing something that they're clearly acknowledging is wrong. In language full of sentiment, these women are gently encouraged to put their own short-term needs first, and not to think about what's best both for their babies and themselves in the long run.

The pink hearts signed "Mommy"; the informal baptism ceremonies that some women hold after their abortions; the stones that the women are told to "imbue . . . with whatever meaning they choose"—all these things meant to heal and comfort are rendered duplicitous by the brutal act taking place. All the pink paper hearts in the world don't change the fact that abortion is taking a life *with* the mother's permission.

Pro-life advocates and counselors have been using the language of help and healing for a long time now and with great results. We need to keep doing that, but we also need to point out that language can be deadly when it is not used in service of the truth. Women do need to know that comfort and forgiveness are always available through Christ, if repentance is sincere. But they also need to understand that a child's life for a pretty, colorful stone is a very bad deal.

From BreakPoint, October 1, 2003, reprinted with permission of Prison Fellowship www.breakpoint.org.

FOR IMMEDIATE ABOLITION

BY WILLIAM LLOYD GARRISON, 1831

William Lloyd Garrison had always advocated the abolition of slavery. In 1829, however, he changed his stance. He had been a gradualist, saying that a slow, steady movement toward freedom would be better for all. Portions of the famous discourse from the Liberator's first issue are reprinted below.

In the month of August I issued proposals for publishing the Liberator in Washington City; but the enterprise, though hailed in different sections of the country, was palsied by public indifference. Since that time, the removal of the Genius of Universal Emancipation to the seat of government has rendered less imperious the establishment of a similar periodical in that quarter.

During my recent tour for the purpose of exciting the minds of the people by a series of discourses on the subject of slavery, every place that I visited gave fresh evidence of the fact that a greater revolution in public sentiment was to be effected in the free states--and particularly in New England--than at the South. I found contempt more bitter, opposition more active, detraction more relentless, prejudice more stubborn, and apathy more frozen than among slaveowners themselves. Of course, there were individual exceptions to the contrary. This state of things afflicted but did not dishearten me. I determined, at every hazard, to lift up the standard of emancipation in the eyes of the nation, within sight of Bunker Hill and in the birthplace of liberty. That standard is now unfurled; and long may it float, unhurt by the spoliations of time or the missiles of a desperate foe--yea, till every chain be broken and every bondman set free! Let Southern oppressors tremble; let their secret abettors tremble; let their Northern apologists tremble; let all the enemies of the persecuted blacks tremble.

I deem the publication of my original prospectus unnecessary, as it has obtained a wide circulation. The principles therein inculcated will be steadily pursued in this paper, excepting that I shall not array myself as the political partisan of any man. In defending the great cause of human rights, I wish to derive the assistance of all religions and of all parties.

Assenting to the "self-evident truth" maintained in the American Declaration of Independence, "that all men are created equal and endowed by their Creator with certain inalienable rights, among which are life, liberty, and the pursuit of happiness," I shall strenuously contend for the immediate enfranchisement of our slave population. In Park Street Church, on the Fourth of July, 1829, in an address on slavery, I unreflectingly assented to the popular but pernicious doctrine of gradual abolition. I seize this opportunity to make a full and unequivocal recantation, and thus publicly to ask pardon my God, of my country, and of my brethren, the poor slaves, for having uttered a sentiment so full of timidity, injustice, and absurdity. A similar recantation from my pen was published in the Genius of Universal Emancipation at Baltimore, in September 1829. My conscience is now satisfied.

I am aware that many object to the severity of my language; but is there not cause for severity? I will be as harsh as truth and as uncompromising as justice. On this subject I do not wish to think, or speak, or write with moderation. No! No! Tell a man whose house is on fire to give a moderate alarm; tell him to moderately rescue his wife from the hands of the ravisher; tell the mother to gradually extricate her baby from the fire into which it has fallen--but urge me not to use moderation in a cause like the present. I am in earnest; I will not equivocate; I will not excuse; I will not retreat a single inch AND I WILL BE HEARD. The apathy of the people is enough to make every statue leap from its pedestal and to hasten the resurrection of the dead.

It is pretended that I am retarding the cause of emancipation by the coarseness of my invective and the precipitancy of my measures. The charge is not true. On this question my influence, humble as it is, is felt at this moment to a considerable extent, and shall be felt in coming years--not perniciously but beneficially: not as a curse but as a blessing--and posterity will bear testimony that I was right. I desire to thank God that He enables me to disregard "the fear of man which bringeth a snare," and to speak His truth in its simplicity and power.

SHE DID GOOD
BY PAUL HARVEY

"Frequently, the lottery winner enjoys his bonanza only a little while before he and it are consumed by excesses, marital problems, and health problems. So often the winners lose. But Catherine McAuley of Dublin, Ireland, multiplied her inheritance. In 1822, Catherine learned that she was sole heir to the estate of her adoptive parents. The inheritance, the equivalent of $1 million, would ensure that she could live out her life in comfort and luxury.

"Catherine had seen others of 17th-century Dublin living lavishly and purposelessly. Instead, this socialite turned social worker; this lady of fashion and culture became a compassionate teacher and healer of the poor. With her inheritance, she bought a huge old home on Baggot Street in fashionable Dublin and converted it into a House of Mercy. There the poor and the sick found healing, the uneducated found teaching, the unloved found love.

"Catherine's life was one of austerity; her time and her resources were all devoted to praying, teaching and visiting the sick. When an ailing baby was left on her doorstep, and she was able to cure its influenza, Catherine decided that her ministry must focus primarily on healing. When friends and relatives chided her for squandering her inheritance on the 'thankless poor,' she not only persisted, but sought to enlist them in her work. And some did volunteer. A few at first, then many.

"Soon the Baggot Street House of Mercy was overcrowded. And, in 1831, Catherine and the volunteers who had embraced her commitment created a Catholic religious congregation and began to extend their spiritual and medical services throughout Ireland and beyond.

"Catherine McAuley lived but 10 years more, yet that was long enough for her to see her ministry spreading throughout the world. Her single House of Mercy is now a worldwide institute of the religious Sisters of Mercy — with more than 100 health care facilities in the United States. Seventy-five percent of our population lives within 25 miles of a Mercy Hospital. Additionally, the Mercy sisters operate 18 colleges and 40 high schools in the United States. Eighteen thousand Sisters of Mercy serve in 30 countries.

"So what would you and I do with $1 million? Catherine McAuley did good."

Paul Harvey, syndicated columnist The Los Angeles Times, 1987

Germany's Claims, delivered February 20, 1938

By Adolf Hitler

Despite the really exemplary discipline, strength and restraint which National Socialists preserved in their revolution, we have seen that a certain portion of the foreign press inundated the new Reich with a virtual flood of lies and calumnies. It was a remarkable mixture of arrogance and deplorable ignorance which led them to act as the judges of people who should be presented as models to these democratic apostles.

The best proof for showing up these lies is success. For if we had acted during these five years like the democratic world citizens of Soviet Russia, that is, like those of the Jewish race, we would not have succeeded in making out of a Germany, which was in the deepest material collapse, a country of material order. For this very reason we claim the right to surround our work with that protection which renders it impossible for criminal elements or for the insane to disturb it.

Whoever disturbs this mission is the enemy of the people, whether he pursues his aim as a bolshevist democrat, a revolutionary terrorist or a reactionary dreamer. In such a time of necessity those who act in the name of God are not those who, citing Bible quotations, wander idly about the country and spend the day partly doing nothing and partly criticizing the work of others; but those whose prayers take the highest form of uniting man with his God, that is the form of work.

I had a right to turn against everyone who, instead of helping, thought his mission was to criticize our work. Foreign nations contributed nothing apart from this spirit, for their rejection was tinged by hate or a spirit of knowing better than we know.

It was the A B C of our creed to find help in our own strength. The standard of living of the nation is the outcome of its total production; in other words, the value of every wage and salary corresponds to the volume of goods produced as a result of the work performed. This is a very unpopular doctrine in a time resounding with cries such as "higher wages and less work."

Next to the United States, Germany today has become the greatest steel country in the world. I could give many more examples. They are documentary proof of the work such as our people never before achieved. To these successes will be added in a few years the gigantic results of the Four-Year Plan. Is it not a joke of history when those very countries which themselves have only crises think they can criticize us and give us advice?

We have given the German nation that weapon of steel which presents a wall at our frontiers against the intentions of the malicious international press campaign.

At the conclusion of the next decade the German people will bear in mind the success of their efficiency and will be filled with a supreme pride. One of these achievements is the construction of a national leadership which is far removed from parliamentary democracy as it is from military dictatorship.

If ever international agitation or poisoning of opinion should attempt to rupture the peace of the Reich, then steel and iron would take the German people and German homesteads under their protection. The world would then see, as quick as lightning, to what extent this Reich, people, party, and these armed forces are fanatically inspired with one spirit, one will.

If Great Britain should suddenly dissolve today and England become dependent solely on her own territory, then the people there would, perhaps, have more understanding of the seriousness of the economic tasks which confront us. If a nation which commands no gold reserves, no foreign exchange--not because National Socialism reigns but because a parliamentary, democratic State was exploited for fifteen years by a world hungry after loot; in other words, if a nation which must feed 140 people to the square kilometer and has no colonies, if a nation which lacks numerous raw materials and is not willing to live an illusory life through credits, reduces the number of its unemployed in five years to nil and improves its standard of living, then all those should remain silent who, despite great economic advantages, scarcely succeed in solving their own unemployment problems.

The claim for German colonial possessions, therefore, will be voiced from year to year with increasing vigor. These possessions, which Germany did not take away from other countries and which today are practically of no value to these powers, are indispensable for our own people.

I should like to refute here the hope that such claims can be averted by granting credits. Above all, we do not wish for naïve assurances that we shall be permitted to buy what we need. We reject such statements once and for all.

You will not expect me to discuss in detail the individual international plans which appear to arouse the varied interests of the various governments. They are too uncertain and they lack the clarity necessary for me to be able to express myself on these questions. Above all, however, take note of my deep-seated distrust of all so-called conferences which may provide interesting hours of conversation for those taking part in them, but generally lead to the disappointment of hopeful mankind.

I cannot allow our natural claims to be coupled with political business. Recently rumors have been cropping up, rumors that Germany was about to revise her opinion concerning her return to the League of Nations. I should like again to declare that in 1919 the peace treaty was forced upon some countries. This treaty brought in its train far-reaching inroads upon the lives of the peoples involved. The rape of national and economic destinies and of the communal lives of the nations took place under a cloud of moralizing phrases which, perhaps, tended to salve the uneasy conscience of those who instituted the affair.

After the revision of the map of the world and of territorial and racial spheres, which was as thorough as it was fundamental, had been effected by means of force, a League of Nations was founded whose task it was to crystallize these crazy, unreasonable proceedings and to coordinate its results into an everlasting and unalterable basis of life.

I notice very often that English politicians would be glad to give back to us our colonies if they were not so disturbed by the thought of the wrong and violence which would thus be done to the native inhabitants.

All those colonial empires have not come into being through plebiscites. They are today naturally integral parts of the States in question and form, as such, part of that world order which always has been designated to us, especially by democratic policies, as the "world order of right."

That right the League of Nations now has been ordered to protect. I cannot understand why a nation which itself has been robbed by force should join such illustrious company and I cannot permit the conclusion to be drawn that we should not be prepared to fight for the principles of justice just because we are not in the League of Nations. On the contrary, we do not belong to the League of Nations because we believe that it is not an institution of justice but an institution for defending the interests of Versailles.

A number of material considerations must, however, be added.

First, we left the League of Nations because--loyal to its origin and obligations--it refused us the right to equal armament and just as equal security.

Second, we will never re-enter it because we do not intend to allow ourselves to be used anywhere by a majority vote of the League of Nations for the defense of an injustice.

Third, we believe we will please all those nations who are misled by misfortune to rely on and trust the League of Nations as a factor of genuine help. We should have regarded it as more correct, for instance, in the case of the Ethiopian war, for the League to have shown more understanding for vital Italian needs and less disposition to help the Ethiopians with promises. This would, perhaps, have enabled a more simple and reasonable solution for the whole problem.

Fourth, on no account will we allow the German nation to become entangled in conflicts in which the nation itself is not interested. We are not willing to stand up for the territorial or economic interests of others without the slightest benefits to Germans being visible. Moreover, we ourselves do not expect such support from others. Germany is determined to impose upon herself wise moderation in her interests and demands. But if German interests should be seriously at stake we shall not expect to receive support from the League of Nations but we shall assume the right from the beginning to shoulder our task ourselves.

Fifth, we do not intend to allow our attitude to be determined in the future by any international institution which, while excluding official recognition of indisputable facts, resembles less the acts of a man of considered judgment than the habits of a certain type of large bird. The interests of nations in so far as their existence or non-existence are ultimately concerned are stronger than formalistic considerations. For in the year 2038 it is possible that new States may have arisen or others disappeared without this new state of affairs having been registered at Geneva.

Germany will not take part in such unreasonable proceedings by being a member of the League of Nations.

With one country alone have we scorned to enter into relations. That State is Soviet Russia. We see in bolshevism more now than before the incarnation of human destructive forces. We do not blame the Russian people as such for this gruesome ideology of destruction. We know it is a small Jewish intellectual group which led a great nation into this position of madness. If this doctrine would confine itself territorially to Russia maybe one could put up with it. Alas, Jewish international bolshevism attempts to hollow out the nation of the world from its Soviet center.

As I have more than once stated Germany has in Europe no more territorial demands to make of France. With the return of the Saar we trust the period of Franco-German territorial differences is finally closed.

Germany also has no quarrel with England apart from her colonial wishes. However, there is no cause for any conceivable conflict. The only thing that has poisoned and thus injured the common life of these two countries is the utterly unendurable press campaign which in these two countries has existed under the motto "freedom of personal opinion."

The British Government desires the limitation of armaments or the prohibition of bombing. I myself proposed this some time ago. However, I also suggested at the time that the most important thing was to prevent the poisoning of the world's public opinion by infamous press articles. That which strengthened our sympathy with Italy, if this were possible, is the fact that in the country State policy and press policy tread the same road.

There are more than 10,000,000 Germans in States adjoining Germany which before 1866 were joined to the bulk of the German nation by a national link. Until 1918 they fought in the great war shoulder to shoulder with the German soldiers of the Reich. Against their own free will they were prevented by peace treaties from uniting with the Reich.

This was painful enough, but there must be no doubt about one thing: Political separation from the Reich may not lead to deprivation of rights, that is the general rights of racial self-determination which were solemnly promised to us in Wilson's fourteen points as a condition for the armistice. We cannot disregard it just because this is a case concerning Germans.

In the long run it is unbearable for a world power, conscious of herself, to know there are citizens at her side who are constantly being inflicted with severest sufferings for their sympathy or unity with the total nation, its faith and philosophy.

We well know there can scarcely be a frontier line in Europe which satisfies all. It should be all the more important to avoid the torture of national minorities in order not to add to the suffering of political separation, the suffering of persecution on account of their belonging to a certain people.

That it is possible to find ways leading to the lessening of tension has been proved. But he who tries to prevent by force such lessening of tension through creating an equilibrium in Europe will some day inevitably conjure up force among the nations themselves. It cannot be denied that Germany herself, as long as she was powerless and defenseless, was compelled to tolerate many of these continual persecutions of the German people on our frontier.

But just as England stands up for her interests all over the globe, present-day Germany will know how to guard its more restricted interests. To these interests of the German Reich belong also the protection of those German peoples who are not in a position to secure along our frontiers their political and philosophical freedom by their own efforts.

I may say that since the League of Nations has abandoned its continuous attempts at disturbance in Danzig and since the advent of the new commissioner this most dangerous place for European peace has entirely lost its menace.

Poland respects the national conditions in the Free City of Danzig and Germany respects Polish rights.

Now I turn to Austria. It is not only the same people but above all a long communal history and culture which bind together the Reich and Austria.

Difficulties which emerged in the carrying out of the agreement of July 11, 1936, made essential an attempt to remove misunderstandings and obstacles to final reconciliation. It is clear that whether we wished it or not an intolerable position might have developed that would have contained the seeds of catastrophe. It does not lie in the power of man to stop the rolling stone of fate which through neglect or lack of wisdom has been set moving.

I am happy to say that these ideas correspond with the viewpoint of the Austrian Chancellor, whom I invited to visit me. The underlying intention was to bring about a détente in our relations which would guarantee to National Socialist sympathizers in Austria within the limits of the law the same rights enjoyed by other citizens.

In connection with it there was to be an act of conciliation in the form of a general amnesty and better understanding between the two States through closer and friendlier relations in the various spheres of cultural, political and economic cooperation. All this is a development within the framework of the treaty of July 11.

I wish to pay tribute to the Austrian Chancellor for his efforts to find together with me a way which is just as much in the interests of both countries as in that of the entire German people whose sons we all are regardless of where we came from. I believe we have thus made a contribution to European peace.

Our satisfactory relations with other countries are known to all. Above all it is to be mentioned our cooperation with those two great powers which, like Germany, have recognized bolshevism as a world danger and are therefore determined to resist the Comintern with a common defense. It is my earnest wish to see this cooperation with Italy and Japan more and more extended.

The German people is no warlike nation. It is a soldierly one which means it does not want a war but does not fear it. It loves peace but it also loves its honor and freedom.

The new Reich shall belong to no class, no profession but to the German people. It shall help the people find an easier road in this world. It shall help them in making their lot a happier one. Party, State, armed forces, economics are institutions and functions which can only be estimated as a means toward an end. They will be judged by history according to the services they render toward this goal. Their purpose, however, is to serve the people.

I now pray to God that He will bless in the years to come our work, our deeds, our foresight, our resolve; that the Almighty may protect us from both arrogance and cowardly servility, that He may help us find the right way which He has laid down for the German people and that He may always give us courage to do the right thing and never to falter or weaken before any power or any danger.

Long live Germany and the German people.

Reichstag Speech, May 4, 1941
By Adolf Hitler

Deputies. Men of the German Reichstag: At a time when only deeds count and words are of little importance, it is not my intention to appear before you, the elected representatives of the German people, more often than absolutely necessary. The first time I spoke to you was at the outbreak of the war when, thanks to the Anglo-French conspiracy against peace, every attempt at an understanding with Poland, which otherwise would have been possible, had been frustrated.

The most unscrupulous men of the present time had, as they admit today, decided as early as 1936 to involve the Reich, which in its peaceful work of reconstruction was becoming too powerful for them, in a new and bloody war and, if possible, to destroy it. They had finally succeeded in finding a State that was prepared for their interests and aims, and that State was Poland.

All my endeavors to come to an understanding with Britain were wrecked by the determination of a small clique which, whether from motives of hate or for the sake of material gain, rejected every German proposal for an understanding due to their resolve, which they never concealed, to resort to war, whatever happened.

The man behind this fanatical and diabolical plan to bring about war at whatever cost was Mr. Churchill. His associates were the men who now form the British Government.

These endeavors received most powerful support, both openly and secretly, from the so-called great democracies on both sides of the Atlantic. At a time when the people were more and more dissatisfied with their deficient statesmanship, the responsible men over there believed that a successful war would be the most likely means of solving problems that otherwise would be beyond their power to solve.

Behind these men there stood the great international Jewish financial interests that control the banks and the Stock Exchange as well as the armament industry. And now, just as before, they scented the opportunity of doing their unsavory business. And so, just as before, there was no scruple about sacrificing the blood of the peoples. That was the beginning of this war. A few weeks later the State that was the third country in Europe, Poland, but had been reckless enough to allow herself to be used for the financial interests of these warmongers, was annihilated and destroyed.

In these circumstances I considered that I owed it to our German people and countless men and women in the opposite camps, who as individuals were as decent as they were innocent of blame, to make yet another appeal to the common sense and the conscience of these statesmen. On October 6, 1939, I therefore once more publicly stated that Germany had neither demanded nor intended to demand anything either from Britain or from France, that it was madness to continue the war and, above all, that the scourge of modern weapons of warfare, once they were brought into action, would inevitably ravage vast territories.

But just as the appeal I made on September 1, 1939, proved to be in vain, this renewed appeal met with indignant rejection. The British and their Jewish capitalist backers could find no other explanation for this appeal, which I had made on humanitarian grounds, than the assumption of weakness on the part of Germany.

They assured the people of Britain and France that Germany dreaded the clash to be expected in the spring of 1940 and was eager to make peace for fear of the annihilation that would then inevitably result.

Already at that time the Norwegian Government, misled by the stubborn insistence of Mr. Churchill's false prophecies, began to toy with the idea of a British landing on their soil, thereby contributing to the destruction of Germany by permitting their harbors and Swedish iron ore fields to be seized.

So sure were Mr. Churchill and Paul Reynaud of the success of their new scheme that finally, whether from sheer recklessness or perhaps under the influence of drink, they deemed it no longer necessary to make a secret of their intentions.

It was thanks to these two gentlemen's tendency to gossip that the German Government at that time gained cognizance of the plans being made against the Reich. A few weeks later this danger to Germany was eliminated. One of the boldest deeds of arms in the whole history of warfare frustrated the attack of the British and French armies against the right flank of our line of defense.

Immediately after the failure of these plans, increased pressure was exerted by the British warmongers upon Belgium and Holland. Now that the attack upon our sources for the supply of iron ore had proved unsuccessful, they aimed to advance the front to the Rhine by involving the Belgian and Dutch States and thus to threaten and paralyze our production centers for iron and steel.

On May 10 of last year perhaps the most memorable struggle in all German history commenced. The enemy front was broken up in a few days and the stage was then set for the operation that culminated in the greatest battle of annihilation in the history of the world. Thus France collapsed, Belgium and Holland were already occupied, and the battered remnants of the British expeditionary force were driven from the European continent, leaving their arms behind.

On July 19, 1940, I then convened the German Reichstag for the third time in order to render that great account which you all still remember. The meeting provided me with the opportunity of expressing the thanks of the nation to its soldiers in a form suited to the uniqueness of the event. Once again I seized the opportunity of urging the world to make peace. And what I foresaw and prophesied at that time happened. My offer of peace was misconstrued as a symptom of fear and cowardice.

The European and American warmongers succeeded once again in befogging the sound common sense of the masses, who can never hope to profit from this war, by conjuring up false pictures of new hope. Thus, finally, under pressure of public opinion, as formed by their press, they once more managed to induce the nation to continue this struggle.

Even my warnings against night bombings of the civilian population, as advocated by Mr. Churchill, were interpreted as a sign of German impotence. He, the most bloodthirsty or amateurish strategist that history has ever known, actually saw fit to believe that the reserve displayed for months by the German Air Force could be looked upon only as proof of their incapacity to fly by night.

So this man for months ordered his paid scribblers to deceive the British people into believing that the Royal Air Force alone - and no others - was in a position to wage war in this way, and that thus ways and means had been found to force the Reich to its knees by the ruthless onslaught of the British Air Force on the German civilian population in conjunction with the starvation blockade.

Again and again I uttered these warnings against this specific type of aerial warfare, and I did so for over three and a half months. That these warnings failed to impress Mr. Churchill does not surprise me in the least. For what does this man care for the lives of others? What does he care for culture or for architecture? When war broke out he stated clearly that he wanted to have his war, even though the cities of England might be reduced to ruins. So now he has got his war.

My assurances that from a given moment every one of his bombs would be returned if necessary a hundredfold failed to induce this man to consider even for an instant the criminal nature of his action. He professes not to be in the least depressed and he even assures us that the British people, too, after such bombing raids, greeted him with a joyous serenity, causing him to return to London refreshed by his visits to the stricken areas.

It is possible that this sight strengthened Mr. Churchill in his firm determination to continue the war in this way, and we are no less determined to continue to retaliate, if necessary, a hundred bombs for every one of his and to go on doing so until the British nation at last gets rid of this criminal and his methods.

The appeal to forsake me, made to the German nation by this fool and his satellites on May Day, of all days, are only to be explained either as symptomatic of a paralytic disease or of a drunkard's ravings. His abnormal state of mind also gave birth to a decision to transform the Balkans into a theater of war.

For over five years this man has been chasing around Europe like a madman in search of something that he could set on fire. Unfortunately, he again and again finds hirelings who open the gates of their country to this international incendiary.

After he had succeeded in the course of the past winter in persuading the British people by a wave of false assertions and pretensions that the German Reich, exhausted by the campaign in the preceding months, was completely spent, he saw himself obliged, in order to prevent an awakening of the truth, to create a fresh conflagration in Europe.

In so doing he returned to the project that had been in his mind as early as the autumn of 1939 and the spring of 1940. It was thought possible at the time to mobilize about 100 divisions in Britain's interest.

The sudden collapse which we witnessed in May and June of the past year forced these plans to be abandoned for the moment. But by the autumn of last year Mr. Churchill began to tackle this problem once again.

In the meantime, however, certain difficulties had arisen. As a result, Rumania, owing to internal changes, dropped out of England's political scheme.

In dealing with these conditions, I shall begin by giving you a brief outline of the aims of Germany's policy in the Balkans. As in the past, the Reich never pursued any territorial or any other selfish political interest in the Balkans. In other words, the Reich has never taken the slightest interest in territorial problems and internal conditions in these States for any selfish reason whatsoever.

On the other hand, the Reich has always endeavored to build up and to strengthen close economic ties with these States in particular. This, however, not only served the interests of the Reich but equally the interests of these countries themselves.

If any two national economic systems ever effectively complemented one another, that is especially the case regarding the Balkan States and Germany. Germany is an industrial country and requires foodstuffs and raw materials. The Balkan States are agrarian countries and are short of these raw materials. At the same time, they require industrial products.

It was therefore hardly surprising when Germany thus became the main business partner of the Balkan States. Nor was this in Germany's interest alone, but also in that of the Balkan peoples themselves.

AND NONE BUT OUR JEW-RIDDEN DEMOCRACIES, WHICH CAN THINK ONLY IN TERMS OF CAPITALISM, CAN MAINTAIN THAT IF ONE STATE DELIVERS MACHINERY TO ANOTHER STATE IT THEREBY DOMINATES THAT OTHER STATE. IN ACTUAL FACT SUCH DOMINATION, IF IT OCCURS, CAN BE ONLY A RECIPROCAL DOMINATION.

It is presumably easier to be without machinery than without food and raw materials. Consequently, the partner in need of raw material and foodstuffs would appear to be more tied down than the recipient of industrial products. IN THIS TRANSACTION THERE WAS NEITHER CONQUEROR NOR CONQUERED. THERE WERE ONLY PARTNERS.

The German Reich of the National Socialist revolution has prided itself on being a fair and decent partner, offering in exchange high-quality products instead of worthless democratic paper money. For these reasons the Reich was interested in only one thing if, indeed, there was any question of political interest, namely, in seeing that internally the business partner was firmly established on a sound and healthy basis.

THE APPLICATION OF THIS IDEA LED IN FACT NOT ONLY TO INCREASING PROSPERITY IN THESE COUNTRIES BUT ALSO TO THE BEGINNING OF MUTUAL CONFIDENCE. All the greater, however, became the endeavor of that world incendiary, Churchill, to put an end to this peaceful development and by shamelessly imposing upon these States utterly worthless British guarantees and promises of assistance to introduce into this peaceable European territory elements of unrest, uncertainty, distrust and, finally, conflict.

Originally, Rumania was first won over by these guarantees and later, of course, Greece. It has, meanwhile, probably been sufficiently demonstrated that he had absolutely no power of any kind to provide real help and that these guarantees were merely intended to rope these States in to follow the dangerous trend of filthy British politics.

RUMANIA HAS HAD TO PAY BITTERLY FOR THE GUARANTEES, WHICH WERE CALCULATED TO ESTRANGE HER FROM THE AXIS POWERS.

Greece, which least of all required such a guarantee, was offered her share to link her destiny to that of the country that provided her King with cash and orders.

EVEN TODAY I FEEL THAT I MUST, AS I BELIEVE IN THE INTEREST OF HISTORICAL ACCURACY, DISTINGUISH BETWEEN THE GREEK PEOPLE AND THAT THIN TOP LAYER OF CORRUPT LEADERS WHO, INSPIRED BY A KING WHO HAD NO EYES FOR THE DUTY OF TRUE LEADERSHIP, PREFERRED INSTEAD TO FURTHER THE AIMS OF BRITISH WAR POLITICS. To me this is a subject of profound regret.

Germany, with the faint hope of still being able to contribute in some way to a solution of the problem, had not severed relations with Greece. But even then I was bound in duty to point out before the whole world that we would not tacitly allow a revival of the old Salonika scheme of the Great War.

Unfortunately, my warning was not taken seriously enough. That we were determined, if the British tried to gain another foothold in Europe, to drive them back into the sea was not taken seriously enough.

The result was that the British began in an increasing degree to establish bases for the formation of a new Salonika army. They began by laying out airdromes and by establishing the necessary ground organization in the firm conviction that the occupation of the airdromes themselves could afterward be carried out very speedily.

Finally a continuous stream of transports brought equipment for an army which, according to Mr. Churchill's idea and plans, was to be landed in Greece. As I have said, already we were aware of this. For months we watched this entire strange procedure with attention, if with restraint.

The reverses suffered by the Italian Army in North Africa, owing to a certain material inferiority of their tanks and anti-tank guns, finally led Mr. Churchill to believe that the time was ripe to transfer the theater of war from Libya to Greece. He ordered the transport of the remaining tanks and of the infantry division, composed mainly of Anzacs, and was convinced that he could now complete his scheme, which was to set the Balkans aflame.

THUS DID MR. CHURCHILL COMMIT ONE OF THE GREATEST STRATEGIC BLUNDERS OF THIS WAR. As soon as there could be no further doubt regarding Britain's intentions of gaining a foothold in the Balkans, I took the necessary steps.

Germany, by keeping pace with these moves, assembled the necessary forces for the purpose of counteracting any possible tricks of that gentleman. In this connection I must state categorically that this action was not directed against Greece.

The Duce did not even request me to place one single German division at his disposal for this purpose. He was convinced that with the advent of good weather his stand against Greece would have been brought to a successful conclusion. I was of the same opinion.

The concentration of German forces was therefore not made for the purpose of assisting the Italians against Greece. It was a precautionary measure against the British attempt under cover of the clamor caused by the Italo-Greek war to intrench themselves secretly in the Balkans in order to force the issue from that quarter on the model of the Salonika army during the World War, and, above all, to draw other elements into the whirlpool.

This hope was founded principally on two States, namely, Turkey and Yugoslavia. But with these very States I have striven during the years since I came into power to establish close co-operation.

The World War actually started from Belgrade. Nevertheless, the German people, who are by nature so ready to forgive and forget, felt no animosity toward that country. Turkey was our ally in the World War. The unfortunate outcome of that struggle weighed upon that country just as heavily as it did upon us.

The great genius who created the new Turkey was the first to set a wonderful example of recovery to our allies whom fortune had at that time deserted and whom fate had dealt so terrible a blow. Whereas Turkey, thanks to the practical attitude of her leaders, preserved her independence in carrying out her own resolutions, Yugolsavia fell a victim to British intrigue.

Most of you, especially my old Party comrades among you, know what efforts I have made to establish a straightforward understanding and indeed friendly relations between Germany and Yugoslavia. In pursuance of this aim Herr von Ribbentrop, our Minister of Foreign Affairs, submitted to the Yugoslav Government proposals that were so outstanding and so fair that at least even the Yugoslav State of that time seemed to become increasingly eager for such close co-operation.

Germany had no intention of starting a war in the Balkans. On the contrary, it was our honest intention as far as possible to contribute to a settlement of the conflict with Greece by means that would be tolerable to the legitimate wishes of Italy.

The Duce not only consented to but lent his full support to our efforts to bring Yugoslavia into a close community of interests with our peace aims. Thus it finally became possible to induce the Yugoslav Government to join the Threepower Pact, which made no demands whatever on Yugoslavia but only offered that country advantages.

Thus on March 26 of this year a pact was signed in Vienna that offered the Yugoslav State the greatest future conceivable and could have assured peace for the Balkans. Believe me, gentlemen, on that day I left the beautiful city of the Danube truly happy not only because it seemed as though almost eight years of foreign policies had received their reward but also because I believed that perhaps at the last moment German intervention in the Balkans might not be necessary.

We were all stunned by the news of that coup, carried through by a handful of bribed conspirators who had brought about the event that caused the British Prime Minister to declare in joyous words that at last he had something good to report.

YOU WILL SURELY UNDERSTAND, GENTLEMEN, THAT WHEN I HEARD THIS I AT ONCE GAVE ORDERS TO ATTACK YUGOSLAVIA. To treat the, German Reich in this way is impossible. One cannot spent years in concluding a treaty that is in the interest of the other party merely to discover that this treaty has not only been broken overnight but also that it has been answered by the insulting of the representative of the German Reich, by the threatening of his military attache, by the injuring of the aide de camp of this attache, by the maltreating of numerous other Germans, by demolishing property, by laying waste the homes of German citizens and by terrorizing.

GOD KNOWS THAT I WANTED PEACE. But I can do nothing but protect the interests of the Reich with those means which, thank God, are at our disposal. I made my decision at that moment all the more calmly because I knew that I was in accord with Bulgaria, who had always remained unshaken in her loyalty to the German Reich, and with the equally justified indignation of Hungary.

Both of our old allies in the World War were bound to regard this action as a provocation emanating from the State that once before had set the whole of Europe on fire and had been guilty of the indescribable sufferings that befell Germany, Hungary, and Bulgaria in consequence.

The general directions of operations issued by me through the Supreme Command of the German forces on March 27 confronted the Army and the Air Force with a formidable task. By a mere turn of the hand an additional campaign had to be prepared. Units that had already arrived had to be moved about. Supplies of armaments had to be assured and the air force had to take over numerous improvised airports part of which were still under water.

WITHOUT THE SYMPATHETIC ASSISTANCE OF HUNGARY AND THE EXTREMELY LOYAL ATTITUDE OF RUMANIA IT WOULD HAVE BEEN VERY DIFFICULT TO CARRY OUT MY ORDERS IN THE SHORT TIME ENVISAGED.

I fixed April 6 as the day on which the attack was to begin. The main plan of operation was: First, to proceed with an army coming from Bulgaria against Thrace in Greece in the direction of the Aegean Sea.

The main striking strength of this army lay in its right wing, which was to force a passage through to Salonika by using mountain divisions and a division of tanks; second, to thrust forward with a second army with the object of establishing connection as speedily as possible with the Italian forces advancing from Albania. These two operations were to begin on April 6.

Third, a further operation, beginning on the eighth, provided for the break-through of an army from Bulgaria with the object of reaching the neighborhood of Belgrade. In conjunction with this, a German army corps was to occupy the Banat on the tenth.

In connection with these operations general agreement had been made with our allies, Italy and Hungary. Agreements as to co-operation had also been reached between the two air forces. The command of the German Armies operating against Macedonia and Greece was placed in the hands of Field Marshal von List, who had already particularly distinguished himself in the previous campaigns. Once more and under the most exacting conditions he carried out the task confronting him in truly superior fashion.

The forces advancing against Yugoslavia from the southwest and from Hungary were commanded by Col. Gen. von Weick. He, too, in a very short time with the forces under his command reached his objective.

ity such as was accorded by Roman senators to generals honorably defeated in battle. It is merely proof of that perpetual blindness with which the gods afflict those whom they are about to destroy.

The consequences of this campaign are extraordinary. In view of the fact that a small set of conspirators in Belgrade again were able to foment trouble in the service of extracontinental interests, the radical elimination of this danger means the removal of an element of tension for the whole of Europe.

The Danube as an important waterway is thus safeguarded against any further act of sabotage. Traffic has been resumed in full.

Apart from the modest correction of its frontiers, which were infringed as a result of the outcome of the World War, the Reich has no special territorial interests in these parts. As far as politics are concerned we are merely interested in safeguarding peace in this region, while in the realm of economics we wish to see an order that will allow the production of goods to be developed and the exchange of products to be resumed in the interests of all.

It is, however, only in accordance with supreme justice if those interests are also taken into account that are founded upon ethnographical, historical, or economic conditions.

I can assure you that I look into the future with perfect tranquility and great confidence. The German Reich and its allies represent power, military, economic and, above all, in moral respects, which is superior to any possible coalition in the world. The German armed forces will always do their part whenever it may be necessary. The confidence of the German people will always accompany their soldiers.

The Church — Not Men, but Christ

By John Huss

This church the Savior calls his church in the Gospel quoted, when he said: "On this rock I will build my church." And that He means this church is plain from the words which follow: "And the gates of hell shall not prevail against it." For seeing that Christ is the rock of that church and also the foundation on whom she is builded in respect to predestination, she cannot finally be overthrown by gates of hell, that is, by the power and the assaults of tyrants who persecute her or the assaults of wicked spirits. For mightier is Christ the king of heaven, the bridegroom of the church, than the prince of this world.

Therefore, in order to show His power and foreknowledge and the predestination wherewith He builds, protects, foreknows, and predestinates His church, and to give persevering hope to His church, He added: "And the gates of hell shall not prevail against it." Here Lyra says: "From this it appears that the church is not composed of men by virtue of any power of ecclesiastical and secular dignity, because there are many princes and high priests and others of lower degree who have been found apostates from the faith."

This comment has its proof, in part, in the case of Judas Iscariot, both apostle and bishop, who was present when Christ said: "On this rock I will build my church, and the gates of hell shall not prevail against it." But he himself was not built upon the rock in respect of predestination, and therefore the gates of hell prevailed against him.

From the aforesaid words of Christ it is evident that the church is taken to mean all, in a special sense, who after his resurrection were to be built upon Him and in Him by faith and perfecting grace. For Christ commended Peter, who bore [represented] the person of the universal church and confessed his faith in the words: "Thou art the Christ, the Son of the living God." And Christ said to him, "Blessed art thou, Simon Bar-Jonah." This commendation befits Peter and the whole church, which from the beginning was blessed in the way, by confessing humbly, obediently, heartily, and constantly that Christ is the Son of the living God.

This faith in regard to that most hidden article, the flesh—that is, the wisdom of the world—does not reveal; nor does blood reveal it, that is, pure philosophical science—but alone God, the Father. And because the confession was so clear and positive, the Rock *(Petra)* said to Peter (the rock): "And I say unto thee that thou art Peter," that is, the confessor of the true Rock *(Petra),* who is Christ; and "on this Rock," which thou hast confessed—that is, upon me—"I will build" by strong faith and perfecting grace "my church"—that is, the company of the predestinate who, the probation being over, are appointed to glory. Wherefore, "the gates of hell shall not prevail against it."

Up to this point it has been deduced from the Saviour's words that there is (1) one church—namely from the very word "church"; (2) that it is Christ's church—from the word "my"; (3) that it is holy—from the words, "the gates of hell shall not prevail against it." The conclusion, therefore, is that there is one holy church of Christ, which in Greek is *katholike* and in Latin *universalis.* She is also called apostolic, *apostolike,* because she was established by the words and deeds of the apostles and founded upon the Rock, Christ, as Jerome says in the Prologue to his *Commentary on the Apocalypse.*

The third foundation, included in the proposition (Matt. 16:18) is touched upon in the words, "On this rock I will build my church." And in view of the fact that in their utterances the popes most of all use this saying of Christ, wishing to draw from it that they themselves are the rock or the foundation upon which the church stands, namely upon Peter, to whom it is was said, "Thou art Peter,"—in view of this fact, in order to understand the Lord's word it must be noted that the foundation of the church by whom it is founded is touched upon in the words, "I will build," and the foundation in which it is laid is referred to in the words, "on this Rock," and the foundation wherewith the church is founded is referred to in the words, "Thou art the Christ, the Son of the living God."

Christ is therefore the foundation by whom primarily and in whom primarily the holy catholic church is founded and faith is the foundation with which it is founded—that faith which works through love, which Peter set forth when he said: "Thou art the Christ, the Son of the living God." The foundation, therefore, of the church is Christ, and He said: "Apart from me ye can do nothing" (John 15:5); that is, apart from me as the prime and principal foundation.

But Christ grounds and builds His church on Himself, the Rock, when He so influences her that she hears and does His words, for then the gates of hell do not prevail against her. Hence Christ says: "Every one that cometh unto me and heareth my words and doeth them, I will show you to whom he is like: he is like a man building a house, who built a house deep and laid the foundation on a rock: and when the flood arose, the stream brake against that house and could not shake it: for it was founded on the rock." (Luke 6:48) And what this foundation is, the apostle Paul shows in I Cor. 3:11: "Other foundation can no man lay than that which is laid, which is Christ Jesus"; and I Cor. 10:4: "But the rock was Christ." Therefore, it is in this foundation and on this rock and from this rock up that holy church is built, for He says: "Upon this Rock I will build my church."

And on this foundation the apostles built the church of Christ. For not to themselves did they call the people, but to Christ, who is the first, the essential and most effectual foundation. For this reason the apostle said: "Other foundation can no man lay." Therefore this apostle, seeing how the Corinthians might err concerning the foundation, condemned them saying: "Each of you saith I am indeed of Paul, and I of Apollos, and I of Cephas, and I of Christ. Is therefore Christ divided, or was Paul crucified for you, or were ye baptized in the name of Paul?" (I Cor. 1:12,13) It is as if he said, No!

Therefore, neither Peter nor Paul nor any other besides Christ is the chief foundation of the church, so that later the holy apostle said: "What then is Apollos and what is Paul? His ministers whom ye believed and each one as the Lord gave to him" to minister to the church. (I Cor. 3:5) He said: "I planted," that is by preaching; "Apollos watered," that is by baptizing, "but God gave the increase," that is through the founding by faith, hope, and love. Therefore, neither he that planteth," as Paul, "is anything, nor he that watereth," like Apollos, "is anything," that is anything upon which the church may be founded, but only God who giveth the increase; He is the church's foundation. And the words follow: "Let every one take heed how he buildeth thereon, for other foundation can no man lay than that is laid, which is Christ Jesus."

Now, this foundation is the rock of righteousness of which Christ spoke in the Gospel to St. Peter: "Thou art Peter, and upon this Rock I will build my church." On these words St. Augustine says, in his *Sermons on Words of the Lord, 13 (Nicene Fathers, 6:340)*: "Our Lord Jesus Christ thus spake to Peter: Thou art Peter and upon this rock I build my church—on this Rock, which thou hast confessed, on this Rock which thou hast recognized, when thou saidest, 'Thou art Christ, the Son of the Living God'—I will build my church': I will build thee upon myself, not myself upon thee. For wishing that men should be built upon men, they were saying, 'I am of Paul, I of Apollos, and I of Cephas,' that is, Peter. And others did not wish to be built upon Peter (*Petrum*) but upon the Rock (*Petram*) said, 'I am of Christ.'"

Again, in his last Homily on John *(Nicene Fathers, 7:450),* Augustine says: "Peter the apostle, because of the primacy of his apostleship, had a symbolic and representative personality, for what belonged to him as an individual was that by nature he was one man, by grace one Christian, and by a more abundant grace he was one and the same chief apostle. But when it was said to him: 'I will give unto thee the keys of the kingdom of heaven, and whatever thou shalt bind on earth shall be bound in heaven, and whatsoever thou shalt loose on earth shall be loosed in heaven,' he represented the universal church which in this world is shaken by divers temptations, even as by torrents of rain, by rivers, and tempests, and yet doth not fall, because it is founded upon the Rock, the word from which Peter got his name. For Rock *(Petra)* does not come from *Peter—(Petrus)* but Peter from Rock, just as the word Christ is not derived from Christian, but Christian from Christ.

"Hence the Lord said: 'On this Rock I will build my church,' because Peter had said before, 'Thou art the Christ, the Son of the living God.' Upon this Rock which thou hast confessed, he said, 'I will build my church.' For Christ was the Rock. Therefore, the church, which is founded on Christ, received from Him the keys of the kingdom of heaven in the person of Peter, that is, the power of binding and loosing sins. For what the church is essentially in Christ, that Peter is symbolically in the Rock *(Petra)* by which symbolism Christ is understood to be the Rock and Peter the church. Therefore, this church which Peter represented, so long as she prospers among evil men, is by loving and by following Christ freed from evil, but much more does she follow in the case of those who fight for the truth even unto death."

These things Augustine teaches throughout, in agreement with the apostle, that Christ alone is the foundation and Rock upon which the church is built. To this the apostle Peter speaks, when he says: "Unto whom coming, a living stone, rejected indeed of men, but of God elect and precious, ye also, as living stones, are built upon into spiritual houses to be a holy priesthood to offer up spiritual sacrifices unto God through Jesus Christ." (I Pet. 2:4,5)

For this reason the Scripture continues: "Behold I lay in Zion a chief cornerstone, elect, precious, and he that believeth on Him shall not be put to shame. For you, therefore, that believe is the honor, but for such as disbelieve, the stone which the builders rejected, the same was made the head of the corner and a stone of stumbling and a Rock of offense. For they stumble at the word and do not believe that whereunto they were appointed." Paul also said: "Israel following after a law of righteousness did not arrive at the law of righteousness. Wherefore? Because they sought it not by faith but by works. They stumbled at the stone of stumbling and a rock of offense, and he that believeth on Him shall not be put to shame." (Rom. 9:31-33)

Behold how these two Roman apostles and bishops, Peter and Paul, prove from Scripture that the Lord Jesus Christ is Himself, the stone and the Rock of foundation, for the Lord says: "Behold I will lay for a foundation in Zion a cornerstone tried and precious, a stone of sure foundation." (Isa. 28:16) And also in the Psalms 118:22: "The stone which the builders rejected has been made the head of the corner." Therefore, Christ Himself is the foundation of the apostles and the whole church, and in Him it is fitly framed together.

From these things it is plain that Christ alone is the chief foundation of the church, and in this sense the apostle thought of that foundation, because he did not dare to speak of anything except what was built upon that foundation. Hence he says: "I will not dare to speak of any thing save those which Christ wrought through me by the obedience of God in word, and in deeds, and in the power of signs and wonders, in the power of the Holy Spirit. And so I have preached this Gospel not where Christ was already known, that I might not build upon another man's foundation." (Rom. 15:18-20) Was not this that apostle, a vessel of election, who said he did not dare to preach anything save those things which Christ spoke through him; for otherwise he would not be building on Christ, the most effectual foundation, if perchance he should say and teach or do anything which did not have its foundation in Jesus Christ. And from this it is plain, that not Peter but the Rock, Christ, was intended in Christ's Gospel, when Christ said: "On this Rock I will build my church."

Therefore, it is not a matter of much doubt to the simple Christian—faithful—that Peter did not dare to claim to be the head of the holy catholic church, for the reason that he did not rule over the whole church and did not excel above the whole church in dignity, nor was he the bridegroom of the catholic church. John the Baptist, than whom, according to the testimony of the truth in Matthew 11:11, "There hath not risen a greater among these born of women," did not dare to call himself the bridegroom, but in humility confessed himself the bridegroom's friend.

And when his disciples in their zeal for him said, "Rabbi, he that was with thee beyond Jordan to whom thou hast borne witness, behold the same baptizeth and all men come to him," John answered them and said; "A man can receive nothing except it have been given from heaven. Ye yourselves bear me witness I have said I am not the Christ, but that I am sent before Him. He that hath the bride is the bridegroom: but it is sufficient for me that I am the bridegroom's friend that standeth and heareth with joy the bridegroom's voice." (John 3:27-29) And the bridegroom said: "Ye are my friends if ye do whatsoever I command you." (John 15:14) Thus it is evident that it would be the highest arrogance and folly for any man, Christ excepted, to call himself the head and the bridegroom of the holy catholic church.

Reprinted with permission.

Inaugural Address by Thomas Jefferson, March 4, 1801

Friends and fellow citizens: Called upon to undertake the duties of the first executive office of our country, I avail myself of the presence of that portion of my fellow-citizens which is here assembled to express my grateful thanks for the favor with which they have been pleased to look toward me, to declare a sincere consciousness that the task is above my talents, and that I approach it with those anxious and awful presentiments which the greatness of the charge and the weakness of my powers so justly inspire. A rising nation, spread over a wide and fruitful land, traversing all the seas with the rich productions of their industry, engaged in commerce with nations who feel power and forget right, advancing rapidly to destinies beyond the reach of mortal eye -- when I contemplate these transcendent objects, and see the honor, the happiness, and the hopes of this beloved country committed to the issue and the auspices of this day, I shrink from the contemplation, and humble myself before the magnitude of the undertaking. Utterly, indeed, should I despair did not the presence of many whom I here see remind me that in the other high authorities provided by our Constitution I shall find resources of wisdom, of virtue, and of zeal on which to rely under all difficulties. To you, then, gentlemen, who are charged with the sovereign functions of legislation, and to those associated with you, I look with encouragement for that guidance and support which may enable us to steer with safety the vessel in which we are all embarked amidst the conflicting elements of a troubled world.

During the contest of opinion through which we have passed the animation of discussions and of exertions has sometimes worn an aspect which might impose on strangers unused to think freely and to speak and to write what they think; but this being now decided by the voice of the nation, announced according to the rules of the Constitution, all will, of course, arrange themselves under the will of the law, and unite in common efforts for the common good. All, too, will bear in mind this sacred principle, that though the will of the majority is in all cases to prevail, that will to be rightful must be reasonable; that the minority possess their equal rights, which equal law must protect, and to violate would be oppression. Let us, then, fellow-citizens, unite with one heart and one mind. Let us restore to social intercourse that harmony and affection without which liberty and even life itself are but dreary things. And let us reflect that, having banished from our land that religious intolerance under which mankind so long bled and suffered, we have yet gained little if we countenance a political intolerance as despotic, as wicked, and capable of as bitter and bloody persecutions. During the throes and convulsions of the ancient world, during the agonizing spasms of infuriated man, seeking through blood and slaughter his long-lost liberty, it was not wonderful that the agitation of the billows should reach even this distant and peaceful shore; that this should be more felt and feared by some and less by others, and should divide opinions as to measures of safety. But every difference of opinion is not a difference of principle. We have called by different names brethren of the same principle. We are all Republicans, we are all Federalists. If there be any among us who would wish to dissolve this Union or to change its republican form, let them stand undisturbed as monuments of the safety with which error of opinion may be tolerated where reason is left free to combat it. I know, indeed, that some honest men fear that a republican government can not be strong, that this Government is not strong enough; but would the honest patriot, in the full tide of successful experiment, abandon a government which has so far kept us free and firm on the theoretic and visionary fear that this Government, the world's best hope, may by possibility want energy to preserve itself? I trust not. I believe this, on the contrary, the strongest Government on earth. I believe it the only one where every man, at the call of the law, would fly to the standard of the law, and would meet invasions of the public order as his own personal concern. Sometimes it is said that man can not be trusted with the government of himself. Can he, then, be trusted with the government of others? Or have we found angels in the forms of kings to govern him? Let history answer this question.

Let us, then, with courage and confidence pursue our own Federal and Republican principles, our attachment to union and representative government. Kindly separated by nature and a wide ocean from the exterminating havoc of one quarter of the globe; too high-minded to endure the degradations of the others; possessing a chosen country, with room enough for our descendants to the thousandth and thousandth generation; entertaining a due sense of our equal right to the use of our own faculties, to the acquisitions of our own industry, to honor and confidence from our fellow-citizens, resulting not from birth, but from our actions and their sense of them; enlightened by a benign religion, professed, indeed, and practiced in various forms, yet all of them inculcating honesty, truth, temperance, gratitude, and the love of man; acknowledging and adoring an overruling Providence, which by all its dispensations proves that it delights in the happiness of man here and his greater happiness hereafter -- with all these blessings, what more is necessary to make us a happy and a prosperous people? Still one thing more, fellow-citizens -- a wise and frugal Government, which shall restrain men from injuring one another, shall leave them otherwise free to regulate their own pursuits of industry and improvement, and shall not take from the mouth of labor the bread it has earned. This is the sum of good government, and this is necessary to close the circle of our felicities.

About to enter, fellow-citizens, on the exercise of duties which comprehend everything dear and valuable to you, it is proper you should understand what I deem the essential principles of our Government, and consequently those which ought to shape its Administration. I will compress them within the narrowest compass they will bear, stating the general principle, but not all its limitations. Equal and exact justice to all men, of whatever state or persuasion, religious or political; peace, commerce, and honest friendship with all nations, entangling alliances with none; the support of the State governments in all their rights, as the most competent administrations for our domestic concerns and the surest bulwarks against anti-republican tendencies; the preservation of the General Government in its whole constitutional vigor, as the sheet anchor of our peace at home and safety abroad; a jealous care of the right of election by the people -- a mild and safe corrective of abuses which are lopped by the sword of revolution where peaceable remedies are unprovided; absolute acquiescence in the decisions of the majority, the vital principle of republics, from which is no appeal but to force, the vital principle and immediate parent of despotism; a well-disciplined militia, our best reliance in peace and for the first moments of war till regulars may relieve them; the supremacy of the civil over the military authority; economy in the public expense, that labor may be lightly burthened; the honest payment of our debts and sacred preservation of the public faith; encouragement of agriculture, and of commerce as its handmaid; the diffusion of information and arraignment of all abuses at the bar of the public reason; freedom of religion; freedom of the press, and freedom of person under the protection of the habeas corpus, and trial by juries impartially selected. These principles form the bright constellation which has gone before us and guided our steps through an age of revolution and reformation. The wisdom of our sages and blood of our heroes have been devoted to their attainment. They should be the creed of our political faith, the text of civic instruction, the touchstone by which to try the services of those we trust; and should we wander from them in moments of error or of alarm, let us hasten to retrace our steps and to regain the road which alone leads to peace, liberty, and safety.

I repair, then, fellow-citizens, to the post you have assigned me. With experience enough in subordinate offices to have seen the difficulties of this the greatest of all, I have learnt to expect that it will rarely fall to the lot of imperfect man to retire from this station with the reputation and the favor which bring him into it. Without pretensions to that high confidence you reposed in our first and greatest revolutionary character, whose preeminent services had entitled him to the first place in his country's love and destined for him the fairest page in the volume of faithful history, I ask so much confidence only as may give firmness and effect to the legal administration of your affairs. I shall often go wrong through defect of judgment. When right, I shall often be thought wrong by those whose positions will not command a view of the whole ground. I ask your indulgence for my own errors, which will never be intentional, and your support against the errors of others, who may condemn what they would not if seen in all its parts. The approbation implied by your suffrage is a great consolation to me for the past, and my future solicitude will be to retain the good opinion of those who have bestowed it in advance, to conciliate that of others by doing them all the good in my power, and to be instrumental to the happiness and freedom of all.

Relying, then, on the patronage of your good will, I advance with obedience to the work, ready to retire from it whenever you become sensible how much better choice it is in your power to make. And may that Infinite Power which rules the destinies of the universe lead our councils to what is best, and give them a favorable issue for your peace and prosperity.

http://www.yale.edu/lawweb/avalon/presiden/inaug/jefinau1.htm

Letter from Birmingham Jail
By Martin Luther King, Jr., April 16,
1963, Birmingham, Alabama

My Dear Fellow Clergymen: While confined here in the Birmingham city jail, I came across your recent statement calling present activities "unwise and untimely." Seldom do I pause to answer criticism of my work and ideas. If I sought to answer all the criticisms that cross my desk, my secretaries would have little time for anything other than such correspondence in the course of the day, and I would have no time for constructive work. But since I feel that you are men of genuine good will and that your criticisms are sincerely set forth, I want to try to answer your statement in what I hope will be patient and reasonable terms.

I think I should indicate why I am here in Birmingham, since you have been influenced by the view which argues against "outsiders coming in." I have the honor of serving as President of the Southern Christian Leadership Conference, an organization operating in every southern state, with headquarters in Atlanta, Georgia. We have some eighty-five affiliated organizations across the South, and one of them is the Alabama Christian Movement for Human Rights. Frequently we share staff, educational and financial resources with our affiliates. Several months ago the affiliate here in Birmingham asked us to be on call to engage in a nonviolent direct-action program if such were deemed necessary. We readily consented, and when the hour came we lived up to our promise. So I, along with several members of my staff, am here because I was invited here. I am here because I have organizational ties here.

But more basically, I am in Birmingham because injustice is here. Just as the prophets of the eighth century B.C. left their villages and carried their "thus saith the Lord" far beyond the boundaries of their home towns, and just as the Apostle Paul left his village of Tarsus and carried the gospel of Jesus Christ to the far corners of the Greco-Roman world, so am I compelled to carry the gospel of freedom beyond my own home town. Like Paul, I must constantly respond to the Macedonian call for aid.

Moreover, I am cognizant of the interrelatedness of all communities and states. I cannot sit idly in Atlanta and not be concerned about what happens in Birmingham. Injustice anywhere is a threat to justice everywhere. We are caught in an inescapable network of mutuality, tied in a single garment of destiny. Whatever affects one directly, affects all indirectly. Never again can we afford to live with the narrow, provincial "outside agitator" idea. Anyone who lives inside the United States can never be considered an outsider anywhere within its bounds.

You deplore the demonstrations taking place in Birmingham. But your statement, I am sorry to say, fails to express a similar concern for the conditions that brought about the demonstrations. I am sure that none of you would want to rest content with the superficial kind of social analysis that deals merely with effects and does not grapple with underlying causes. It is unfortunate that demonstrations are taking place in Birmingham, but it is even more unfortunate that the city's white power structure left the Negro community with no alternative.

In any nonviolent campaign there are four basic steps: collection of the facts to determine whether injustices exist; negotiation; self purification; and direct action. We have gone through all these steps in Birmingham. There can be no gain saying the fact that racial injustice engulfs this community. Birmingham is probably the most thoroughly segregated city in the United States. Its ugly record of brutality is widely known. Negroes have experienced grossly unjust treatment in the courts. There have been more unsolved bombings of Negro homes and churches in Birmingham that in any other city in the nation. These are the hard, brutal facts of the case. On the basis of these conditions, Negro leaders sought to negotiate with the city fathers. But the latter consistently refused to engage in good-faith negotiation.

Then, last September, came the opportunity to talk with leaders of Birmingham's economic community. In the course of the negotiations, certain promises were made by the merchants -- for example, to remove the stores' humiliating racial signs. On the basis of these promises, the Reverend Fred Shuttlesworth and the leaders of the Alabama Christian Movement for Human Rights agreed to a moratorium on all demonstrations. As the weeks and months went by, we realized that we were the victims of a broken promise. A few signs, briefly removed, returned; the others remained.

As in so many past experiences, our hopes had been blasted, and the shadow of deep disappointment settled upon us. We had no alternative except to prepare for direct action, whereby we would present our very bodies as a means of laying our case before the conscience of the local and the national community. Mindful of the difficulties involved, we decided to undertake a process of self-purification. We began a series of workshops on nonviolence, and we repeatedly asked ourselves: "Are you able to accept blows without retaliation?" "are you able to endure the ordeal of jail?" We decided to schedule our direct-action program for the Easter season, realizing that except for Christmas, this is the main shopping period of the year. Knowing that a strong economic withdrawal program would be the by-product of direct action, we felt that this would be the best time to bring pressure to bear on the merchants for the needed change.

Then it occurred to us that Birmingham's mayoralty election was coming up in March, and we speedily decided to postpone action until after election day. When we discovered that the Commissioner of Public Safety, Eugene "Bill" Connor, had piled up enough votes to be in the run-off, we decided again to postpone action until the day after the run-off so that the demonstrations could not be used to cloud the issues. Like many others, we waited to see Mr. Connor defeated, and to this end we endured postponement after postponement. Having aided in this community need, we felt that our direct-action program could be delayed no longer.

You may well ask: "Why direct action? Why sit-ins, marches, and so forth? Isn't negotiation a better path?" You are quite right in calling for negotiation. Indeed, this is the very purpose of direct action. Nonviolent direct action seeks to create such a crisis and foster such a tension that a community which has constantly refused to negotiate is forced to confront the issue. It seeks so to dramatize the issue that it can no longer be ignored. My citing the creation of tension as part of the work of the nonviolent-resister may sound rather shocking. But I must confess that I am not afraid of the word "tension." I have earnestly opposed violent tension, but there is a type of constructive, nonviolent tension which is necessary for growth. Just as Socrates felt that it was necessary to create a tension in the mind so that individuals could rise from the bondage of myths and halftruths to the unfettered realm of creative analysis and objective appraisal, so must we see the need for nonviolent gadflies to create the kind of tension in society that will help men rise from the dark depths of prejudice and racism to the majestic heights of understanding and brotherhood.

The purpose of our direct-action program is to create a situation so crisis-packed that it will inevitably open the door to negotiation. I therefore concur with you in your call for negotiation. Too long has our beloved Southland been bogged down in a tragic effort to live in monologue rather than dialogue.

One of the basic points in your statement is that the action that I and my associates have taken in Birmingham is untimely. Some have asked: "Why didn't you give the new city administration time to act?" The only answer that I can give to this query is that the new Birmingham administration must be prodded about as much as the outgoing one, before it will act. We are sadly mistaken if we feel that the election of Albert Boutwell as mayor will bring the millennium to Birmingham. While Mr. Boutwell is a much more gentle person that Mr. Connor, they are both segregationists, dedicated to maintenance of the status quo. I have hoped that Mr. Boutwell will be reasonable enough to see the futility of massive resistance to desegregation. But he will not see this without pressure from devotees of civil rights. My friends, I must say to you that we have not made a single gain in civil rights without determined legal and nonviolent pressure. Lamentably, it is an historical fact that privileged groups seldom give up their privileges voluntarily. Individuals may see the moral light and voluntarily give up their unjust posture; but as Reinhold Niebuhr has reminded us, groups tend to be more immoral than individuals.

We know through painful experience that freedom is never voluntarily given by the oppressor, it must be demanded by the oppressed. Frankly, I have yet to engage in a direct-action campaign that was "well timed" in view of those who have not suffered unduly from the disease of segregation. For years now I have heard the word "wait!" It rings in the ear of every Negro with piercing familiarity. This "Wait" has almost always meant "Never." We must come to see, with one of our distinguished jurists, that "justice too long delayed is justice denied."

We have waited for more than 340 years for our constitutional and God given rights. The nations of Asia and Africa are moving with jet like speed toward gaining political independence, but we still creep at horse-and-buggy pace toward gaining a cup of coffee at a lunch counter. Perhaps it is easy for those who have never felt the stinging darts of segregation to say, "Wait." But when you have seen vicious mobs lynch your mothers and fathers at will and drown your sisters and brothers at whim; when you have seen hate-filled policemen curse, kick, and even kill your black brothers and sisters; when you see the vast majority of your twenty million Negro brothers smothering in an airtight cage of poverty in the midst of an affluent society; when you suddenly find your tongue twisted and your speech stammering as you seek to explain to your six-year-old daughter why she can't go to the public amusement park that has just been advertised on television, and see tears welling up in her eyes when she is told that Funtown is closed to colored children, and see ominous clouds of inferiority beginning to form in her little mental sky, and see her beginning to distort her personality by developing an unconscious bitterness toward white people; when you have to concoct an answer for a five-year-old son who is asking, "Daddy, why do white people treat colored people so mean?"; when you take a cross-country drive and find it necessary to sleep night after night in the uncomfortable corners of your automobile because no motel will accept you; when you are humiliated day in and day out by nagging signs reading "white" and "colored" when your first name becomes "Nigger," your middle name becomes "boy" (however old you are) and your last name becomes "John," and your wife and mother are never given the respected title "Mrs."; when your are harried by day and haunted by night by the fact that you are a Negro, living constantly at tiptoe stance, never quite knowing what to expect next, and are plagued with inner fears and outer resentments; when you are forever fighting a degenerating sense of "nobodiness" then you will understand why we find it difficult to wait. There comes a time when the cup of endurance runs over, and men are no longer willing to be plunged into the abyss of despair. I hope, sirs, you can understand our legitimate and unavoidable impatience.

You express a great deal of anxiety over our willingness to break laws. This is certainly a legitimate concern. Since we so diligently urge people to obey the Supreme Court's decision of 1954 outlawing segregation in the public schools, at first glance it may seem rather paradoxical for us consciously to break laws. One may ask: "How can you advocate breaking some laws and obeying others?" The answer lies in the fact that there are two types of laws: just and unjust. I would be the first to advocate obeying just laws. One has not only a legal but a moral responsibility to obey just laws. Conversely, one has a moral responsibility to disobey unjust laws. I would agree with St. Augustine that "an unjust law is no law at all."

Now, what is the difference between the two? How does one determine whether a law is just or unjust? A just law is a man-made code that squares with the moral law or the law of God. An unjust law is a code that is out of Harmony with the moral law. To put it in the terms of St. Thomas Aquinas: An unjust law is a human law that is not rooted in eternal law and natural law. Any law that uplifts human personality is just. Any law that degrades human personality is unjust. All segregation statutes are unjust because segregation distorts the soul and damages the personality. It gives the segregator a false sense of superiority and the segregated a false sense of inferiority. Segregation, to use the terminology of the Jewish philosopher Martin Buber, substitutes an "I-it" relationship for an "I-thou" relationship and ends up relegating persons to the status of things. Hence segregation is not only politically, economically and sociologically unsound, it is morally wrong and sinful. Paul Tillich has said that sin is separation. Is not segregation an existential expression of man's tragic separation, his awful estrangement, his terrible sinfulness? Thus is it that I can urge men to obey the 1954 decision of the Supreme Court, for it is morally right; and I can urge them to disobey segregation ordinances, for they are morally wrong.

Let us consider a more concrete example of just and unjust laws. An unjust law is a code that a numerical or power majority group compels a minority group to obey but does not make binding on itself. This is difference made legal. By the same token, a just law is a code that a majority compels a minority to follow and that it is willing to follow itself. This is sameness made legal.

Let me give another explanation. A law is unjust if it is inflicted on a minority that, as a result of being denied the right to vote, had no part in enacting or devising the law. Who can say that the legislature of Alabama which set up that state's segregation laws was democratically elected? Throughout Alabama all sorts of devious methods are used to prevent Negroes from becoming registered voters, and there are some counties in which, even though Negroes constitute a majority of the population, not a single Negro is registered. Can any law enacted under such circumstances be considered democratically structured?

Sometimes a law is just on its face and unjust in its application. For instance, I have been arrested on a charge of parading without a permit. Now, there is nothing wrong in having an ordinance which requires a permit for a parade. But such an ordinance becomes unjust when it is used to maintain segregation and to deny citizens the First-Amendment privilege of peaceful assembly and protest.

I hope you are able to see the distinction I am trying to point out. In no sense do I advocate evading or defying the law, as would the rabid segregationist. That would lead to anarchy. One who breaks an unjust law must do so openly, lovingly, and with a willingness to accept the penalty. I submit that an individual who breaks a law that conscience tells him is unjust, and who willingly accepts the penalty of imprisonment in order to arouse the conscience of the community over its injustice, is in reality expressing the highest respect for law.

Of course, there is nothing new about this kind of civil disobedience. It was evidenced sublimely in the refusal of Shadrach, Meshach, and Abednego to obey the laws of Nebuchadnezzar, on the ground that a higher moral law was at stake. It was practiced superbly by the early Christians, who were willing to face hungry lions and the excruciating pain of chopping blocks rather than submit to certain unjust laws of the Roman Empire. To a degree, academic freedom is a reality today because Socrates practiced civil disobedience. In our own nation, the Boston Tea Party represented a massive act of civil disobedience.

We should never forget that everything Adolf Hitler did in Germany was "legal" and everything the Hungarian freedom fighters did in Hungary was "illegal." It was "illegal" to aid and comfort a Jew in Hitler's Germany. 'Even so, I am sure that, had I lived in Germany at the time, I would have aided and comforted my Jewish brothers. If today I lived in a Communist country where certain principles dear to the Christian faith are suppressed, I would openly advocate disobeying that country's anti-religious laws.

I must make two honest confessions to you, my Christian and Jewish brothers. First, I must confess that over the past few years I have been gravely disappointed with the white moderate. I have almost reached the regrettable conclusion that the Negro's great stumbling block in his stride toward freedom is not the White Citizen's Councilor or the Ku Klux Klanner, but the white moderate, who is more devoted to "order" than to justice; who prefers a negative peace which is the absence of tension to a positive peace which is the presence of justice; who constantly says, "I agree with you in the goal you seek, but I cannot agree with your methods of direct action"; who paternalistically believes he can set the timetable for another man's freedom; who lives by a mythical concept of time and who constantly advises the Negro to wait for a "more convenient season." Shallow understanding from people of good will is more frustrating than absolute misunderstanding from people of ill will. Lukewarm acceptance is much more bewildering than outright rejection.

I had hoped that the white moderate would understand that law and order exist for the purpose of establishing justice and that when they fail in this purpose they become the dangerously structured dams that block the flow of social progress. I had hoped that the white moderate would understand that the present tension in the South is a necessary phase of the transition from an obnoxious negative peace, in which the Negro passively accepted his unjust plight, to a substantive and positive peace, in which all men will respect the dignity and worth of human personality. Actually, we who engage in nonviolent direct action are not the creators of tension. We merely bring to the surface the hidden tension that is already alive. We bring it out in the open, where it can be seen and dealt with. Like a boil that can never be cured so long as it is covered up but must be opened with all its ugliness to the natural medicines of air and light injustice must be exposed with all the tension its exposure creates, to the light of human conscience and the air of national opinion, before it can be cured.

In your statement you assert that our actions, even though peaceful, must be condemned because they precipitate violence. But is this a logical assertion? Isn't this like condemning a robbed man because his possession of money precipitated the evil act of robbery? Isn't this like condemning Socrates because his unswerving commitment to truth and his philosophical inquiries precipitated the act by the misguided populace in which they made him drink hemlock? Isn't this like condemning Jesus because his unique God-consciousness and never-ceasing devotion to God's will precipitated the evil act of crucifixion? We must come to see that, as the federal courts have consistently affirmed, it is wrong to urge an individual to cease his efforts to gain his basic constitutional rights because the quest may precipitate violence. Society must protect the robbed and punish the robber.

I had also hoped that the white moderate would reject the myth concerning time in relations to the struggle for freedom. I have just received a letter from a white brother in Texas. He writes: "All Christians know that the colored people will receive equal rights eventually, but it is possible that you are in too great a religious hurry. It has taken Christianity almost two thousand years to accomplish what it has. The teachings of Christ take time to come to earth." Such an attitude stems from a tragic misconception of time, from the strangely irrational notion that there is something in the very flow of time will inevitably cure all ills. Actually, time itself is neutral; it can be used either destructively or constructively. More and more I feel that the people of ill will have used time much more effectively than have the people of good will. We will have to repent in the generation not merely for the hateful words and actions of the bad people, but for the appalling silence of the good people. Human progress never rolls in on wheels of inevitability; it comes through the tireless efforts of men willing to be co-workers with God, and without this hard work, time itself becomes an ally of the forces of stagnation. We must use time creatively, in the knowledge that the time is always ripe to do right. Now is the time to make real the promise of democracy and transform our pending national elegy into a creative psalm of brotherhood. Now is the time to lift our national policy from the quicksand of racial injustice to the solid rock of human dignity.

You speak of our activity in Birmingham as extreme. At first I was rather disappointed that fellow clergyman would see my nonviolent efforts as those of an extremist. I began thinking about the fact that I stand in the middle of two opposing forces in the Negro community. One is a force of complacency, made up in part of Negroes who, as a result of long years of oppression, are so drained of self-respect and a sense of "somebodiness" that they have adjusted to segregation; and in part of a few middle-class Negroes who, because of a degree of academic and economic security and because in some ways they profit by segregation, have become insensitive to the problems of the masses. The other force is one of bitterness and hatred, and it comes perilously closed on advocating violence. It is expressed in the various black nationalist groups that are springing up across the nation, the largest and best-known being Elijah Muhammad's Muslim movement. Nourished by the Negro's frustration over the continued existence of racial discrimination, this movement is made up of people who have lost faith in America, who have absolutely repudiated Christianity, and who have concluded that the white man is an incorrigible "devil."

I have tried to stand between these two forces, saying that we need emulate neither the "do-nothingism" of the complacent nor the hatred and despair of the black nationalist. For there is the more excellent way of love and nonviolent protest. I am grateful to God that, through the influence of the Negro church, the way of nonviolence became an integral part of our struggle.

If this philosophy had not emerged, by now many streets of the South would, I am convinced, be flowing with blood. And I am further convinced that if our white brothers dismiss as "rabble-rousers" and "outside agitators" those of us who employ nonviolent direct action, and if they refuse to support our nonviolent efforts, millions of Negroes will, out of frustration and despair, seek solace and security in black nationalist ideologies -- a development that would inevitably lead to a frightening racial nightmare.

Oppressed people cannot remain oppressed forever. The yearning for freedom eventually manifests itself, and that is what has happened to the American Negro. Something within has reminded him of his birthright of freedom, and something without has reminded him that it can be gained. Consciously or unconsciously, he has been caught up by the Zeitgeist, and with his black brothers of Africa and his brown and yellow brothers of Asia, South America, and the Caribbean, the United States Negro is moving with a sense of great urgency toward the promised land of racial justice. If one recognizes this vital urge that has engulfed the Negro community, one should readily understand why public demonstrations are taking place. The Negro has many pent-up resentments and latent frustrations, and he must release them. So let him march; let him make prayer pilgrimages to the city hall; let him go on freedom rides -- and try to understand why he must do so. If his repressed emotions are not released in nonviolent ways, they will seek expression through violence; this is not a threat but a fact of history. So I have not said to my people, "Get rid of your discontent." Rather, I have tried to say that this normal and healthy discontent can be channeled into the creative outlet of nonviolent direct action. And now this approach is being termed extremist.

But though I was initially disappointed at being categorized as an extremist, as I continued to think about the matter I gradually gained a measure of satisfaction from the label. Was not Jesus an extremist for love: "Love your enemies, bless them that curse you, do good to them that hate you, and pray for them which despitefully use you, and persecute you." Was not Amos an extremist for justice: "Let justice roll down like waters and righteousness like an ever-flowing stream." Was not Paul an extremist for the Christian gospel: "I bear in my body the marks of the Lord Jesus." Was not Martin Luther an extremist: "Here I stand; I cannot do otherwise, so help me God." And John Bunyan: "I will stay in jail to the end of my days before I make a butchery of my conscience." And Abraham Lincoln: "This nation cannot survive half slave and half free." And Thomas Jefferson: "We hold these truths to be self-evident, that all men are created equal . . . ." So the question is not whether we will be extremists, but what kind of extremists we will be. Will we be extremists for hate or for love? Will we be extremists for the preservation of injustice or for the extension of justice? In that dramatic scene on Calvary's hill three men were crucified. We must never forget that all three were crucified for the same crime -- the crime of extremism. Two were extremists for immorality, and thus fell below their environment. The other, Jesus Christ, was an extremist for love, truth, and goodness, and thereby rose above his environment. Perhaps the South, the nation, and the world are in dire need of creative extremists.

I had hoped that the white moderate would see this need. Perhaps I was too optimistic; perhaps I expected too much. I suppose I should have realized that few members of the oppressor race can understand the deep groans and passionate yearnings of the oppressed race, and still fewer have the vision to see that injustice must be rooted out by strong, persistent, and determined action. I am thankful, however, that some of our white brothers in the South have grasped the meaning of this social revolution and committed themselves to it. They are still all too few in quantity, but they are big in quality. Some -- such as Ralph McGill, Lillian Smith, Harry Golden, James McBride Dabbs, Ann Braden, and Sarah Patton Boyle -- have written about our struggle in eloquent and prophetic terms. Others have marched with us down nameless streets of the South. They have languished in filthy, roach-infested jails, suffering the abuse and brutality of policemen who view them as "dirty nigger-lovers." Unlike so many of their moderate brothers and sisters, they have recognized the urgency of the moment and sensed the need for powerful "action" antidotes to combat the disease of segregation.

Let me take note of my other major disappointment. I have been so greatly disappointed with the white church and its leadership. Of course, there are some notable exceptions. I am not unmindful of the fact that each of you has taken some significant stands on this issue. I commend you, Reverend Stallings, for your Christian stand on this past Sunday, in welcoming Negroes to your worship service on a nonsegregated basis. I commend the Catholic leaders of this state for integrating Spring Hill College several years ago.

But despite these notable exceptions, I must honestly reiterate that I have been disappointed with the church. I do not say this as one of those negative critics who can always find something wrong with the church. I say this as a minister of the gospel, who loves the church; who was nurtured in its bosom; who has been sustained by its spiritual blessings and who will remain true to it as long as the cord of life shall lengthen.

When I was suddenly catapulted into the leadership of the bus protest in Montgomery, Alabama, a few years ago, I felt we would be supported by the white church. I felt that the ministers, priests, and rabbis of the South would be among our strongest allies. Instead, some have been outright opponents, refusing to understand the freedom movement and misrepresenting its leaders; all too many others have been more cautious than courageous and have remained silent behind the anesthetizing security of stained-glass windows.

In spite of my shattered dreams, I came to Birmingham with the hope that the white religious leadership of this community would see the justice of our cause and, with deep moral concern, would serve as the channel through which our just grievances could reach the power structure. I had hoped that each of you would understand. But again I have been disappointed.

I have heard numerous southern religious leaders admonish their worshipers to comply with a desegregation decision because it is the law, but I have longed to hear white ministers declare: "Follow this decree because integration is morally right and because the Negro is your brother." In the midst of blatant injustices inflicted upon the Negro, I have watched white churchmen stand on the sideline and mouth pious irrelevancies and sanctimonious trivialities. In the midst of a mighty struggle to rid our nation of racial and economic injustice, I have heard many ministers say: "Those are social issues, with which the gospel has no real concern." And I have watched many churches commit themselves to a completely otherworldly religion which makes a strange, un-Biblical distinction between body and soul, between the sacred and the secular.

I have traveled the length and breadth of Alabama, Mississippi, and all the other southern states. On sweltering summer days and crisp autumn mornings I have looked at the South's beautiful churches with their lofty spires pointing heavenward. I have beheld the impressive outlines of her massive religious-education buildings. Over and over I have found myself asking: "What kind of people worship here? Who is their God? Where were their voices when the lips for Governor Barnett dripped with words of interposition and nullification? Where were they when Governor Wallace gave a clarion call defiance and hatred? Where were their voices of support when bruised and weary Negro men and women decided to rise from the dark dungeons of complacency to the bright hills of creative protest?"

Yes, these questions are still in my mind. In deep disappointment I have wept over the laxity of the church. But be assured that my tears have been tears of love. Yes, I love the church. How could I do otherwise? I am in the rather unique position of being the son, the grandson, and the great-grandson of preachers. Yes, I see the church as the body of Christ. But, oh! How we have blemished and scarred that body through social neglect and through fear of being nonconformists.

There was a time when the church was very powerful -- in the time when the early Christians rejoiced at being deemed worthy to suffer for what they believed. In those days the church was not merely a thermometer that recorded the ideas and principles of popular opinion; it was a thermostat that transformed the mores of society. Whenever the early Christians entered a town, the people in power became disturbed and immediately sought to convict the Christians for being "disturbers of the peace" and "outside agitators." But the Christians pressed on, in the conviction that they were "a colony of heaven," called to obey Gad rather than man. Small in number, they were big in commitment. They were too God-intoxicated to be "astronomically intimidated." By their effort and example they brought an end to such ancient evils as infanticide and gladiatorial contests.

Things are different now. So often the contemporary church is a weak, ineffectual voice with an uncertain sound. So often it is an archdefender of the status quo. Far from being disturbed by the presence of the church, the power structure of the average community is consoled by the church's silent -- and often even vocal -- sanction of things as they are.

But the judgment of God is upon the church as never before. If today's church does not recapture the sacrificial spirit of the early church, it will lose its authenticity, forfeit the loyalty of millions, and be dismissed as an irrelevant social club with no meaning for the twentieth century. Every day I meet young people whose disappointment with the church has turned into outright disgust.

Perhaps I have once again been too optimistic. Is organized religion too inextricably bound to the status quo to save our nation and the world? Perhaps I must turn my faith to the inner spiritual church, the church within the church, as the true ekklesia and the hope of the world. But again I am thankful to God that some noble souls from the ranks of organized religion have broken loose from the paralyzing chains of conformity and joined us as active partners in the struggle for freedom. They have left their secure congregations and walked the streets of Albany, Georgia, with us. They have gone down the highways of the South on tortuous rides for freedom. Yes, they have gone to jail with us. Some have been dismissed from their churches, have lost the support of their bishops and fellow ministers. But they have acted in the faith that right defeated is stronger than evil triumphant. Their witness has been the spiritual salt that has preserved the true meaning of the gospel in these troubled times. They have carved a tunnel of hope through the dark mountain of disappointment.

I hope the church as a whole will meet the challenge of this decisive hour. But even if the church does not come to the aid of justice, I have no despair about the future. I have no fear about the outcome of our struggle in Birmingham, even if our motives are at present misunderstood. We will reach the goal of freedom in Birmingham and all over the nation, because the goal of America is freedom. Abused and scorned though we may be, our destiny is tied up with America's destiny. Before the pilgrims landed at Plymouth, we were here. For more than two centuries our forebears labored in this country without wages; they made cotton king; they built the homes of their masters while suffering gross injustice and shameful humiliation -- and yet out of bottomless vitality they continued to thrive and develop. If the inexpressible cruelties of slavery could not stop us, the opposition we now face will surely fail. We will win our freedom because the sacred heritage of our nation and the eternal will of God are embodied in our echoing demands.

Before closing I feel impelled to mention one other point in your statement that has troubled me profoundly. You warmly commended the Birmingham police force for keeping "order" and "preventing violence." I doubt that you would so quickly commend the policemen if you were to observe their ugly and inhumane treatment of Negroes here in the city jail; if you were to watch them push and curse old Negro women and young Negro girls; if you were to see them slap and kick Negro men and young boys; if you were to observe them, as they did on two occasions, refuse to give us food because we wanted to sing our grace together. I cannot join you in your praise of the Birmingham police department.

It is true that the police have exercised a degree of discipline in handling the demonstrations. In this sense they have conducted themselves rather "nonviolently" in public. But for what purpose? To preserve the evil system of segregation. Over the past few years I have consistently preached that nonviolence demands that the means we use must be as pure as the ends we seek. I have tried to make clear that it is wrong to use immoral means to attain moral ends. But now I must affirm that it is just as wrong, or perhaps even more so, to use moral means to preserve immoral ends. Perhaps Mr. Connor and his policemen have been rather nonviolent in public, as was Chief Pritchett in Albany, Georgia, but they have used the moral means of nonviolence to maintain the immoral end of racial injustice. As T.S. Eliot has said, "The last temptation is the greatest treason: To do the right deed for the wrong reason."

I wish you had commended the Negro sit-inners and demonstrators of Birmingham for their sublime courage, their willingness to suffer, and their amazing discipline in the midst of great provocation. One day the South will recognize its real heroes. They will be the James Merediths, with the noble sense of purpose that enables them to face jeering and hostile mobs, and with the agonizing loneliness that characterizes the life of the pioneer. They will be old, oppressed, battered Negro women, symbolized in a seventy-two-year-old woman in Montgomery, Alabama, who rose up with a sense of dignity and when her people decided not to ride segregated buses, and who responded with ungrammatical profundity to one who inquired about her weariness: "My feets is tired, but my soul is at rest." They will be the young high school and college students, the young ministers of the gospel and a host of their elders, courageously and nonviolently sitting in at lunch counters and willingly going to jail for conscience' sake. One day the South will know that when these disinherited children of God sat down at lunch counters, they were in reality standing up for what is best in the American dream and for the most sacred values in our Judaeo-Christian heritage, thereby bringing our nation back to those great wells of democracy which were dug deep by the founding fathers in their formulation of the Constitution and the Declaration of Independence.

Never before have I written so long a letter. I'm afraid it is much too long to take your precious time. I can assure you that it would have been much shorter if I had been writing from a comfortable desk, but what else can one do when he is alone in a narrow jail cell, other than write long letters, think long thoughts, and pray long prayers?

If I have said anything in this letter that overstates the truth and indicates an unreasonable impatience, I beg you to forgive me. If I have said anything that understates the truth and indicates my having a patience that allows me to settle for anything less than brotherhood, I beg God to forgive me.

I hope this letter finds you strong in the faith. I also hope that circumstances will soon make it possible for me to meet each of you, not as an integrationist or a civil-rights leader but as a fellow clergyman and a Christian brother. Let us all hope that the dark clouds of racial prejudice will soon pass away and the deep fog of misunderstanding will be lifted from our fear-drenched communities, and in some not too distant tomorrow the radiant stars of love and brotherhood will shine over our great nation with all their scintillating beauty.

Yours for the cause of Peace and Brotherhood, Martin Luther King, Jr.

They're Smiling in Heaven Today - A Reflection on Charles Schulz

By Don Lindman Syndicated Columnist

They're smiling in heaven today.

Well, if not today, tomorrow, or at least by next week. Charles Schulz has joined the folks up there, and while there are no tears or crying in heaven, he will enrich even their days as soon as he takes hold of a pencil and paper.

And we are the poorer. For over five decades Schulz's "Peanuts" cartoon strip has made us mortals smile, chuckle and at times even laugh. An inspiration to his peers, Schulz was a role model for the rest of us as a man who combined success in the nation's press with an uncompromising Christian faith.

Like many real-life kids but unlike most other cartoon children, the Peanuts characters went to Sunday School and could quote Bible verses. But that didn't make them angels.

If Schulz does start drawing again, for Heaven's Herald, I doubt that Charlie Brown will wear a halo. His characters have always just been ordinary people. We have seen ourselves reflected in them, which is what gave them their appeal and their lasting quality.

Charlie Brown touched the eternal optimist in all of us. We get stepped on and beaten down and oftentimes keep coming back to try just one more time, whether we're dealing with a kite-eating tree or a Lucy Van Pelt who keeps pulling the football away every time we try to kick it. Other kids may have had more prestigious fathers, but Charlie's dad-the-barber was just fine in the eyes of that "little round-headed kid."

We saw the cynical and self-centered side of ourselves and others in the person of Lucy. That's why, when she appears in Heaven's Herald, she won't be sporting horns and a tail. There is a Lucy in most of us, and if we can reach heaven by God's grace, so can she.

Schulz's characters reflected the simpler time of the 50s and early 60s, when morality was expected and families stayed together. Some critics might want to argue that they are now hopelessly out of date, a pleasant and nostalgic anachronism in today's world.

But while circumstances have indeed changed, people haven't. Honesty, integrity, and loving, caring relationships are still valued, and they can be a part of our lives if we choose to live them. In that sense Charlie Brown is less an anachronism than a call to personal responsibility.

Schulz changed the face of cartooning, according to colleague Gary Trudeau in a moving tribute written when his mentor announced his retirement. The simple, line-drawing style with minimal background is reflected in Trudeau's "Doonesbury" and Bill Watterson's "Calvin and Hobbes," two immensely popular strips over the past years.

There is nothing we can say in tribute that will enhance Schulz's greatness. We can only try to express our sorrow and our sense of loss.

But this much can be said. Schulz, in his life, exemplified these words from the Scriptures that he loved so much: "Whatever you do, in word or deed, do it all in the name of the Lord Jesus, giving thanks to God the Father through Him."

And there is one who already has said to him, "Well done, good and faithful servant. Enter into the joy of your Lord." That's the only tribute that matters for any of us.

Reprinted with permission of The Amy Foundation Internet Syndicate. To contact the author or The Amy Foundation, write or E-mail to: P.O. Box 16091, Lansing, MI 48901-6091; amyfoundtn@aol.com. Visit our website at www.amyfound.org.

Lord Clive, 1843
By Thomas Babington Macaulay

This is part of a very long communication regarding an uprising of Indians in Calcutta.

Then was committed that great crime, memorable for its singular atrocity, memorable for the tremendous retribution by which it was followed. The English captives were left to the mercy of the guards, and the guards determined to secure them for the night in the prison of the garrison, a chamber known by the fearful name of the Black Hole. Even for a single European malefactor, that dungeon would, in such a climate, have been too close and narrow. The space was only twenty feet square. The air holes were small and obstructed. It was the summer solstice, the season when the fierce heat of Bengal can scarcely be rendered tolerable to natives of England by lofty halls and by the constant waving of fans. The number of the prisoners was one hundred and forty-six. When they were ordered to enter the cell, they imagined that the soldiers were joking; and, being in high spirits on account of the promise of the Nabob to spare their lives, they laughed and jested at the absurdity of the notion. They soon discovered their mistake. They expostulated; they entreated; but in vain. The guards threatened to cut down all who hesitated. The captives were driven into the cell at the point of the sword, and the door was instantly shut and locked upon them.

Nothing in history or fiction, not even the story which Ugolino told in the sea of everlasting ice, after he had wiped his bloody lips on the scalp of his murderer, approaches the horrors which were recounted by the few survivors of that night. They cried for mercy. They strove to burst the door. Holwell, who, even in that extremity, retained some presence of mind, offered large bribes to the gaolers. But the answer was that nothing could be done without the Nabob's orders, that the Nabob was asleep, and that he would be angry if anybody woke him. Then the prisoners went mad with despair. They trampled each other down, fought for the places at the windows, fought for the pittance of water with which the cruel mercy of the murderers mocked their agonies, raved, prayed, blasphemed, implored the guards to fire among them. The gaolers in the meantime held lights to the bars, and shouted with laughter at the frantic struggles of their victims. At length the tumult died away in low gaspings and moanings. The day broke. The Nabob had slept off his debauch, and permitted the door to be opened. But it was some time before the soldiers could make a lane for the survivors, by piling up on each side the heaps of corpses on which the burning climate had already begun to do its loathsome work. When at length a passage was made, twenty-three ghastly figures, such as their own mothers would not have known, staggered one by one out of the charnel-house. A pit was instantly dug. The dead bodies, a hundred and twenty-three in number, were flung into it promiscuously and covered up.

From Thomas Babington Macaulay, "Lord Clive," Classical Rhetoric for the Modern Student.
Reprinted with permission

MANIFESTO OF THE COMMUNIST PARTY, 1848

BY KARL MARX AND FREDERICK ENGELS

A spectre is haunting Europe -- the spectre of communism. All the powers of old Europe have entered into a holy alliance to exorcise this spectre: Pope and Tsar, Metternich and Guizot, French Radicals and German police-spies.

Where is the party in opposition that has not been decried as communistic by its opponents in power? Where is the opposition that has not hurled back the branding reproach of communism, against the more advanced opposition parties, as well as against its reactionary adversaries?

Two things result from this fact:

I. Communism is already acknowledged by all European powers to be itself a power.

II. It is high time that Communists should openly, in the face of the whole world, publish their views, their aims, their tendencies, and meet this nursery tale of the spectre of communism with a manifesto of the party itself.

To this end, Communists of various nationalities have assembled in London and sketched the following manifesto, to be published in the English, French, German, Italian, Flemish and Danish languages.

I -- BOURGEOIS AND PROLETARIANS [1]

The history of all hitherto existing society [2] is the history of class struggles.

Freeman and slave, patrician and plebian, lord and serf, guild-master [3] and journeyman, in a word, oppressor and oppressed, stood in constant opposition to one another, carried on an uninterrupted, now hidden, now open fight, a fight that each time ended, either in a revolutionary reconstitution of society at large, or in the common ruin of the contending classes.

In the earlier epochs of history, we find almost everywhere a complicated arrangement of society into various orders, a manifold gradation of social rank. In ancient Rome we have patricians, knights, plebians, slaves; in the Middle Ages, feudal lords, vassals, guild-masters, journeymen, apprentices, serfs; in almost all of these classes, again, subordinate gradations.

The modern bourgeois society that has sprouted from the ruins of feudal society has not done away with class antagonisms. It has but established new classes, new conditions of oppression, new forms of struggle in place of the old ones.

Our epoch, the epoch of the bourgeoisie, possesses, however, this distinct feature: it has simplified class antagonisms. Society as a whole is more and more splitting up into two great hostile camps, into two great classes directly facing each other -- bourgeoisie and proletariat.

From the serfs of the Middle Ages sprang the chartered burghers of the earliest towns. From these burgesses the first elements of the bourgeoisie were developed.

The discovery of America, the rounding of the Cape, opened up fresh ground for the rising bourgeoisie. The East-Indian and Chinese markets, the colonisation of America, trade with the colonies, the increase in the means of exchange and in commodities generally, gave to commerce, to navigation, to industry, an impulse never before known, and thereby, to the revolutionary element in the tottering feudal society, a rapid development.

The feudal system of industry, in which industrial production was monopolized by closed guilds, now no longer suffices for the growing wants of the new markets. The manufacturing system took its place. The guild-masters were pushed aside by the manufacturing middle class; division of labor between the different corporate guilds vanished in the face of division of labor in each single workshop.

Meantime, the markets kept ever growing, the demand ever rising. Even manufacturers no longer sufficed. Thereupon, steam and machinery revolutionized industrial production. The place of manufacture was taken by the giant, MODERN INDUSTRY; the place of the industrial middle class by industrial millionaires, the leaders of the whole industrial armies, the modern bourgeois.

Modern industry has established the world market, for which the discovery of America paved the way. This market has given an immense development to commerce, to navigation, to communication by land. This development has, in turn, reacted on the extension of industry; and in proportion as industry, commerce, navigation, railways extended, in the same proportion the bourgeoisie developed, increased its capital, and pushed into the background every class handed down from the Middle Ages.

We see, therefore, how the modern bourgeoisie is itself the product of a long course of development, of a series of revolutions in the modes of production and of exchange.

Each step in the development of the bourgeoisie was accompanied by a corresponding political advance in that class. An oppressed class under the sway of the feudal nobility, an armed and self-governing association of medieval commune [4]: here independent urban republic (as in Italy and Germany); there taxable "third estate" of the monarchy (as in France); afterward, in the period of manufacturing proper, serving either the semi-feudal or the absolute monarchy as a counterpoise against the nobility, and, in fact, cornerstone of the great monarchies in general -- the bourgeoisie has at last, since the establishment of Modern Industry and of the world market, conquered for itself, in the modern representative state, exclusive political sway. The executive of the modern state is but a committee for managing the common affairs of the whole bourgeoisie. The bourgeoisie, historically, has played a most revolutionary part.

The bourgeoisie, wherever it has got the upper hand, has put an end to all feudal, patriarchal, idyllic relations. It has pitilessly torn asunder the motley feudal ties that bound man to his "natural superiors", and has left no other nexus between people than naked self-interest, than callous "cash payment". It has drowned out the most heavenly ecstacies of religious fervor, of chivalrous enthusiasm, of philistine sentimentalism, in the icy water of egotistical calculation. It has resolved personal worth into exchange value, and in place of the numberless indefeasible chartered freedoms, has set up that single, unconscionable freedom -- Free Trade. In one word, for exploitation, veiled by religious and political illusions, it has substituted naked, shameless, direct, brutal exploitation.

The bourgeoisie has stripped of its halo every occupation hitherto honored and looked up to with reverent awe. It has converted the physician, the lawyer, the priest, the poet, the man of science, into its paid wage laborers.

The bourgeoisie has torn away from the family its sentimental veil, and has reduced the family relation into a mere money relation.

The bourgeoisie has disclosed how it came to pass that the brutal display of vigor in the Middle Ages, which reactionaries so much admire, found its fitting complement in the most slothful indolence. It has been the first to show what man's activity can bring about. It has accomplished wonders far surpassing Egyptian pyramids, Roman aqueducts, and Gothic cathedrals; it has conducted expeditions that put in the shade all former exoduses of nations and crusades.

The bourgeoisie cannot exist without constantly revolutionizing the instruments of production, and thereby the relations of production, and with them the whole relations of society. Conservation of the old modes of production in unaltered form, was, on the contrary, the first condition of existence for all earlier industrial classes. Constant revolutionizing of production, uninterrupted disturbance of all social conditions, everlasting uncertainty and agitation distinguish the bourgeois epoch from all earlier ones. All fixed, fast frozen relations, with their train of ancient and venerable prejudices and opinions, are swept away, all new-formed ones become antiquated before they can ossify. All that is solid melts into air, all that is holy is profaned, and man is at last compelled to face with sober senses his real condition of life and his relations with his kind.

The need of a constantly expanding market for its products chases the bourgeoisie over the entire surface of the globe. It must nestle everywhere, settle everywhere, establish connections everywhere.

The bourgeoisie has, through its exploitation of the world market, given a cosmopolitan character to production and consumption in every country. To the great chagrin of reactionaries, it has drawn from under the feet of industry the national ground on which it stood. All old-established national industries have been destroyed or are daily being destroyed. They are dislodged by new industries, whose introduction becomes a life and death question for all civilized nations, by industries that no longer work up indigenous raw material, but raw material drawn from the remotest zones; industries whose products are consumed, not only at home, but in every quarter of the globe. In place of the old wants, satisfied by the production of the country, we find new wants, requiring for their satisfaction the products of distant lands and climes. In place of the old local and national seclusion and self-sufficiency, we have intercourse in every direction, universal inter-dependence of nations. And as in material, so also in intellectual production. The intellectual creations of individual nations become common property. National one-sidedness and narrow-mindedness become more and more impossible, and from the numerous national and local literatures, there arises a world literature.

The bourgeoisie, by the rapid improvement of all instruments of production, by the immensely facilitated means of communication, draws all, even the most barbarian, nations into civilization. The cheap prices of commodities are the heavy artillery with which it forces the barbarians' intensely obstinate hatred of foreigners to capitulate. It compels all nations, on pain of extinction, to adopt the bourgeois mode of production; it compels them to introduce what it calls civilization into their midst, i.e., to become bourgeois themselves. In one word, it creates a world after its own image.

The bourgeoisie has subjected the country to the rule of the towns. It has created enormous cities, has greatly increased the urban population as compared with the rural, and has thus rescued a considerable part of the population from the idiocy of rural life. Just as it has made the country dependent on the towns, so it has made barbarian and semi-barbarian countries dependent on the civilized ones, nations of peasants on nations of bourgeois, the East on the West.

The bourgeoisie keeps more and more doing away with the scattered state of the population, of the means of production, and of property. It has agglomerated population, centralized the means of production, and has concentrated property in a few hands. The necessary consequence of this was political centralization. Independent, or but loosely connected provinces, with separate interests, laws, governments, and systems of taxation, became lumped together into one nation, with one government, one code of laws, one national class interest, one frontier, and one customs tariff.

The bourgeoisie, during its rule of scarce one hundred years, has created more massive and more colossal productive forces than have all preceding generations together. Subjection of nature's forces to man, machinery, application of chemistry to industry and agriculture, steam navigation, railways, electric telegraphs, clearing of whole continents for cultivation, canalization or rivers, whole populations conjured out of the ground -- what earlier century had even a presentiment that such productive forces slumbered in the lap of social labor?

We see then: the means of production and of exchange, on whose foundation the bourgeoisie built itself up, were generated in feudal society. At a certain stage in the development of these means of production and of exchange, the conditions under which feudal society produced and exchanged, the feudal organization of agriculture and manufacturing industry, in one word, the feudal relations of property became no longer compatible with the already developed productive forces; they became so many fetters. They had to be burst asunder; they were burst asunder.

Into their place stepped free competition, accompanied by a social and political constitution adapted in it, and the economic and political sway of the bourgeois class.

A similar movement is going on before our own eyes. Modern bourgeois society, with its relations of production, of exchange and of property, a society that has conjured up such gigantic means of production and of exchange, is like the sorcerer who is no longer able to control the powers of the nether world whom he has called up by his spells. For many a decade past, the history of industry and commerce is but the history of the revolt of modern productive forces against modern conditions of production, against the property relations that are the conditions for the existence of the bourgeois and of its rule. It is enough to mention the commercial crises that, by their periodical return, put the existence of the entire bourgeois society on its trial, each time more threateningly. In these crises, a great part not only of the existing products, but also of the previously created productive forces, are periodically destroyed. In these crises, there breaks out an epidemic that, in all earlier epochs, would have seemed an absurdity -- the epidemic of over-production. Society suddenly finds itself put back into a state of momentary barbarism; it appears as if a famine, a universal war of devastation, had cut off the supply of every means of subsistence; industry and commerce seem to be destroyed. And why? Because there is too much civilization, too much means of subsistence, too much industry, too much commerce. The productive forces at the disposal of society no longer tend to further the development of the conditions of bourgeois property; on the contrary, they have become too powerful for these conditions, by which they are fettered, and so soon as they overcome these fetters, they bring disorder into the whole of bourgeois society, endanger the existence of bourgeois property. The conditions of bourgeois society are too narrow to comprise the wealth created by them. And how does the bourgeoisie get over these crises? On the one hand, by enforced destruction of a mass of productive forces; on the other, by the conquest of new markets, and by the more thorough exploitation of the old ones. That is to say, by paving the way for more extensive and more destructive crises, and by diminishing the means whereby crises are prevented.

The weapons with which the bourgeoisie felled feudalism to the ground are now turned against the bourgeoisie itself.

But not only has the bourgeoisie forged the weapons that bring death to itself; it has also called into existence the men who are to wield those weapons -- the modern working class -- the proletarians.

In proportion as the bourgeoisie, i.e., capital, is developed, in the same proportion is the proletariat, the modern working class, developed -- a class of laborers, who live only so long as they find work, and who find work only so long as their labor increases capital. These laborers, who must sell themselves piecemeal, are a commodity, like every other article of commerce, and are consequently exposed to all the vicissitudes of competition, to all the fluctuations of the market.

Owing to the extensive use of machinery, and to the division of labor, the work of the proletarians has lost all individual character, and, consequently, all charm for the workman. He becomes an appendage of the machine, and it is only the most simple, most monotonous, and most easily acquired knack, that is required of him. Hence, the cost of production of a workman is restricted, almost entirely, to the means of subsistence that he requires for maintenance, and for the propagation of his race. But the price of a commodity, and therefore also of labor, is equal to its cost of production. In proportion, therefore, as the repulsiveness of the work increases, the wage decreases. What is more, in proportion as the use of machinery and division of labor increases, in the same proportion the burden of toil also increases, whether by prolongation of the working hours, by the increase of the work exacted in a given time, or by increased speed of machinery, etc.

Modern Industry has converted the little workshop of the patriarchal master into the great factory of the industrial capitalist. Masses of laborers, crowded into the factory, are organized like soldiers. As privates of the industrial army, they are placed under the command of a perfect hierarchy of officers and sergeants. Not only are they slaves of the bourgeois class, and of the bourgeois state; they are daily and hourly enslaved by the machine, by the overlooker, and, above all, in the individual bourgeois manufacturer himself. The more openly this despotism proclaims gain to be its end and aim, the more petty, the more hateful and the more embittering it is.

The less the skill and exertion of strength implied in manual labor, in other words, the more modern industry becomes developed, the more is the labor of men superseded by that of women.

Differences of age and sex have no longer any distinctive social validity for the working class. All are instruments of labor, more or less expensive to use, according to their age and sex.

No sooner is the exploitation of the laborer by the manufacturer, so far at an end, that he receives his wages in cash, than he is set upon by the other portion of the bourgeoisie, the landlord, the shopkeeper, the pawnbroker, etc.

The lower strata of the middle class -- the small tradespeople, shopkeepers, and retired tradesmen generally, the handicraftsmen and peasants -- all these sink gradually into the proletariat, partly because their diminutive capital does not suffice for the scale on which Modern Industry is carried on, and is swamped in the competition with the large capitalists, partly because their specialized skill is rendered worthless by new methods of production. Thus, the proletariat is recruited from all classes of the population.

The proletariat goes through various stages of development. With its birth begins its struggle with the bourgeoisie. At first, the contest is carried on by individual laborers, then by the work of people of a factory, then by the operative of one trade, in one locality, against the individual bourgeois who directly exploits them. They direct their attacks not against the bourgeois condition of production, but against the instruments of production themselves; they destroy imported wares that compete with their labor, they smash to pieces machinery, they set factories ablaze, they seek to restore by force the vanished status of the workman of the Middle Ages.

At this stage, the laborers still form an incoherent mass scattered over the whole country, and broken up by their mutual competition. If anywhere they unite to form more compact bodies, this is not yet the consequence of their own active union, but of the union of the bourgeoisie, which class, in order to attain its own political ends, is compelled to set the whole proletariat in motion, and is moreover yet, for a time, able to do so. At this stage, therefore, the proletarians do not fight their enemies, but the enemies of their enemies, the remnants of absolute monarchy, the landowners, the non-industrial bourgeois, the petty bourgeois. Thus, the whole historical movement is concentrated in the hands of the bourgeoisie; every victory so obtained is a victory for the bourgeoisie.

But with the development of industry, the proletariat not only increases in number; it becomes concentrated in greater masses, its strength grows, and it feels that strength more. The various interests and conditions of life within the ranks of the proletariat are more and more equalized, in proportion as machinery obliterates all distinctions of labor, and nearly everywhere reduces wages to the same low level. The growing competition among the bourgeois, and the resulting commercial crises, make the wages of the workers ever more fluctuating. The increasing improvement of machinery, ever more rapidly developing, makes their livelihood more and more precarious; the collisions between individual workmen and individual bourgeois take more and more the character of collisions between two classes. Thereupon, the workers begin to form combinations (trade unions) against the bourgeois; they club together in order to keep up the rate of wages; they found permanent associations in order to make provision beforehand for these occasional revolts. Here and there, the contest breaks out into riots.

Now and then the workers are victorious, but only for a time. The real fruit of their battles lie not in the immediate result, but in the ever expanding union of the workers. This union is helped on by the improved means of communication that are created by Modern Industry, and that place the workers of different localities in contact with one another. It was just this contact that was needed to centralize the numerous local struggles, all of the same character, into one national struggle between classes. But every class struggle is a political struggle. And that union, to attain which the burghers of the Middle Ages, with their miserable highways, required centuries, the modern proletarian, thanks to railways, achieve in a few years.

This organization of the proletarians into a class, and, consequently, into a political party, is continually being upset again by the competition between the workers themselves. But it ever rises up again, stronger, firmer, mightier. It compels legislative recognition of particular interests of the workers, by taking advantage of the divisions among the bourgeoisie itself. Thus, the Ten-Hours Bill in England was carried.

Altogether, collisions between the classes of the old society further in many ways the course of development of the proletariat. The bourgeoisie finds itself involved in a constant battle. At first with the aristocracy; later on, with those portions of the bourgeoisie itself, whose interests have become antagonistic to the progress of industry; at all time with the bourgeoisie of foreign countries. In all these battles, it sees itself compelled to appeal to the proletariat, to ask for help, and thus to drag it into the political arena. The bourgeoisie itself, therefore, supplies the proletariat with its own elements of political and general education, in other words, it furnishes the proletariat with weapons for fighting the bourgeoisie.

Further, as we have already seen, entire sections of the ruling class are, by the advance of industry, precipitated into the proletariat, or are at least threatened in their conditions of existence. These also supply the proletariat with fresh elements of enlightenment and progress.

Finally, in times when the class struggle nears the decisive hour, the progress of dissolution going on within the ruling class, in fact within the whole range of old society, assumes such a violent, glaring character, that a small section of the ruling class cuts itself adrift, and joins the revolutionary class, the class that holds the future in its hands. Just as, therefore, at an earlier period, a section of the nobility went over to the bourgeoisie, so now a portion of the bourgeoisie goes over to the proletariat, and in particular, a portion of the bourgeois ideologists, who have raised themselves to the level of comprehending theoretically the historical movement as a whole.

Of all the classes that stand face to face with the bourgeoisie today, the proletariat alone is a genuinely revolutionary class. The other classes decay and finally disappear in the face of Modern Industry; the proletariat is its special and essential product.

The lower middle class, the small manufacturer, the shopkeeper, the artisan, the peasant, all these fight against the bourgeoisie, to save from extinction their existence as fractions of the middle class. They are therefore not revolutionary, but conservative. Nay, more, they are reactionary, for they try to roll back the wheel of history. If, by chance, they are revolutionary, they are only so in view of their impending transfer into the proletariat; they thus defend not their present, but their future interests; they desert their own standpoint to place themselves at that of the proletariat.

The "dangerous class", the social scum, that passively rotting mass thrown off by the lowest layers of the old society, may, here and there, be swept into the movement by a proletarian revolution; its conditions of life, however, prepare it far more for the part of a bribed tool of reactionary intrigue.

In the condition of the proletariat, those of old society at large are already virtually swamped. The proletarian is without property; his relation to his wife and children has no longer anything in common with the bourgeois family relations; modern industry labor, modern subjection to capital, the same in England as in France, in America as in Germany, has stripped him of every trace of national character. Law, morality, religion, are to him so many bourgeois prejudices, behind which lurk in ambush just as many bourgeois interests. All the preceding classes that got the upper hand sought to fortify their already acquired status by subjecting society at large to their conditions of appropriation. The proletarians cannot become masters of the productive forces of society, except by abolishing their own previous mode of appropriation, and thereby also every other previous mode of appropriation. They have nothing of their own to secure and to fortify; their mission is to destroy all previous securities for, and insurances of, individual property.

All previous historical movements were movements of minorities, or in the interest of minorities. The proletarian movement is the self-conscious, independent movement of the immense majority, in the interest of the immense majority. The proletariat, the lowest stratum of our present society, cannot stir, cannot raise itself up, without the whole superincumbent strata of official society being sprung into the air.

Though not in substance, yet in form, the struggle of the proletariat with the bourgeoisie is at first a national struggle. The proletariat of each country must, of course, first of all settle matters with its own bourgeoisie.

In depicting the most general phases of the development of the proletariat, we traced the more or less veiled civil war, raging within existing society, up to the point where that war breaks out into open revolution, and where the violent overthrow of the bourgeoisie lays the foundation for the sway of the proletariat.

Hitherto, every form of society has been based, as we have already seen, on the antagonism of oppressing and oppressed classes. But in order to oppress a class, certain conditions must be assured to it under which it can, at least, continue its slavish existence. The serf, in the period of serfdom, raised himself to membership in the commune, just as the petty bourgeois, under the yoke of the feudal absolutism, managed to develop into a bourgeois. The modern laborer, on the contrary, instead of rising with the process of industry, sinks deeper and deeper below the conditions of existence of his own class. He becomes a pauper, and pauperism develops more rapidly than population and wealth. And here it becomes evident that the bourgeoisie is unfit any longer to be the ruling class in society, and to impose its conditions of existence upon society as an overriding law. It is unfit to rule because it is incompetent to assure an existence to its slave within his slavery, because it cannot help letting him sink into such a state, that it has to feed him, instead of being fed by him. Society can no longer live under this bourgeoisie, in other words, its existence is no longer compatible with society.

The essential conditions for the existence and for the sway of the bourgeois class is the formation and augmentation of capital; the condition for capital is wage labor. Wage labor rests exclusively on competition between the laborers. The advance of industry, whose involuntary promoter is the bourgeoisie, replaces the isolation of the laborers, due to competition, by the revolutionary combination, due to association. The development of Modern Industry, therefore, cuts from under its feet the very foundation on which the bourgeoisie produces and appropriates products. What the bourgeoisie therefore produces, above all, are its own grave-diggers. Its fall and the victory of the proletariat are equally inevitable.

FOOTNOTES

[1] By bourgeoisie is meant the class of modern capitalists, owners of the means of social production and employers of wage labor.

By proletariat, the class of modern wage laborers who, having no means of production of their own, are reduced to selling their labor power in order to live. [Note by Engels - 1888 English edition]

[2] That is, all _written_ history. In 1847, the pre-history of society, the social organization existing previous to recorded history, all but unknown. Since then, August von Haxthausen (1792-1866) discovered common ownership of land in Russia, Georg Ludwig von Maurer proved it to be the social foundation from which all Teutonic races started in history, and, by and by, village communities were found to be, or to have been, the primitive form of society everywhere from India to Ireland. The inner organization of this primitive communistic society was laid bare, in its typical form, by Lewis Henry Morgan's (1818-1861) crowning discovery of the true nature of the gens and its relation to the tribe. With the dissolution of the primeaval communities, society begins to be differentiated into separate and finally antagonistic classes. I have attempted to retrace this dissolution in _Der Ursprung der Familie, des Privateigenthumus und des Staats_, second edition, Stuttgart, 1886. [Engels, 1888 English edition]

[3] Guild-master, that is, a full member of a guild, a master within, not a head of a guild. [Engels: 1888 English edition]

[4] This was the name given their urban communities by the townsmen of Italy and France, after they had purchased or conquered their initial rights of self-government from their feudal lords. [Engels: 1890 German edition]

"Commune" was the name taken in France by the nascent towns even before they had conquered from their feudal lords and masters local self-government and political rights as the "Third Estate". Generally speaking, for the economical development of the bourgeoisie, England is here taken as the typical country, for its political development, France. [Engels: 1888 English edition]

II -- PROLETARIANS AND COMMUNISTS

In what relation do the Communists stand to the proletarians as a whole? The Communists do not form a separate party opposed to the other working-class parties.

They have no interests separate and apart from those of the proletariat as a whole.

They do not set up any sectarian principles of their own, by which to shape and mold the proletarian movement. The Communists are distinguished from the other working-class parties by this only:

(1) In the national struggles of the proletarians of the different countries, they point out and bring to the front the common interests of the entire proletariat, independently of all nationality.

(2) In the various stages of development which the struggle of the working class against the bourgeoisie has to pass through, they always and everywhere represent the interests of the movement as a whole.

The Communists, therefore, are on the one hand practically, the most advanced and resolute section of the working-class parties of every country, that section which pushes forward all others; on the other hand, theoretically, they have over the great mass of the proletariat the advantage of clearly understanding the lines of march, the conditions, and the ultimate general results of the proletarian movement.

The immediate aim of the Communists is the same as that of all other proletarian parties: Formation of the proletariat into a class, overthrow of the bourgeois supremacy, conquest of political power by the proletariat.

The theoretical conclusions of the Communists are in no way based on ideas or principles that have been invented, or discovered, by this or that would-be universal reformer.

They merely express, in general terms, actual relations springing from an existing class struggle, from a historical movement going on under our very eyes. The abolition of existing property relations is not at all a distinctive feature of communism.

All property relations in the past have continually been subject to historical change consequent upon the change in historical conditions.

The French Revolution, for example, abolished feudal property in favor of bourgeois property.

The distinguishing feature of communism is not the abolition of property generally, but the abolition of bourgeois property. But modern bourgeois private property is the final and most complete expression of the system of producing and appropriating products that is based on class antagonisms, on the exploitation of the many by the few.

In this sense, the theory of the Communists may be summed up in the single sentence: Abolition of private property.

We Communists have been reproached with the desire of abolishing the right of personally acquiring property as the fruit of a man's own labor, which property is alleged to be the groundwork of all personal freedom, activity and independence.

Hard-won, self-acquired, self-earned property! Do you mean the property of petty artisan and of the small peasant, a form of property that preceded the bourgeois form? There is no need to abolish that; the development of industry has to a great extent already destroyed it, and is still destroying it daily.

Or do you mean the modern bourgeois private property?

But does wage labor create any property for the laborer? Not a bit. It creates capital, i.e., that kind of property which exploits wage labor, and which cannot increase except upon conditions of begetting a new supply of wage labor for fresh exploitation. Property, in its present form, is based on the antagonism of capital and wage labor. Let us examine both sides of this antagonism.

To be a capitalist, is to have not only a purely personal, but a social STATUS in production. Capital is a collective product, and only by the united action of many members, nay, in the last resort, only by the united action of all members of society, can it be set in motion.

Capital is therefore not only personal; it is a social power.

When, therefore, capital is converted into common property, into the property of all members of society, personal property is not thereby transformed into social property. It is only the social character of the property that is changed. It loses its class character.

Let us now take wage labor.

The average price of wage labor is the minimum wage, i.e., that quantum of the means of subsistence which is absolutely requisite to keep the laborer in bare existence as a laborer. What, therefore, the wage laborer appropriates by means of his labor merely suffices to prolong and reproduce a bare existence. We by no means intend to abolish this personal appropriation of the products of labor, an appropriation that is made for the maintenance and reproduction of human life, and that leaves no surplus wherewith to command the labor of others. All that we want to do away with is the miserable character of this appropriation, under which the laborer lives merely to increase capital, and is allowed to live only in so far as the interest of the ruling class requires it.

In bourgeois society, living labor is but a means to increase accumulated labor. In communist society, accumulated labor is but a means to widen, to enrich, to promote the existence of the laborer.

In bourgeois society, therefore, the past dominates the present; in communist society, the present dominates the past. In bourgeois society, capital is independent and has individuality, while the living person is dependent and has no individuality.

And the abolition of this state of things is called by the bourgeois, abolition of individuality and freedom! And rightly so. The abolition of bourgeois individuality, bourgeois independence, and bourgeois freedom is undoubtedly aimed at.

By freedom is meant, under the present bourgeois conditions of production, free trade, free selling and buying.

But if selling and buying disappears, free selling and buying disappears also. This talk about free selling and buying, and all the other "brave words" of our bourgeois about freedom in general, have a meaning, if any, only in contrast with restricted selling and buying, with the fettered traders of the Middle Ages, but have no meaning when opposed to the communist abolition of buying and selling, or the bourgeois conditions of production, and of the bourgeoisie itself.

You are horrified at our intending to do away with private property. But in your existing society, private property is already done away with for nine-tenths of the population; its existence for the few is solely due to its non-existence in the hands of those nine-tenths. You reproach us, therefore, with intending to do away with a form of property, the necessary condition for whose existence is the non-existence of any property for the immense majority of society.

In one word, you reproach us with intending to do away with your property. Precisely so; that is just what we intend.

From the moment when labor can no longer be converted into capital, money, or rent, into a social power capable of being monopolized, i.e., from the moment when individual property can no longer be transformed into bourgeois property, into capital, from that moment, you say, individuality vanishes.

You must, therefore, confess that by "individual" you mean no other person than the bourgeois, than the middle-class owner of property. This person must, indeed, be swept out of the way, and made impossible.

Communism deprives no man of the power to appropriate the products of society; all that it does is to deprive him of the power to subjugate the labor of others by means of such appropriations.

It has been objected that upon the abolition of private property, all work will cease, and universal laziness will overtake us.

According to this, bourgeois society ought long ago to have gone to the dogs through sheer idleness; for those who acquire anything, do not work. The whole of this objection is but another expression of the tautology: There can no longer be any wage labor when there is no longer any capital.

All objections urged against the communistic mode of producing and appropriating material products, have, in the same way, been urged against the communistic mode of producing and appropriating intellectual products. Just as to the bourgeois, the disappearance of class property is the disappearance of production itself, so the disappearance of class culture is to him identical with the disappearance of all culture.

That culture, the loss of which he laments, is, for the enormous majority, a mere training to act as a machine.

But don't wrangle with us so long as you apply, to our intended abolition of bourgeois property, the standard of your bourgeois notions of freedom, culture, law, etc. Your very ideas are but the outgrowth of the conditions of your bourgeois production and bourgeois property, just as your jurisprudence is but the will of your class made into a law for all, a will whose essential character and direction are determined by the economical conditions of existence of your class.

The selfish misconception that induces you to transform into eternal laws of nature and of reason the social forms stringing from your present mode of production and form of property -- historical relations that rise and disappear in the progress of production -- this misconception you share with every ruling class that has preceded you. What you see clearly in the case of ancient property, what you admit in the case of feudal property, you are of course forbidden to admit in the case of your own bourgeois form of property.

Abolition of the family! Even the most radical flare up at this infamous proposal of the Communists.

On what foundation is the present family, the bourgeois family, based? On capital, on private gain. In its completely developed form, this family exists only among the bourgeoisie. But this state of things finds its complement in the practical absence of the family among proletarians, and in public prostitution.

The bourgeois family will vanish as a matter of course when its complement vanishes, and both will vanish with the vanishing of capital.

Do you charge us with wanting to stop the exploitation of children by their parents? To this crime we plead guilty.

But, you say, we destroy the most hallowed of relations, when we replace home education by social.

And your education! Is not that also social, and determined by the social conditions under which you educate, by the intervention direct or indirect, of society, by means of schools, etc.? The Communists have not intended the intervention of society in education; they do but seek to alter the character of that intervention, and to rescue education from the influence of the ruling class.

The bourgeois claptrap about the family and education, about the hallowed correlation of parents and child, becomes all the more disgusting, the more, by the action of Modern Industry, all the family ties among the proletarians are torn asunder, and their children transformed into simple articles of commerce and instruments of labor.

But you Communists would introduce community of women, screams the bourgeoisie in chorus.

The bourgeois sees his wife a mere instrument of production. He hears that the instruments of production are to be exploited in common, and, naturally, can come to no other conclusion that the lot of being common to all will likewise fall to the women.

He has not even a suspicion that the real point aimed at is to do away with the status of women as mere instruments of production.

For the rest, nothing is more ridiculous than the virtuous indignation of our bourgeois at the community of women which, they pretend, is to be openly and officially established by the Communists. The Communists have no need to introduce free love; it has existed almost from time immemorial.

Our bourgeois, not content with having wives and daughters of their proletarians at their disposal, not to speak of common prostitutes, take the greatest pleasure in seducing each other's wives. (Ah, those were the days!)

Bourgeois marriage is, in reality, a system of wives in common and thus, at the most, what the Communists might possibly be reproached with is that they desire to introduce, in substitution for a hypocritically concealed, an openly legalized system of free love. For the rest, it is self-evident that the abolition of the present system of production must bring with it the abolition of free love springing from that system, i.e., of prostitution both public and private.

The Communists are further reproached with desiring to abolish countries and nationality.

The workers have no country. We cannot take from them what they have not got. Since the proletariat must first of all acquire political supremacy, must rise to be the leading class of the nation, must constitute itself **the** nation, it is, so far, itself national, though not in the bourgeois sense of the word.

National differences and antagonism between peoples are daily more and more vanishing, owing to the development of the bourgeoisie, to freedom of commerce, to the world market, to uniformity in the mode of production and in the conditions of life corresponding thereto.

The supremacy of the proletariat will cause them to vanish still faster. United action of the leading civilized countries at least is one of the first conditions for the emancipation of the proletariat.

In proportion as the exploitation of one individual by another will also be put an end to, the exploitation of one nation by another will also be put an end to. In proportion as the antagonism between classes within the nation vanishes, the hostility of one nation to another will come to an end.

The charges against communism made from a religious, a philosophical and, generally, from an ideological standpoint, are not deserving of serious examination.

Does it require deep intuition to comprehend that man's ideas, views, and conception, in one word, man's consciousness, changes with every change in the conditions of his material existence, in his social relations and in his social life?

What else does the history of ideas prove, than that intellectual production changes its character in proportion as material production is changed? The ruling ideas of each age have ever been the ideas of its ruling class.

When people speak of the ideas that revolutionize society, they do but express that fact that within the old society the elements of a new one have been created, and that the dissolution of the old ideas keeps even pace with the dissolution of the old conditions of existence.

When the ancient world was in its last throes, the ancient religions were overcome by Christianity. When Christian ideas succumbed in the eighteenth century to rationalist ideas, feudal society fought its death battle with the then revolutionary bourgeoisie. The ideas of religious liberty and freedom of conscience merely gave expression to the sway of free competition within the domain of knowledge.

"Undoubtedly," it will be said, "religious, moral, philosophical, and juridicial ideas have been modified in the course of historical development. But religion, morality, philosophy, political science, and law, constantly survived this change."

"There are, besides, eternal truths, such as Freedom, Justice, etc., that are common to all states of society. But communism abolishes eternal truths, it abolishes all religion, and all morality, instead of constituting them on a new basis; it therefore acts in contradiction to all past historical experience."

What does this accusation reduce itself to? The history of all past society has consisted in the development of class antagonisms, antagonisms that assumed different forms at different epochs.

But whatever form they may have taken, one fact is common to all past ages, viz., the exploitation of one part of society by the other. No wonder, then, that the social consciousness of past ages, despite all the multiplicity and variety it displays, moves within certain common forms, or general ideas, which cannot completely vanish except with the total disappearance of class antagonisms.

The communist revolution is the most radical rupture with traditional relations; no wonder that its development involved the most radical rupture with traditional ideas.

But let us have done with the bourgeois objections to communism.

We have seen above that the first step in the revolution by the working class is to raise the proletariat to the position of ruling class to win the battle of democracy.

The proletariat will use its political supremacy to wrest, by degree, all capital from the bourgeoisie, to centralize all instruments of production in the hands of the state, i.e., of the proletariat organized as the ruling class; and to increase the total productive forces as rapidly as possible.

Of course, in the beginning, this cannot be effected except by means of despotic inroads on the rights of property, and on the conditions of bourgeois production; by means of measures, therefore, which appear economically insufficient and untenable, but which, in the course of the movement, outstrip themselves, necessitate further inroads upon the old social order, and are unavoidable as a means of entirely revolutionizing the mode of production.

These measures will, of course, be different in different countries.

Nevertheless, in most advanced countries, the following will be pretty generally applicable.

Abolition of property in land and application of all rents of land to public purposes.

2. A heavy progressive or graduated income tax.

3. Abolition of all rights of inheritance.

4. Confiscation of the property of all emigrants and rebels.

5. Centralization of credit in the banks of the state, by means of a national bank with state capital and an exclusive monopoly.

6. Centralization of the means of communication and transport in the hands of the state.

7. Extension of factories and instruments of production owned by the state; the bringing into cultivation of waste lands, and the improvement of the soil generally in accordance with a common plan.

8. Equal obligation of all to work. Establishment of industrial armies, especially for agriculture.

9. Combination of agriculture with manufacturing industries; gradual abolition of all the distinction between town and country by a more equable distribution of the populace over the country.

10. Free education for all children in public schools. Abolition of children's factory labor in its present form. Combination of education with industrial production, etc.

When, in the course of development, class distinctions have disappeared, and all production has been concentrated in the hands of a vast association of the whole nation, the public power will lose its political character. Political power, properly so called, is merely the organized power of one class for oppressing another. If the proletariat during its contest with the bourgeoisie is compelled, by the force of circumstances, to organize itself as a class; if, by means of a revolution, it makes itself the ruling class, and, as such, sweeps away by force the old conditions of production, then it will, along with these conditions, have swept away the conditions for the existence of class antagonisms and of classes generally, and will thereby have abolished its own supremacy as a class.

In place of the old bourgeois society, with its classes and class antagonisms, we shall have an association in which the free development of each is the condition for the free development of all.

III -- SOCIALIST AND COMMUNIST LITERATURE
1. REACTIONARY SOCIALISM
a. Feudal Socialism

Owing to their historical position, it became the vocation of the aristocracies of France and England to write pamphlets against modern bourgeois society. In the French Revolution of July 1830, and in the English reform agitation, these aristocracies again succumbed to the hateful upstart. Thenceforth, a serious political struggle was altogether out of the question. A literary battle alone remained possible. But even in the domain of literature, the old cries of the restoration period had become impossible. [1]

In order to arouse sympathy, the aristocracy was obliged to lose sight, apparently, of its own interests, and to formulate its indictment against the bourgeoisie in the interest of the exploited working class alone. Thus, the aristocracy took their revenge by singing lampoons on their new masters and whispering in his ears sinister prophesies of coming catastrophe.

In this way arose feudal socialism: half lamentation, half lampoon; half an echo of the past, half menace of the future; at times, by its bitter, witty and incisive criticism, striking the bourgeoisie to the very heart's core, but always ludicrous in its effect, through total incapacity to comprehend the march of modern history.

The aristocracy, in order to rally the people to them, waved the proletarian alms-bag in front for a banner. But the people, so often as it joined them, saw on their hindquarters the old feudal coats of arms, and deserted with loud and irreverent laughter.

One section of the French Legitimists and "Young England" exhibited this spectacle:

In pointing out that their mode of exploitation was different to that of the bourgeoisie, the feudalists forget that they exploited under circumstances and conditions that were quite different and that are now antiquated. In showing that, under their rule, the modern proletariat never existed, they forget that the modern bourgeoisie is the necessary offspring of their own form of society.

For the rest, so little do they conceal the reactionary character of their criticism that their chief accusation against the bourgeois amounts to this: that under the bourgeois regime a class is being developed which is destined to cut up, root and branch, the old order of society.

What they upbraid the bourgeoisie with is not so much that it creates a proletariat as that it creates a _revolutionary_ proletariat.

In political practice, therefore, they join in all corrective measures against the working class; and in ordinary life, despite their high falutin' phrases, they stoop to pick up the golden apples dropped from the tree of industry, and to barter truth, love, and honor, for traffic in wool, beetroot-sugar, and potato spirits. [2]

As the parson has ever gone hand in hand with the landlord, so has clerical socialism with feudal socialism.

Nothing is easier than to give Christian asceticism a socialist tinge. Has not Christianity declaimed against private property, against marriage, against the state? Has it not preached in the place of these, charity and poverty, celibacy and mortification of the flesh, monastic life and Mother Church? Christian socialism is but the holy water with which the priest consecrates the heart-burnings of the aristocrat.

b. Petty-Bourgeois Socialism

The feudal aristocracy was not the only class that was ruined by the bourgeoisie, not the only class whose conditions of existence pined and perished in the atmosphere of modern bourgeois society. The medieval burgesses and the small peasant proprietors were the precursors of the modern bourgeoisie. In those countries which are but little developed, industrially and commercially, these two classes still vegetate side by side with the rising bourgeoisie.

In countries where modern civilization has become fully developed, a new class of petty bourgeois has been formed, fluctuating between proletariat and bourgeoisie, and ever renewing itself a supplementary part of bourgeois society. The individual members of this class, however, as being constantly hurled down into the proletariat by the action of competition, and, as Modern Industry develops, they even see the moment approaching when they will completely disappear as an independent section of modern society, to be replaced in manufactures, agriculture and commerce, by overlookers, bailiffs and shopmen.

In countries like France, where the peasants constitute far more than half of the population, it was natural that writers who sided with the proletariat against the bourgeoisie should use, in their criticism of the bourgeois regime, the standard of the peasant and petty bourgeois, and from the standpoint of these intermediate classes, should take up the cudgels for the working class. Thus arose petty-bourgeois socialism. Sismondi was the head of this school, not only in France but also in England.

This school of socialism dissected with great acuteness the contradictions in the conditions of modern production. It laid bare the hypocritical apologies of economists. It proved, incontrovertibly, the disastrous effects of machinery and division of labor; the concentration of capital and land in a few hands; overproduction and crises; it pointed out the inevitable ruin of the petty bourgeois and peasant, the misery of the proletariat, the anarchy in production, the crying inequalities in the distribution of wealth, the industrial war of extermination between nations, the dissolution of old moral bonds, of the old family relations, of the old nationalities.

In it positive aims, however, this form of socialism aspires either to restoring the old means of production and of exchange, and with them the old property relations, and the old society, or to cramping the modern means of production and of exchange within the framework of the old property relations that have been, and were bound to be, exploded by those means. In either case, it is both reactionary and Utopian.

Its last words are: corporate guilds for manufacture; patriarchal relations in agriculture.

Ultimately, when stubborn historical facts had dispersed all intoxicating effects of self-deception, this form of socialism ended in a miserable hangover.

c. German or "True" Socialism

The socialist and communist literature of France, a literature that originated under the pressure of a bourgeoisie in power, and that was the expressions of the struggle against this power, was introduced into Germany at a time when the bourgeoisie in that country had just begun its contest with feudal absolutism.

German philosophers, would-be philosophers, and beaux esprits (men of letters), eagerly seized on this literature, only forgetting that when these writings immigrated from France into Germany, French social conditions had not immigrated along with them. In contact with German social conditions, this French literature lost all its immediate practical significance and assumed a purely literary aspect. Thus, to the German philosophers of the eighteenth century, the demands of the first French Revolution were nothing more than the demands of "Practical Reason" in general, and the utterance of the will of the revolutionary French bourgeoisie signified, in their eyes, the laws of pure will, of will as it was bound to be, of true human will generally.

The work of the German literati consisted solely in bringing the new French ideas into harmony with their ancient philosophical conscience, or rather, in annexing the French ideas without deserting their own philosophic point of view.

This annexation took place in the same way in which a foreign language is appropriated, namely, by translation.

It is well known how the monks wrote silly lives of Catholic saints _over_ the manuscripts on which the classical works of ancient heathendom had been written. The German literati reversed this process with the profane French literature. They wrote their philosophical nonsense beneath the French original. For instance, beneath the French criticism of the economic functions of money, they wrote "alienation of humanity", and beneath the French criticism of the bourgeois state they wrote "dethronement of the category of the general", and so forth.

The introduction of these philosophical phrases at the back of the French historical criticisms, they dubbed "Philosophy of Action", "True Socialism", "German Science of Socialism", "Philosophical Foundation of Socialism", and so on.

The French socialist and communist literature was thus completely emasculated. And, since it ceased, in the hands of the German, to express the struggle of one class with the other, he felt conscious of having overcome "French one-sidedness" and of representing, not true requirements, but the requirements of truth; not the interests of the proletariat, but the interests of human nature, of man in general, who belongs to no class, has no reality, who exists only in the misty realm of philosophical fantasy.

This German socialism, which took its schoolboy task so seriously and solemnly, and extolled its poor stock-in-trade in such a mountebank fashion, meanwhile gradually lost its pedantic innocence.

The fight of the Germans, and especially of the Prussian bourgeoisie, against feudal aristocracy and absolute monarchy, in other words, the liberal movement, became more earnest.

By this, the long-wished for opportunity was offered to "True" Socialism of confronting the political movement with the socialistic demands, of hurling the traditional anathemas against liberalism, against representative government, against bourgeois competition, bourgeois freedom of the press, bourgeois legislation, bourgeois liberty and equality, and of preaching to the masses that they had nothing to gain, and everything to lose, by this bourgeois movement. German socialism forgot, in the nick of time, that the French criticism, whose silly echo it was, presupposed the existence of modern bourgeois society, with its corresponding economic conditions of existence, and the political constitution adapted thereto, the very things whose attainment was the object of the pending struggle in Germany.

To the absolute governments, with their following of parsons, professors, country squires, and officials, it served as a welcome scarecrow against the threatening bourgeoisie.

It was a sweet finish, after the bitter pills of flogging and bullets, with which these same governments, just at that time, dosed the German working-class risings.

While this "True" Socialism thus served the government as a weapon for fighting the German bourgeoisie, it, at the same time, directly represented a reactionary interest, the interest of German philistines. In Germany, the petty-bourgeois class, a relic of the sixteenth century, and since then constantly cropping up again under the various forms, is the real social basis of the existing state of things.

To preserve this class is to preserve the existing state of things in Germany. The industrial and political supremacy of the bourgeoisie threatens it with certain destruction -- on the one hand, from the concentration of capital; on the other, from the rise of a revolutionary proletariat. "True" Socialism appeared to kill these two birds with one stone. It spread like an epidemic.

The robe of speculative cobwebs, embroidered with flowers of rhetoric, steeped in the dew of sickly sentiment, this transcendental robe in which the German Socialists wrapped their sorry "eternal truths", all skin and bone, served to wonderfully increase the sale of their goods amongst such a public. And on its part German socialism recognized, more and more, its own calling as the bombastic representative of the petty-bourgeois philistine.

It proclaimed the German nation to be the model nation, and the German petty philistine to be the typical man. To every villainous meanness of this model man, it gave a hidden, higher, socialistic interpretation, the exact contrary of its real character. It went to the extreme length of directly opposing the "brutally destructive" tendency of communism, and of proclaiming its supreme and impartial contempt of all class struggles. With very few exceptions, all the so-called socialist and communist publications that now (1847) circulate in Germany belong to the domain of this foul and enervating literature. [3]

2. CONSERVATIVE OR BOURGEOIS SOCIALISM

A part of the bourgeoisie is desirous of redressing social grievances in order to secure the continued existence of bourgeois society.

To this section belong economists, philanthropists, humanitarians, improvers of the condition of the working class, organizers of charity, members of societies for the prevention of cruelty to animals, temperance fanatics, hole-and-corner reformers of every imaginable kind. This form of socialism has, moreover, been worked out into complete systems.

We may cite Proudhon's **Philosophy of Poverty** as an example of this form.

The socialistic bourgeois want all the advantages of modern social conditions without the struggles and dangers necessarily resulting therefrom. They desire the existing state of society, minus its revolutionary and disintegrating elements. They wish for a bourgeoisie without a proletariat. The bourgeoisie naturally conceives the world in which it is supreme to be the best; and bourgeois socialism develops this comfortable conception into various more or less complete systems. In requiring the proletariat to carry out such a system, and thereby to march straightaway into the social New Jerusalem, it but requires in reality that the proletariat should remain within the bounds of existing society, but should cast away all its hateful ideas concerning the bourgeoisie.

A second, and more practical, but less systematic, form of this socialism sought to depreciate every revolutionary movement in the eyes of the working class by showing that no mere political reform, but only a change in the material conditions of existence, in economical relations, could be of any advantage to them. By changes in the material conditions of existence, this form of socialism, however, by no means understands abolition of the bourgeois relations of production, an abolition that can be affected only by a revolution, but administrative reforms, based on the continued existence of these relations; reforms, therefore, that in no respect affect the relations between capital and labor, but, at the best, lessen the cost, and simplify the administrative work of bourgeois government.

Bourgeois socialism attains adequate expression when, and only when, it becomes a mere figure of speech.

Free trade: for the benefit of the working class. Protective duties: for the benefit of the working class. Prison reform: for the benefit of the working class. This is the last word and the only seriously meant word of bourgeois socialism.

It is summed up in the phrase: the bourgeois is a bourgeois -- for the benefit of the working class.

3. CRITICAL-UTOPIAN SOCIALISM AND COMMUNISM

We do not here refer to that literature which, in every great modern revolution, has always given voice to the demands of the proletariat, such as the writings of Babeuf [4] and others.

The first direct attempts of the proletariat to attain its own ends, made in times of universal excitement, when feudal society was being overthrown, necessarily failed, owing to the then undeveloped state of the proletariat, as well as to the absence of the economic conditions for its emancipation, conditions that had yet to be produced, and could be produced by the impending bourgeois epoch alone. The revolutionary literature that accompanied these first movements of the proletariat had necessarily a reactionary character. It inculcated universal asceticism and social levelling in its crudest form.

The socialist and communist systems, properly so called, those of Saint-Simon [5], Fourier [6], Owen [7], and others, spring into existence in the early undeveloped period, described above, of the struggle between proletariat and bourgeoisie (see Section 1. Bourgeois and Proletarians).

The founders of these systems see, indeed, the class antagonisms, as well as the action of the decomposing elements in the prevailing form of society. But the proletariat, as yet in its infancy, offers to them the spectacle of a class without any historical initiative or any independent political movement.

Since the development of class antagonism keeps even pace with the development of industry, the economic situation, as they find it, does not as yet offer to them the material conditions for the emancipation of the proletariat. They therefore search after a new social science, after new social laws, that are to create these conditions.

Historical action is to yield to their personal inventive action; historically created conditions of emancipation to fantastic ones; and the gradual, spontaneous class organization of the proletariat to an organization of society especially contrived by these inventors. Future history resolves itself, in their eyes, into the propaganda and the practical carrying out of their social plans.

In the formation of their plans, they are conscious of caring chiefly for the interests of the working class, as being the most suffering class. Only from the point of view of being the most suffering class does the proletariat exist for them.

The undeveloped state of the class struggle, as well as their own surroundings, causes Socialists of this kind to consider themselves far superior to all class antagonisms. They want to improve the condition of every member of society, even that of the most favored. Hence, they habitually appeal to society at large, without the distinction of class; nay, by preference, to the ruling class. For how can people when once they understand their system, fail to see in it the best possible plan of the best possible state of society?

Hence, they reject all political, and especially all revolutionary action; they wish to attain their ends by peaceful means, necessarily doomed to failure, and by the force of example, to pave the way for the new social gospel.

Such fantastic pictures of future society, painted at a time when the proletariat is still in a very undeveloped state and has but a fantastic conception of its own position, correspond with the first instinctive yearnings of that class for a general reconstruction of society.

But these socialist and communist publications contain also a critical element. They attack every principle of existing society. Hence, they are full of the most valuable materials for the enlightenment of the working class. The practical measures proposed in them -- such as the abolition of the distinction between town and country, of the family, of the carrying on of industries for the account of private individuals, and of the wage system, the proclamation of social harmony, the conversion of the function of the state into a more superintendence of production -- all these proposals point solely to the disappearance of class antagonisms which were, at that time, only just cropping up, and which, in these publications, are recognized in their earliest indistinct and undefined forms only. These proposals, therefore, are of a purely utopian character.

The significance of critical-utopian socialism and communism bears an inverse relation to historical development. In proportion as the modern class struggle develops and takes definite shape, this fantastic standing apart from the contest, these fantastic attacks on it, lose all practical value and all theoretical justifications. Therefore, although the originators of these systems were, in many respects, revolutionary, their disciples have, in every case, formed mere reactionary sects. They hold fast by the original views of their masters, in opposition to the progressive historical development of the proletariat. They, therefore, endeavor, and that consistently, to deaden the class struggle and to reconcile the class antagonisms. They still dream of experimental realization of their social utopias, of founding isolated **phalansteres**, of establishing "Home Colonies", or setting up a "Little Icaria" [8] -- pocket editions of the New Jerusalem -- and to realize all these castles in the air, they are compelled to appeal to the feelings and purses of the bourgeois. By degrees, they sink into the category of the reactionary conservative socialists depicted above, differing from these only by more systematic pedantry, and by their fanatical and superstitious belief in the miraculous effects of their social science.

They, therefore, violently oppose all political action on the part of the working class; such action, according to them, can only result from blind unbelief in the new gospel.

The Owenites in England, and the Fourierists in France, respectively, oppose the Chartists and the Reformistes.

FOOTNOTES
[1] NOTE by Engels to 1888 English edition: Not the English Restoration (1660-1689), but the French Restoration (1814-1830).

[2] NOTE by Engels to 1888 English edition: This applies chiefly to Germany, where the landed aristocracy and squirearchy have large portions of their estates cultivated for their own account by stewards, and are, moreover, extensive beetroot-sugar manufacturers and distillers of potato spirits. The wealthier british aristocracy are, as yet, rather above that; but they, too, know how to make up for declining rents by lending their names to floaters or more or less shady joint-stock companies.

[3] NOTE by Engels to 1888 German edition: The revolutionary storm of 1848 swept away this whole shabby tendency and cured its protagonists of the desire to dabble in socialism. The chief representative and classical type of this tendency is Mr Karl Gruen.

[4] Francois Noel Babeuf (1760-1797): French political agitator; plotted unsuccessfully to destroy the Directory in revolutionary France and established a communistic system.

[5] Comte de Saint-Simon, Claude Henri de Rouvroy (1760-1825): French social philosopher; generally regarded as founder of French socialism. He thought society should be reorganized along industrial lines and that scientists should be the new spiritual leaders. His most important work is _Nouveau_Christianisme_ (1825).

[6] Charles Fourier (1772-1837): French social reformer; propounded a system of self-sufficient cooperatives known as Fourierism, especially in his work _Le_Nouveau_Monde_industriel_ (1829-30)

[7] Richard Owen (1771-1858): Welsh industrialist and social reformer. He formed a model industrial community at New Lanark, Scotland, and pioneered cooperative societies. His books include _New_View_Of_Society_ (1813).

[8] NOTE by Engels to 1888 English edition: "Home Colonies" were what Owen called his communist model societies. _Phalansteres_ were socialist colonies on the plan of Charles Fourier; Icaria was the name given by Caber to his utopia and, later on, to his American communist colony.

IV -- POSITION OF THE COMMUNISTS IN RELATION TO THE VARIOUS EXISTING OPPOSITION PARTIES

Section II has made clear the relations of the Communists to the existing working-class parties, such as the Chartists in England and the Agrarian Reformers in America.

The Communists fight for the attainment of the immediate aims, for the enforcement of the momentary interests of the working class; but in the movement of the present, they also represent and take care of the future of that movement. In France, the Communists ally with the Social Democrats* against the conservative and radical bourgeoisie, reserving, however, the right to take up a critical position in regard to phases and illusions traditionally handed down from the Great Revolution.

In Switzerland, they support the Radicals, without losing sight of the fact that this party consists of antagonistic elements, partly of Democratic Socialists, in the French sense, partly of radical bourgeois.

In Poland, they support the party that insists on an agrarian revolution as the prime condition for national emancipation, that party which fomented the insurrection of Krakow in 1846.

In Germany, they fight with the bourgeoisie whenever it acts in a revolutionary way, against the absolute monarchy, the feudal squirearchy, and the petty-bourgeoisie.

But they never cease, for a single instant, to instill into the working class the clearest possible recognition of the hostile antagonism between bourgeoisie and proletariat, in order that the German workers may straightway use, as so many weapons against the bourgeoisie, the social and political conditions that the bourgeoisie must necessarily introduce along with its supremacy, and in order that, after the fall of the reactionary classes in Germany, the fight against the bourgeoisie itself may immediately begin.

The Communists turn their attention chiefly to Germany, because that country is on the eve of a bourgeois revolution that is bound to be carried out under more advanced conditions of European civilization and with a much more developed proletariat than that of England was in the seventeenth, and France in the eighteenth century, and because the bourgeois revolution in Germany will be but the prelude to an immediately following proletarian revolution.

In short, the Communists everywhere support every revolutionary movement against the existing social and political order of things.

In all these movements, they bring to the front, as the leading question in each, the property question, no matter what its degree of development at the time.

Finally, they labor everywhere for the union and agreement of the democratic parties of all countries.

The Communists disdain to conceal their views and aims. They openly declare that their ends can be attained only by the forcible overthrow of all existing social conditions. Let the ruling classes tremble at a communist revolution. The proletarians have nothing to lose but their chains. They have a world to win.

Proletarians of all countries, unite!

FOOTNOTES
* NOTE by Engels to 1888 English edition: The party then represented in Parliament by Ledru-Rollin, in literature by Louis Blanc (1811-82), in the daily press by the **Reforme**. The name of Social-Democracy signifies, with these its inventors, a section of the Democratic or Republican Party more or less tinged with socialism.

Reprinted from http://www.anu.edu.au/polsci/marx/classics/manifesto.html (accessed 7/2008)

CHECKERS SPEECH

BY RICHARD M. NIXON - SEPTEMBER 23, 1952

At the 1952 Republican national convention, young Senator Richard M. Nixon was chosen to be the running mate of presidential candidate Dwight D. Eisenhower.

Nixon had enjoyed a spectacular rise in national politics. Elected to Congress in 1946, he quickly made a name for himself as a militant anti-Communist while serving on the House Un-American Activities Committee. In 1950, at age 38, he was elected to the U.S. Senate and became an outspoken critic of President Truman's conduct of the Korean War, wasteful spending by the Democrats, and also alleged Communists were in the government.

But Nixon's rapid rise in American politics came to a crashing halt after a sensational headline appeared in the New York Post stating, "Secret Rich Men's Trust Fund Keeps Nixon in Style Far Beyond His Salary." The headline appeared just a few days after Eisenhower had chosen him as his running mate. Amid the shock and outrage that followed, many Republicans urged Eisenhower to remove Nixon from the ticket before it was too late.

Nixon, however, in a brilliant political maneuver, took his case directly to the American people via the new medium of television in a nationwide hookup. With his wife sitting stoically nearby, Nixon offered an apologetic explanation of all of his finances, including the now-famous lines regarding his wife's "respectable Republican cloth coat" and the tale of a little dog named Checkers given as a present to his young daughters. "...I want to say right now that regardless of what they say, we're going to keep it."

He turned the last section of his address into a political attack, making veiled accusations about the finances of his opponents and challenging them to provide the same kind of open explanation.

Although it would forever be known as Nixon's "Checkers Speech," it was actually a political triumph for Nixon at the time it was given. Eisenhower requested Nixon to come to West Virginia where he was campaigning and greeted Nixon at the airport with, "Dick, you're my boy." The Republicans went on to win the election by a landslide.

My Fellow Americans, I come before you tonight as a candidate for the Vice-presidency and as a man whose honesty and integrity has been questioned.

Now, the usual political thing to do when charges are made against you is to either ignore them or to deny them without giving details. I believe we have had enough of that in the United States, particularly with the present administration in Washington D.C.

To me, the office of the Vice-presidency of the United States is a great office, and I feel that the people have got to have confidence in the integrity of the men who run for that office and who might attain them.

I have a theory, too, that the best and only answer to a smear or an honest misunderstanding of the facts is to tell the truth. And that is why I am here tonight. I want to tell you my side of the case.

I am sure that you have read the charges, and you have heard it, that I, Senator Nixon, took $18,000 from a group of my supporters.

Now, was that wrong? And let me say that it was wrong. I am saying it, incidentally, that it was wrong, just not illegal, because it isn't a question of whether it was legal or illegal, that isn't enough. The question is, was it morally wrong? I say that it was morally wrong if any of that $18,000 went to Senator Nixon, for my personal use. I say that it was morally wrong if it was secretly given and secretly handled.

And I say that it was morally wrong if any of the contributors got special favors for the contributions that they made.

And to answer those questions let me say this--not a cent of the $18,000 or any other money of that type ever went to me for my personal use. Every penny of it was used to pay for political expenses that I did not think should be charged to the taxpayers of the United States.

It was not a secret fund. As a matter of fact, when I was on "Meet the Press"--some of you may have seen it last Sunday--Peter Edson came up to me after the program, and he said, "Dick, what about this fund we hear about?" And I said, "Well, there is no secret about it. Go out and see Dana Smith who was the administrator of the fund," and I gave him his address. And I said you will find that the purpose of the fund simply was to defray political expenses that I did not feel should be charged to the government.

And third, let me point out, and I want to make this particularly clear, that no contributor to this fund, no contributor to any of my campaigns, has ever received any consideration that he would not have received as an ordinary constituent.

I just don't believe in that, and I can say that never, while I have been in the Senate of the United States, as far as the people that contributed to this fund are concerned, have I made a telephone call to an agency, nor have I gone down to an agency on their behalf.

And the records will show that--the records which are in the hands of the administration.

Well, then, some of you will say, and rightly, "Well, what did you use the fund for, Senator? Why did you have to have it?"

Let me tell you in just a word how a Senate office operates. First of all, the Senator gets $15,000 a year in salary. He gets enough money to pay for one trip a year, a round trip, that is, for himself, and his family between his home and Washington D.C. And then he gets an allowance to handle the people that work in his office to handle his mail.

And the allowance for my State of California, is enough to hire 13 people. And let me say, incidentally, that this allowance is not paid to the Senator.

It is paid directly to the individuals, that the Senator puts on his payroll, but all of these people and all of these allowances are for strictly official business--business, for example, when a constituent writes in and wants you to go down to the Veteran's Administration and get some information about his GI policy--items of that type for example. But there are other expenses that are not covered by the government. And I think I can best discuss those expenses by asking you some questions.

Do you think that when I or any other Senator makes a political speech, has it printed, should charge the printing of that speech and the mailing of that speech to the taxpayers?

Do you think, for example, when I or any other Senator makes a trip to his home state to make a purely political speech that the cost of that trip should be charged to the taxpayers?

Do you think when a Senator makes political broadcasts or political television broadcasts, radio or television, that the expense of those broadcasts should be charged to the taxpayers?

I know what your answer is. It is the same answer that audiences give me whenever I discuss this particular problem.

The answer is no. The taxpayers should not be required to finance items which are not official business but which are primarily political business.

Well, then the question arises, you say, "Well, how do you pay for these and how can you do it legally?" And there are several ways, that it can be done, incidentally, and it is done legally in the United States Senate and in the Congress.

The first way is to be a rich man. So I couldn't use that.

Another way that is used is to put your wife on the payroll. Let me say, incidentally, that my opponent, my opposite number for the Vice-presidency on the Democratic ticket, does have his wife on the payroll and has had her on his payroll for the past ten years. Now let me just say this--That is his business, and I am not critical of him for doing that. You will have to pass judgment on that particular point, but I have never done that for this reason:

I have found that there are so many deserving stenographers and secretaries in Washington that needed the work that I just didn't feel it was right to put my wife on the payroll--My wife sitting over there.

She is a wonderful stenographer. She used to teach stenography and she used to teach shorthand in high school. That was when I met her. And I can tell you folks that she has worked many hours on Saturdays and Sundays in my office, and she has done a fine job, and I am proud to say tonight that in the six years I have been in the Senate of the United States, Pat Nixon has never been on the government payroll.

What are the other ways that these finances can be taken care of? Some who are lawyers, and I happen to be a lawyer, continue to practice law, but I haven't been able to do that.

I am so far away from California and I have been so busy with my senatorial work that I have not engaged in any legal practice, and, also, as far as law practice is concerned, it seemed to me that the relationship between an attorney and the client was so personal that you couldn't possibly represent a man as an attorney and then have an unbiased view when he presented his case to you in the event that he had one before government.

And so I felt that the best way to handle these necessary political expenses of getting my message to the American people and the speeches I made--the speeches I had printed for the most part concerned this one message of exposing this administration, the Communism in it, the corruption in it--the only way I could do that was to accept the aid which people in my home state of California, who contributed to my campaign and who continued to make these contributions after I was elected, were glad to make.

And let me say that I am proud of the fact that not one of them has ever asked me for a special favor. I am proud of the fact that not one of them has ever asked me to vote on a bill other than my own conscience would dictate. And I am proud of the fact that the taxpayers by subterfuge or otherwise have never paid one dime for expenses which I thought were political and should not be charged to the taxpayers.

Let me say, incidentally, that some of you may say, "Well, that is all right, Senator, that is your explanation, but have you got any proof?" And I would like to tell you this evening that just an hour ago we received an independent audit of this entire fund. I suggested to Governor Sherman Adams, who is the chief of staff of the Eisenhower campaign, that an independent audit and legal report be obtained, and I have that audit in my hand.

It is an audit made by Price Waterhouse & Co. firm, and the legal opinion by Gibson, Dunn, & Crutcher, lawyers in Los Angeles, the biggest law firm, and incidentally, one of the best ones in Los Angeles.

I am proud to report to you tonight that this audit and legal opinion is being forwarded to General Eisenhower and I would like to read to you the opinion that was prepared by Gibson, Dunn, & Crutcher, based on all the pertinent laws, and statutes, together with the audit report prepared by the certified public accountants.

It is our conclusion that Senator Nixon did not obtain any financial gain from the collection and disbursement of the funds by Dana Smith; that Senator Nixon did not violate any federal or state law by reason of the operation of the fund; and that neither the portion of the fund paid by Dana Smith directly to third persons, nor the portion paid to Senator Nixon, to reimburse him for office expenses, constituted income in a sense which was either reportable or taxable as income under income tax laws.

Signed--Gibson, Dunn, & Crutcher, by Elmo Conley

That is not Nixon speaking, but it is an independent audit which was requested because I want the American people to know all the facts and I am not afraid of having independent people go in and check the facts, and that is exactly what they did.

But then I realized that there are still some who may say, and rightly so--and let me say that I recognize that some will continue to smear regardless of what the truth may be--but that there has been understandably, some honest misunderstanding on this matter, and there are some that will say, "Well, maybe you were able, Senator, to fake the thing. How can we believe what you say--after all, is there a possibility that maybe you got some sums in cash? Is there a possibility that you might have feathered your own nest?" And so now, what I am going to do--and incidentally this is unprecedented in the history of American politics--I am going at this time to give to this television and radio audience, a complete financial history, everything I have earned, everything I have spent and everything I own, and I want you to know the facts.

I will have to start early, I was born in 1913. Our family was one of modest circumstances, and most of my early life was spent in a store out in East Whittier. It was a grocery store, one of those family enterprises.

The only reason we were able to make it go was because my mother and dad had five boys, and we all worked in the store. I worked my way through college, and, to a great extent, through law school. And then in 1940, probably the best thing that ever happened to me happened. I married Pat who is sitting over here.

We had a rather difficult time after we were married, like so many of the young couples who might be listening to us. I practiced law. She continued to teach school.

Then, in 1942, I went into the service. Let me say that my service record was not a particularly unusual one. I went to the South Pacific. I guess I'm entitled to a couple of battle stars. I got a couple of letters of commendation. But I was just there when the bombs were falling. And then I returned. I returned to the United States, and in 1946, I ran for Congress. When we came out of the war--Pat and I--Pat during the war had worked as a stenographer, and in a bank, and as an economist for a government agency--and when we came out, the total of our savings, from both my law practice, her teaching and all the time I was in the war, the total for that entire period was just less than $10,000--every cent of that, incidentally, was in government bonds--well, that's where we start, when I go into politics.

Now, whatever I earned since I went into politics--well, here it is. I jotted it down. Let me read the notes.

First of all, I have had my salary as a Congressman and as a Senator.

Second, I have received a total in this past six years of $1,600 from estates which were in my law firm at the time that I severed my connection with it. And, incidentally, as I said before, I have not engaged in any legal practice, and have not accepted any fees from business that came into the firm after I went into politics.

I have made an average of approximately $1,500 a year from nonpolitical speaking engagements and lectures.

And then, unfortunately, we have inherited little money. Pat sold her interest in her father's estate for $3,000, and I inherited $1,500 from my grandfather. We lived rather modestly.

For four years we lived in an apartment in Parkfairfax, Alexandria Virginia. The rent was $80 a month. And we saved for a time when we could buy a house. Now that was what we took in.

What did we do with this money? What do we have today to show for it? This will surprise you because it is so little. I suppose as standards generally go of people in public life.

First of all, we've got a house in Washington, which cost $41,000 and on which we owe $20,000. We have a house in Whittier, California which cost $13,000 and on which we owe $3,000. My folks are living there at the present time.

I have just $4,000 in life insurance, plus my GI policy which I have never been able to convert, and which will run out in two years.

I have no life insurance whatever on Pat. I have no life insurance on our two youngsters, Patricia and Julie.

I own a 1950 Oldsmobile car. We have our furniture. We have no stocks and bonds of any type. We have no interest, direct or indirect, in any business. Now that is what we have. What do we owe?

Well, in addition to the mortgages, the $20,000 mortgage on the house in Washington and the $10,000 mortgage on the house in Whittier, I owe $4,000 to the Riggs Bank in Washington D.C. with an interest at 4 percent.

I owe $3,500 to my parents, and the interest on that loan, which I pay regularly, because it is a part of the savings they made through the years they were working so hard--I pay regularly 4 percent interest. And then I have a $500 loan, which I have on my life insurance. Well, that's about it. That's what we have. And that's what we owe. It isn't very much.

But Pat and I have the satisfaction that every dime that we have got is honestly ours.

I should say this, that Pat doesn't have a mink coat. But she does have a respectable Republican cloth coat, and I always tell her she would look good in anything.

One other thing I probably should tell you, because if I don't they will probably be saying this about me, too. We did get something, a gift, after the election.

A man down in Texas heard Pat on the radio mention the fact that our two youngsters would like to have a dog, and, believe it or not, the day before we left on this campaign trip we got a message from Union Station in Baltimore, saying they had a package for us. We went down to get it. You know what it was?

It was a little cocker spaniel dog, in a crate that he had sent all the way from Texas, black and white, spotted, and our little girl Tricia, the six year old, named it Checkers.

And you know, the kids, like all kids, loved the dog, and I just want to say this, right now, that regardless of what they say about it, we are going to keep it.

It isn't easy to come before a nation-wide audience and bare your life, as I have done. But I want to say some things before I conclude, that I think most of you will agree on.

Mr. Mitchell, the Chairman of the Democratic National Committee, made this statement that if a man couldn't afford to be in the United States Senate, he shouldn't run for senate. And I just want to make my position clear.

I don't agree with Mr. Mitchell when he says that only a rich man should serve his government in the United States Senate or Congress. I don't believe that represents the thinking of the Democratic Party, and I know it doesn't represent the thinking of the Republican Party.

I believe that it's fine that a man like Governor Stevenson, who inherited a fortune from his father, can run for President. But I also feel that it is essential in this country of ours that a man of modest means can also run for President, because, you know--remember Abraham Lincoln--you remember what he said--"God must have loved the common people, he made so many of them."

And now I'm going to suggest some courses of conduct.

First of all, you have read in the papers about other funds, now, Mr. Stevenson apparently had a couple. One of them in which a group of business people paid and helped to supplement the salaries of state employees. Here is where the money went directly into their pockets, and I think that what Mr. Stevenson should do should be to come before the American people, as I have, give the names of the people that contributed to that fund, give the names of the people who put this money into their pockets, at the same time that they were receiving money from their state government and see what favors, if any, they gave out for that.

I don't condemn Mr. Stevenson for what he did, but until the facts are in, there is a doubt that would be raised. And as far as Mr. Sparkman is concerned, I would suggest the same thing. He's had his wife on the payroll. I don't condemn him for that, but I think that he should come before the American people and indicate what outside sources of income he has had. I would suggest that under the circumstances both Mr. Sparkman and Mr. Stevenson should come before the American people, as I have, and make a complete financial statement as to their financial history, and if they don't, it will be an admission that they have something to hide.

And I think you will agree with me--because, folks, remember, a man that's to be President of the United States, a man that is to be Vice President of the United States, must have the confidence of all the people. And that's why I'm doing what I'm doing. And that is why I suggest that Mr. Stevenson and Mr. Sparkman, if they are under attack, that should be what they are doing.

Now let me say this: I know this is not the last of the smears. In spite of my explanation tonight, other smears will be made. Others have been made in the past. And the purpose of the smears, I know, is this, to silence me, to make me let up.

Well, they just don't know who they are dealing with. I'm going to tell you this: I remember in the dark days of the Hiss trial some of the same columnists, some of the same radio commentators who are attacking me now and misrepresenting my position, were violently opposing me at the time I was after Alger Hiss. But I continued to fight because I knew I was right, and I can say to this great television and radio audience that I have no apologies to the American people for my part in putting Alger Hiss where he is today. And as far as this is concerned, I intend to continue to fight.

Why do I feel so deeply? Why do I feel that in spite of the smears, the misunderstanding, the necessity for a man to come up here and bare his soul? And I want to tell you why.

Because, you see, I love my country. And I think my country is in danger. And I think the only man that can save America at this time is the man that's running for President, on my ticket, Dwight Eisenhower.

You say, why do I think it is in danger? And I say look at the record. Seven years of the Truman-Acheson administration, and what's happened? Six hundred million people lost to Communists.

And a war in Korea in which we have lost 117,000 American casualties, and I say that those in the State Department that made the mistakes which caused that war and which resulted in those losses should be kicked out of the State Department just as fast as we can get them out of there.

And let me say that I know Mr. Stevenson won't do that because he defends the Truman policy, and I know that Dwight Eisenhower will do that, and he will give America the leadership that it needs.

Take the problem of corruption. You have read about the mess in Washington. Mr. Stevenson can't clean it up because he was picked by the man, Truman, under whose Administration the mess was made.

You wouldn't trust the man who made the mess to clean it up. That is Truman. And by the same token you can't trust the man who was picked by the man who made the mess to clean it up and that's Stevenson. And so I say, Eisenhower who owes nothing to Truman, nothing to the big city bosses--he is the man who can clean up the mess in Washington.

Take Communism. I say as far as that subject is concerned the danger is greater to America. In the Hiss case they got the secrets which enabled them to break the American secret State Department code.

They got secrets in the atomic bomb case which enabled them to get the secret of the atomic bomb five years before they would have gotten it by their own devices. And I say that any man who called the Alger Hiss case a red herring isn't fit to be President of the United States.

I say that a man who, like Mr. Stevenson, has pooh-poohed and ridiculed the Communist threat in the United States--he has accused us, that they have attempted to expose the Communists, of looking for Communists in the Bureau of Fisheries and Wildlife. I say that a man who says that isn't qualified to be President of the United States.

And I say that the only man who can lead us into this fight to rid the government of both those who are Communists and those who have corrupted this government is Eisenhower, because General Eisenhower, you can be sure, recognizes the problem, and knows how to handle it.

Let me say this, finally. This evening I want to read to you just briefly excerpts from a letter that I received, a letter, which after all this is over, no one can take away from us. It reads as follows:

Dear Senator Nixon, Since I am only 19 years of age, I can't vote in this presidential election, but believe me if I could, you and General Eisenhower would certainly get my vote. My husband is in the Fleet Marines in Korea. He is in the front lines. And we have a two month old son he has never seen. And I feel confident that with great Americans like you and General Eisenhower in the White House, lonely Americans like myself will be united with their loved ones now in Korea. I only pray to God that you won't be too late. Enclosed is a small check to help you with your campaign. Living on $85 a month it is all I can do.

Folks, it is a check for $10, and it is one that I shall never cash. And let me just say this: We hear a lot about prosperity these days, but I say why can't we have prosperity built on peace, rather than prosperity built on war? Why can't we have prosperity and an honest government in Washington D.C. at the same time?

Believe me, we can. And Eisenhower is the man that can lead the crusade to bring us that kind of prosperity.

And now, finally, I know that you wonder whether or not I am going to stay on the Republican ticket or resign. Let me say this: I don't believe that I ought to quit, because I am not a quitter. And, incidentally, Pat is not a quitter. After all, her name is Patricia Ryan and she was born on St. Patrick's day, and you know the Irish never quit.

But the decision, my friends, is not mine. I would do nothing that would harm the possibilities of Dwight Eisenhower to become President of the United States. And for that reason I am submitting to the Republican National Committee tonight through this television broadcast the decision which it is theirs to make. Let them decide whether my position on the ticket will help or hurt. And I am going to ask you to help them decide. Wire and write the Republican National Committee whether you think I should stay on or whether I should get off. And whatever their decision, I will abide by it.

But let me just say this last word. Regardless of what happens, I am going to continue this fight. I am going to campaign up and down America until we drive the crooks and the Communists and those that defend them out of Washington, and remember folks, Eisenhower is a great man. Folks, he is a great man, and a vote for Eisenhower is a vote for what is good for America.

Reprinted with permission from the Richard Nixon Library and Birthplace, www.nixonlibrary.org.

Funeral Oration, 431 BC
By Pericles

At the end of the first year of war, the Athenians held, as was their custom, an elaborate funeral for all those killed in the war. The funeral oration over these dead was delivered by the brilliant and charismatic politician and general, Pericles, who perished a little bit later in the horrifying plague that decimated Athens the next year. The Funeral Oration is the classic statement of Athenian ideology, containing practically in full the patriotic sentiment felt by most Athenians.

Most of those who have spoken here before me have commended the lawgiver who added this oration to our other funeral customs. It seemed to them a worthy thing that such an honor should be given at their burial to the dead who have fallen on the field of battle. But I should have preferred that, when men's deeds have been brave, they should be honored in deed only, and with such an honor as this public funeral, which you are now witnessing. Then the reputation of many would not have been imperiled on the eloquence or want of eloquence of one, and their virtues believed or not as he spoke well or ill. For it is difficult to say neither too little nor too much; and even moderation is apt not to give the impression of truthfulness. The friend of the dead who knows the facts is likely to think that the words of the speaker fall short of his knowledge and of his wishes; another who is not so well informed, when he hears of anything which surpasses his own powers, will be envious and will suspect exaggeration. Mankind are tolerant of the praises of others so long as each hearer thinks that he can do as well or nearly as well himself, but, when the speaker rises above him, jealousy is aroused and he begins to be incredulous. However, since our ancestors have set the seal of their approval upon the practice, I must obey, and to the utmost of my power shall endeavor to satisfy the wishes and beliefs of all who hear me.

I will speak first of our ancestors, for it is right and seemly that now, when we are lamenting the dead, a tribute should be paid to their memory. There has never been a time when they did not inhabit this land, which by their valor they will have handed down from generation to generation, and we have received from them a free state. But if they were worthy of praise, still more were our fathers, who added to their inheritance, and after many a struggle transmitted to us their sons this great empire. And we ourselves assembled here today, who are still most of us in the vigor of life, have carried the work of improvement further, and have richly endowed our city with all things, so that she is sufficient for herself both in peace and war. Of the military exploits by which our various possessions were acquired, or of the energy with which we or our fathers drove back the tide of war, Hellenic or Barbarian, I will not speak; for the tale would be long and is familiar to you. But before I praise the dead, I should like to point out by what principles of action we rose ~ to power, and under what institutions and through what manner of life our empire became great. For I conceive that such thoughts are not unsuited to the occasion, and that this numerous assembly of citizens and strangers may profitably listen to them.

Our form of government does not enter into rivalry with the institutions of others. Our government does not copy our neighbors', but is an example to them. It is true that we are called a democracy, for the administration is in the hands of the many and not of the few. But while there exists equal justice to all and alike in their private disputes, the claim of excellence is also recognized; and when a citizen is in any way distinguished, he is preferred to the public service, not as a matter of privilege, but as the reward of merit. Neither is poverty an obstacle, but a man may benefit his country whatever the obscurity of his condition. There is no exclusiveness in our public life, and in our private business we are not suspicious of one another, nor angry with our neighbor if he does what he likes; we do not put on sour looks at him which, though harmless, are not pleasant. While we are thus unconstrained in our private business, a spirit of reverence pervades our public acts; we are prevented from doing wrong by respect for the authorities and for the laws, having a particular regard to those which are ordained for the protection of the injured as well as those unwritten laws which bring upon the transgressor of them the reprobation of the general sentiment.

And we have not forgotten to provide for our weary spirits many relaxations from toil; we have regular games and sacrifices throughout the year; our homes are beautiful and elegant; and the delight which we daily feel in all these things helps to banish sorrow. Because of the greatness of our city the fruits of the whole earth flow in upon us; so that we enjoy the goods of other countries as freely as our own.

Then, again, our military training is in many respects superior to that of our adversaries. Our city is thrown open to the world, though and we never expel a foreigner and prevent him from seeing or learning anything of which the secret if revealed to an enemy might profit him. We rely not upon management or trickery, but upon our own hearts and hands. And in the matter of education, whereas they from early youth are always undergoing laborious exercises which are to make them brave, we live at ease, and yet are equally ready to face the perils which they face. And here is the proof: The Lacedaemonians come into Athenian territory not by themselves, but with their whole confederacy following; we go alone into a neighbor's country; and although our opponents are fighting for their homes and we on a foreign soil, we have seldom any difficulty in overcoming them. Our enemies have never yet felt our united strength, the care of a navy divides our attention, and on land we are obliged to send our own citizens everywhere. But they, if they meet and defeat a part of our army, are as proud as if they had routed us all, and when defeated they pretend to have been vanquished by us all.

If then we prefer to meet danger with a light heart but without laborious training, and with a courage which is gained by habit and not enforced by law, are we not greatly the better for it? Since we do not anticipate the pain, although, when the hour comes, we can be as brave as those who never allow themselves to rest; thus our city is equally admirable in peace and in war. For we are lovers of the beautiful in our tastes and our

strength lies, in our opinion, not in deliberation and discussion, but that knowledge which is gained by discussion preparatory to action. For we have a peculiar power of thinking before we act, and of acting, too, whereas other men are courageous from ignorance but hesitate upon reflection. And they are surely to be esteemed the bravest spirits who, having the clearest sense both of the pains and pleasures of life, do not on that account shrink from danger. In doing good, again, we are unlike others; we make our friends by conferring, not by receiving favors. Now he who confers a favor is the firmer friend, because he would rather by kindness keep alive the memory of an obligation; but the recipient is colder in his feelings, because he knows that in requiting another's generosity he will not be winning gratitude but only paying a debt. We alone do good to our neighbors not upon a calculation of interest, but in the confidence of freedom and in a frank and fearless spirit. To sum up: I say that Athens is the school of Hellas, and that the individual Athenian in his own person seems to have the power of adapting himself to the most varied forms of action with the utmost versatility and grace. This is no passing and idle word, but truth and fact; and the assertion is verified by the position to which these qualities have raised the state. For in the hour of trial Athens alone among her contemporaries is superior to the report of her. No enemy who comes against her is indignant at the reverses which he sustains at the hands of such a city; no subject complains that his masters are unworthy of him. And we shall assuredly not be without witnesses; there are mighty monuments of our power which will make us the wonder of this and of succeeding ages; we shall not need the praises of Homer or of any other panegyrist whose poetry may please for the moment, although his representation of the facts will not bear the light of day. For we have compelled every land and every sea to open a path for our valor, and have everywhere planted eternal memorials of our friendship and of our enmity. Such is the city for whose sake these men nobly fought and died; they could not bear the thought that she might be taken from them; and every one of us who survive should gladly toil on her behalf.

I have dwelt upon the greatness of Athens because I want to show you that we are contending for a higher prize than those who enjoy none of these privileges, and to establish by manifest proof the merit of these men whom I am now commemorating. Their loftiest praise has been already spoken. For in magnifying the city I have magnified them, and men like them whose virtues made her glorious. And of how few Hellenes can it be said as of them, that their deeds when weighed in the balance have been found equal to their fame! I believe that a death such as theirs has been the true measure of a man's worth; it may be the first revelation of his virtues, but is at any rate their final seal. For even those who come short in other ways may justly plead the valor with which they have fought for their country; they have blotted out the evil with the good, and have benefited the state more by their public services than they have injured her by their private actions. None of these men were enervated by wealth or hesitated to resign the pleasures of life; none of them put off the evil day in the hope, natural to poverty, that a man, though poor, may one day become rich. But, deeming that the punishment of their enemies was sweeter than any of these things, and that they could fall in no nobler cause, they determined at the hazard of their lives to be honorably avenged, and to leave the rest. They resigned to hope their unknown chance of happiness; but in the face of death they resolved to rely upon themselves alone. And when the moment came they were minded to resist and suffer, rather than to fly and save their lives; they ran away from the word of dishonor, but on the battlefield their feet stood fast, and in an instant, at the height of their fortune, they passed away from the scene, not of their fear, but of their glory.

Such was the end of these men; they were worthy of Athens, and the living need not desire to have a more heroic spirit, although they may pray for a less fatal issue. The value of such a spirit is not to be expressed in words. Any one can discourse to you for ever about the advantages of a brave defense, which you know already. But instead of listening to him I would have you day by day fix your eyes upon the greatness of Athens, until you become filled with the love of her; and when you are impressed by the spectacle of her glory, reflect that this empire has been acquired by men who knew their duty and had the courage to do it, who in the hour of conflict had the fear of dishonor always present to them, and who, if ever they failed in an enterprise, would not allow their virtues to be lost to their country, but freely gave their lives to her as the fairest offering which they could present at her feast. The sacrifice which they collectively made was individually repaid to them; for they received again each one for himself a praise which grows not old, and the noblest of all tombs, I speak not of that in which their remains are laid, but of that in which their glory survives, and is proclaimed always and on every fitting occasion both in word and deed. For the whole earth is the tomb of famous men; not only are they commemorated by columns and inscriptions in their own country, but in foreign lands there dwells also an unwritten memorial of them, graven not on stone but in the hearts of men. Make them your examples, and, esteeming courage to be freedom and freedom to be happiness, do not weigh too nicely the perils of war. The unfortunate who has no hope of a change for the better has less reason to throw away his life than the prosperous who, if he survive, is always liable to a change for the worse, and to whom any accidental fall makes the most serious difference. To a man of spirit, cowardice and disaster coming together are far more bitter than death striking him unperceived at a time when he is full of courage and animated by the general hope.

Wherefore I do not now pity the parents of the dead who stand here; I would rather comfort them. You know that your dead have passed away amid manifold vicissitudes; and that they may be deemed fortunate who have gained their utmost honor, whether an honorable death like theirs, or an honorable sorrow like yours, and whose share of happiness has been so ordered that the term of their happiness is likewise the term of their life. I know how hard it is to make you feel this, when the good fortune of others will too often remind you of the gladness which once lightened your hearts. And sorrow is felt at the want of those blessings, not which a man never knew, but which were a part of his life before they were taken from him. Some of you are of an age at which they may hope to have other children, and they ought to bear their sorrow better; not only will the children who may hereafter be born make them forget their own lost ones, but the city will be doubly a gainer. She will not be left desolate, and she will be safer. For a man's counsel cannot have equal weight or worth, when he alone has no children to risk in the general danger. To those of you who have passed their prime, I say: "Congratulate yourselves that you have been happy during the greater part of your days; remember that your life of sorrow will not last long, and be comforted by the glory of those who are gone. For the love of honor alone is ever young, and not riches, as some say, but honor is the delight of men when they are old and useless.

To you who are the sons and brothers of the departed, I see that the struggle to emulate them will be an arduous one. For all men praise the dead, and, however preeminent your virtue may be, I do not say even to approach them, and avoid living their rivals and detractors, but when a man is out of the way, the honor and goodwill which he receives is unalloyed. And, if I am to speak of womanly virtues to those of you who will henceforth be widows, let me sum them up in one short admonition: To a woman not to show more weakness than is natural to her sex is a great glory, and not to be talked about for good or for evil among men.

I have paid the required tribute, in obedience to the law, making use of such fitting words as I had. The tribute of deeds has been paid in part; for the dead have them in deeds, and it remains only that their children should be maintained at the public charge until they are grown up: this is the solid prize with which, as with a garland, Athens crowns her sons living and dead, after a struggle like theirs. For where the rewards of virtue are greatest, there the noblest citizens are enlisted in the service of the state. And now, when you have duly lamented, every one his own dead, you may depart.

http://www.wsu.edu/~dee/GREECE/PERICLES.HTM (accessed 7/2008)

BRANDENBURG GATE SPEECH

BY PRESIDENT RONALD REAGAN, JUNE 12, 1987, BERLIN

Thank you. Thank you, very much. Chancellor Kohl, Governing Mayor Diepgen, ladies and gentlemen: Twenty four years ago, President John F. Kennedy visited Berlin, and speaking to the people of this city and the world at the city hall. Well since then two other presidents have come, each in his turn to Berlin. And today, I, myself, make my second visit to your city.

We come to Berlin, we American Presidents, because it's our duty to speak in this place of freedom. But I must confess, we're drawn here by other things as well; by the feeling of history in this city -- more than 500 years older than our own nation; by the beauty of the Grunewald and the Tiergarten; most of all, by your courage and determination. Perhaps the composer, Paul Linke, understood something about American Presidents. You see, like so many Presidents before me, I come here today because wherever I go, whatever I do: *"Ich hab noch einen Koffer in Berlin"* [I still have a suitcase in Berlin.]

Our gathering today is being broadcast throughout Western Europe and North America. I understand that it is being seen and heard as well in the East. To those listening throughout Eastern Europe, I extend my warmest greetings and the good will of the American people. To those listening in East Berlin, a special word: Although I cannot be with you, I address my remarks to you just as surely as to those standing here before me. For I join you, as I join your fellow countrymen in the West, in this firm, this unalterable belief: *Es gibt nur ein Berlin*. [There is only one Berlin.]

Behind me stands a wall that encircles the free sectors of this city, part of a vast system of barriers that divides the entire continent of Europe. From the Baltic South, those barriers cut across Germany in a gash of barbed wire, concrete, dog runs, and guard towers. Farther south, there may be no visible, no obvious wall. But there remain armed guards and checkpoints all the same -- still a restriction on the right to travel, still an instrument to impose upon ordinary men and women the will of a totalitarian state.

Yet, it is here in Berlin where the wall emerges most clearly; here, cutting across your city, where the news photo and the television screen have imprinted this brutal division of a continent upon the mind of the world.

Standing before the Brandenburg Gate, every man is a German separated from his fellow men. Every man is a Berliner, forced to look upon a scar.

President Von Weizsäcker has said, "The German question is open as long as the Brandenburg Gate is closed." Well today -- today I say: As long as this gate is closed, as long as this scar of a wall is permitted to stand, it is not the German question alone that remains open, but the question of freedom for all mankind.

Yet, I do not come here to lament. For I find in Berlin a message of hope, even in the shadow of this wall, a message of triumph.

In this season of spring in 1945, the people of Berlin emerged from their air-raid shelters to find devastation. Thousands of miles away, the people of the United States reached out to help. And in 1947 Secretary of State -- as you've been told -- George Marshall announced the creation of what would become known as the Marshall Plan. Speaking precisely 40 years ago this month, he said: "Our policy is directed not against any country or doctrine, but against hunger, poverty, desperation, and chaos."

In the Reichstag a few moments ago, I saw a display commemorating this 40th anniversary of the Marshall Plan. I was struck by a sign -- the sign on a burnt-out, gutted structure that was being rebuilt. I understand that Berliners of my own generation can remember seeing signs like it dotted throughout the western sectors of the city. The sign read simply: "The Marshall Plan is helping here to strengthen the free world." A strong, free world in the West -- that dream became real. Japan rose from ruin to become an economic giant. Italy, France, Belgium -- virtually every nation in Western Europe saw political and economic rebirth; the European Community was founded.

In West Germany and here in Berlin, there took place an economic miracle, the Wirtschaftswunder. Adenauer, Erhard, Reuter, and other leaders understood the practical importance of liberty--that just as truth can flourish only when the journalist is given freedom of speech, so prosperity can come about only when the farmer and businessman enjoy economic freedom. The German leaders--the German leaders reduced tariffs, expanded free trade, lowered taxes. From 1950 to 1960 alone, the standard of living in West Germany and Berlin doubled.

Where four decades ago there was rubble, today in West Berlin there is the greatest industrial output of any city in Germany: busy office blocks, fine homes and apartments, proud avenues, and the spreading lawns of parkland. Where a city's culture seemed to have been destroyed, today there are two great universities, orchestras and an opera, countless theaters, and museums. Where there was want, today there's abundance -- food, clothing, automobiles -- the wonderful goods of the Kudamm.[1] From devastation, from utter ruin, you Berliners have, in freedom, rebuilt a city that once again ranks as one of the greatest on earth. Now the Soviets may have had other plans. But my friends, there were a few things the Soviets didn't count on: *Berliner Herz, Berliner Humor, ja, und Berliner Schnauze.* [Berliner heart, Berliner humor, yes, and a Berliner Schnauze.[2]]

In the 1950s Khrushchev predicted: "We will bury you." But in the West today, we see a free world that has achieved a level of prosperity and well-being unprecedented in all human history. In the Communist world, we see failure, technological backwardness, declining standards of health, even want of the most basic kind -- too little food. Even today, the Soviet Union still cannot feed itself. After these four decades, then, there stands before the entire world one great and inescapable conclusion: Freedom leads to prosperity. Freedom replaces the ancient hatreds among the nations with comity and peace. Freedom is the victor.

And now -- now the Soviets themselves may, in a limited way, be coming to understand the importance of freedom. We hear much from Moscow about a new policy of reform and openness. Some political prisoners have been released. Certain foreign news broadcasts are no longer being jammed. Some economic enterprises have been permitted to operate with greater freedom from state control.

Are these the beginnings of profound changes in the Soviet state? Or are they token gestures intended to raise false hopes in the West, or to strengthen the Soviet system without changing it? We welcome change and openness; for we believe that freedom and security go together, that the advance of human liberty -- the advance of human liberty can only strengthen the cause of world peace.

There is one sign the Soviets can make that would be unmistakable, that would advance dramatically the cause of freedom and peace.

General Secretary Gorbachev, if you seek peace, if you seek prosperity for the Soviet Union and Eastern Europe, if you seek liberalization: Come here to this gate.

Mr. Gorbachev, open this gate. Mr. Gorbachev -- Mr. Gorbachev, tear down this wall!

I understand the fear of war and the pain of division that afflict this continent, and I pledge to you my country's efforts to help overcome these burdens. To be sure, we in the West must resist Soviet expansion. So, we must maintain defenses of unassailable strength. Yet we seek peace; so we must strive to reduce arms on both sides.

Beginning 10 years ago, the Soviets challenged the Western alliance with a grave new threat, hundreds of new and more deadly SS-20 nuclear missiles capable of striking every capital in Europe. The Western alliance responded by committing itself to a counter-deployment (unless the Soviets agreed to negotiate a better solution)--namely, the elimination of such weapons on both sides. For many months, the Soviets refused to bargain in earnestness. As the alliance, in turn, prepared to go forward with its counter-deployment, there were difficult days, days of protests like those during my 1982 visit to this city; and the Soviets later walked away from the table.

But through it all, the alliance held firm. And I invite those who protested then -- I invite those who protest today -- to mark this fact: Because we remained strong, the Soviets came back to the table. Because we remained strong, today we have within reach the possibility, not merely of limiting the growth of arms, but of eliminating, for the first time, an entire class of nuclear weapons from the face of the earth.

As I speak, NATO ministers are meeting in Iceland to review the progress of our proposals for eliminating these weapons. At the talks in Geneva, we have also proposed deep cuts in strategic offensive weapons. And the Western allies have likewise made far-reaching proposals to reduce the danger of conventional war and to place a total ban on chemical weapons.

While we pursue these arms reductions, I pledge to you that we will maintain the capacity to deter Soviet aggression at any level at which it might occur. And in cooperation with many of our allies, the United States is pursuing the Strategic Defense Initiative -- research to base deterrence not on the threat of offensive retaliation, but on defenses that truly defend; on systems, in short, that will not target populations, but shield them. By these means we seek to increase the safety of Europe and all the world. But we must remember a crucial fact: East and West do not mistrust each other because we are armed; we are armed because we mistrust each other. And our differences are not about weapons but about liberty. When President Kennedy spoke at the City Hall those 24 years ago, freedom was encircled; Berlin was under siege. And today, despite all the pressures upon this city, Berlin stands secure in its liberty. And freedom itself is transforming the globe.

In the Philippines, in South and Central America, democracy has been given a rebirth. Throughout the Pacific, free markets are working miracle after miracle of economic growth. In the industrialized nations, a technological revolution is taking place, a revolution marked by rapid, dramatic advances in computers and telecommunications.

In Europe, only one nation and those it controls refuse to join the community of freedom. Yet in this age of redoubled economic growth, of information and innovation, the Soviet Union faces a choice: It must make fundamental changes, or it will become obsolete.

Today, thus, represents a moment of hope. We in the West stand ready to cooperate with the East to promote true openness, to break down barriers that separate people, to create a safer, freer world. And surely there is no better place than Berlin, the meeting place of East and West, to make a start.

Free people of Berlin: Today, as in the past, the United States stands for the strict observance and full implementation of all parts of the Four Power Agreement of 1971. Let us use this occasion, the 750th anniversary of this city, to usher in a new era, to seek a still fuller, richer life for the Berlin of the future. Together, let us maintain and develop the ties between the Federal Republic and the Western sectors of Berlin, which is permitted by the 1971 agreement.

And I invite Mr. Gorbachev: Let us work to bring the Eastern and Western parts of the city closer together, so that all the inhabitants of all Berlin can enjoy the benefits that come with life in one of the great cities of the world.

To open Berlin still further to all Europe, East and West, let us expand the vital air access to this city, finding ways of making commercial air service to Berlin more convenient, more comfortable, and more economical. We look to the day when West Berlin can become one of the chief aviation hubs in all central Europe.

With our French and British partners, the United States is prepared to help bring international meetings to Berlin. It would be only fitting for Berlin to serve as the site of United Nations meetings, or world conferences on human rights and arms control, or other issues that call for international cooperation.

There is no better way to establish hope for the future than to enlighten young minds, and we would be honored to sponsor summer youth exchanges, cultural events, and other programs for young Berliners from the East. Our French and British friends, I'm certain, will do the same. And it's my hope that an authority can be found in East Berlin to sponsor visits from young people of the Western sectors.

One final proposal, one close to my heart: Sport represents a source of enjoyment and ennoblement, and you may have noted that the Republic of Korea -- South Korea -- has offered to permit certain events of the 1988 Olympics to take place in the North. International sports competitions of all kinds could take place in both parts of this city. And what better way to demonstrate to the world the openness of this city than to offer in some future year to hold the Olympic games here in Berlin, East and West.

In these four decades, as I have said, you Berliners have built a great city. You've done so in spite of threats -- the Soviet attempts to impose the East-mark, the blockade. Today the city thrives in spite of the challenges implicit in the very presence of this wall. What keeps you here? Certainly there's a great deal to be said for your fortitude, for your defiant courage. But I believe there's something deeper, something that involves Berlin's whole look and feel and way of life -- not mere sentiment. No one could live long in Berlin without being completely disabused of illusions. Something, instead, that has seen the difficulties of life in Berlin but chose to accept them, that continues to build this good and proud city in contrast to a surrounding totalitarian presence, that refuses to release human energies or aspirations, something that speaks with a powerful voice of affirmation, that says "yes" to this city, yes to the future, yes to freedom. In a word, I would submit that what keeps you in Berlin -- is "love." Love both profound and abiding.

Perhaps this gets to the root of the matter, to the most fundamental distinction of all between East and West. The totalitarian world produces backwardness because it does such violence to the spirit, thwarting the human impulse to create, to enjoy, to worship. The totalitarian world finds even symbols of love and of worship an affront.

Years ago, before the East Germans began rebuilding their churches, they erected a secular structure: the television tower at Alexander Platz. Virtually ever since, the authorities have been working to correct what they view as the tower's one major flaw: treating the glass sphere at the top with paints and chemicals of every kind. Yet even today when the sun strikes that sphere, that sphere that towers over all Berlin, the light makes the sign of the cross. There in Berlin, like the city itself, symbols of love, symbols of worship, cannot be suppressed.

As I looked out a moment ago from the Reichstag, that embodiment of German unity, I noticed words crudely spray-painted upon the wall, perhaps by a young Berliner (quote):

"This wall will fall. Beliefs become reality." Yes, across Europe, this wall will fall, for it cannot withstand faith; it cannot withstand truth. The wall cannot withstand freedom.

And I would like, before I close, to say one word. I have read, and I have been questioned since I've been here about certain demonstrations against my coming. And I would like to say just one thing, and to those who demonstrate so. I wonder if they have ever asked themselves that if they should have the kind of government they apparently seek, no one would ever be able to do what they're doing again.

Thank you and God bless you all. Thank you.

[1] Very exclusive shopping district in Berlin.

[2] "Berliner Schnauze" is a standard expression used in Germany to describe the way people in and around Berlin talk to each other. Interestingly enough, the sound and choice of words among these folks is slightly more rude as compared to similar expressions found in other regions n Germany."Schnauze" is the German word for "mouth of dogs" and is comparable to the word "snout." [My thanks to Mr. Arndt Ulland for the above information.]

www.americanrhetoric.com

"Tear Down This Wall"--President Reagan's most famous line was almost deleted. An insider's story.

By Peter Robinson

The call of a trumpet. Many of Ronald Reagan's speeches sounded that way to me. During his long political career he used simple, direct, forceful language to make his points, developing his own unique sound. So when I joined his speechwriting staff in 1983 -- at age 26, its youngest member -- my goal was to help Reagan go on sounding like Reagan. One big challenge was the speech at the Berlin Wall, which Reagan would visit during a 1987 trip to Berlin to help commemorate the city's 750th anniversary. I was told only that he would speak at the wall, that he'd likely draw a crowd of about 10,000, and that, given the setting, he probably ought to talk about foreign policy.

One day in late April 1987, I met the ranking American diplomat in Berlin, hoping to get some material. The diplomat knew what Reagan *shouldn't say*. Since West Berliners were intellectually and politically sophisticated, he would have to watch himself. So no chest-thumping. No Soviet bashing. And no inflammatory statements about the wall. People who lived here, the diplomat said, had long ago become used to the structure that encircled them.

After meeting the diplomat, I flew over Berlin in a U.S. Army helicopter. From the sky, the wall seemed less to cut Berlin in two than to separate two modes of existence. On one side I saw movement, color, crowded sidewalks. On the other, buildings were pockmarked from shelling during the war; pedestrians were poorly dressed. The East Berlin side was lined with guard posts, dog runs, rows of barbed wire.

That night, I went to a dinner party hosted by Dieter and Ingeborg Elz, native Germans who had retired to West Berlin after Dieter completed his career at the World Bank. We had friends in common, and they were hosting this party to help give me a feel for their city. They had invited Berliners of many walks of life -- businessmen, academics, homemakers. We talked about the weather, about German wine. And then I related what the diplomat had told me. "Is it true?" I asked. "Have you gotten used to the wall?"

The Elzes and their guests glanced at one another uneasily. My heart sank. *Had I come across as brash, tactless?* Finally one man raised an arm and pointed. "My sister lives 20 miles in that direction," he explained. "I haven't seen her in more than two decades. Do you think I can get used to that?" Another man spoke up. Each morning on his way to work, he said, he walked past a guard tower. Each morning, the same soldier gazed down at him through binoculars. "That soldier and I speak the same language," he said. "We share the same history. But one of us is a zookeeper and the other is an animal, and I'm never certain which one is which."

Our hostess now broke in. "If this man Gorbachev is serious with his talk of glasnost and perestroika," she said angrily, pounding her fist, "he can prove it. He can get rid of this wall."

One Day?

Back in Washington, I told Tony Dolan, who oversaw Presidential speechwriting, that I wanted to make Ingeborg Elz's comment the central passage in Reagan's speech. I thought the passion and decency it conveyed sounded a lot like Reagan -- like that trumpet again. But when I sat down to write, the words didn't exactly flow.

In one draft I wrote, "Herr Gorbachev, bring down this wall," using "Herr" because I thought it would please the President's German audience, and "bring" because it was the only verb I could think of. I also swapped "bring" for "take," as if that were some sort of an improvement.

By week's end I'd produced nothing but a first draft that even I considered banal. I can still hear the *clomp-clomp-clomp* of Tony's cowboy boots as he walked down the hallway from his office to toss that draft onto my desk. "It's no good," he said.

"What's wrong with it?" I asked.

"I just told you. It's no good."

"Which paragraphs, Tony?"

"The whole thing is no good."

The next week I wrote another draft. This time I framed the challenge to the Soviet leader in stronger language, urging Gorbachev to "tear down the wall." On Friday, May 15, the speeches for the President's trip to Rome, Venice and Berlin were sent to him, and on Monday, May 18, the speechwriters joined him in the Oval Office. My speech was the last to be discussed. When Tom Griscom, the director of communications, asked Reagan for his comments, the President replied simply that he liked it.

"Mr. President," I said to him, "I learned that your speech will not only be heard in West Berlin but throughout East Germany." Radios might be able to pick up the speech as far east as Moscow. "Is there anything you'd like to say to people on the other side of the Berlin Wall?" I asked.

"Well, there's that passage about tearing down the wall," he replied. "That wall has to come down. That's what I'd like to say to them."

With three weeks to go, the speech was circulated to the State Department and the National Security Council. Both tried to squelch it. The draft was naive, they said. It was clumsy. It was provocative. State and the NSC submitted their own drafts -- no fewer than seven in all. In each, the call to "tear down the wall" was missing.

In principle, State and the NSC had no objection to a call for the wall's destruction. One draft, for example, contained the line, "One day, this ugly wall will disappear." I looked at that for a while. *"One day"*? One day the lion would lie down with the lamb, too, but you wouldn't want to hold your breath. "This ugly wall will disappear" was another line. What did that mean? The wall would disappear only when the Soviets knocked it down. What State and the NSC were saying was that Reagan could call for the wall's demise, but only if he used language so vague and euphemistic everyone could see he didn't mean it.

"The Right Thing to Do"

A few days before the President was to leave for Europe, Tom Griscom got a call from the chief of staff, Howard Baker, asking Griscom to step into his office. "It was Baker and the Secretary of State -- just the two of them," recalls Griscom. Secretary of State George Shultz objected to the speech. "He said, 'I think that line about tearing down the wall is going to be an affront to Mr. Gorbachev.' I said, 'Mr. Secretary, the President has commented on this line. He's comfortable with it.' "

When the traveling party reached Italy, Shultz objected again, to deputy chief of staff Ken Duberstein. So on June 5, Duberstein briefed Reagan on the objections and asked him to reread the speech's central passage. He did. Duberstein told Reagan that he thought the line about tearing down the wall sounded good. "Then," says Duberstein, "he got that wonderful, knowing smile on his face and said, 'Let's leave it in.' "

When Reagan arrived in Berlin, State and the NSC submitted still another draft. Yet the President was determined to deliver the controversial line. "The boys at State are going to kill me," he told Duberstein, smiling, "but it's the right thing to do."

So at the end of this long, messy process -- what? The President stood before the Berlin Wall on June 12, 1987, the Brandenburg Gate behind him, the crowd hanging on his every word. Then came the line: "Mr. Gorbachev, tear down this wall." There it was. No euphemisms. No wishful thinking. The truth. Reagan sounding like Reagan.

And that's my point. Though I flailed around a bit as I composed the speech, I knew I simply had to write something with the same trumpetlike sound Reagan himself always made. We speechwriters weren't attempting to fabricate an image. We were attempting to meet the standard Reagan himself had long ago established.

After the President delivered the speech, people felt he'd been correct to do so. As Tom Griscom recalls, "The Secretary of State found me after the speech and said, 'You were right.' "

From Reader's Digest - February 2004

*http://www.rd.com/your-america-inspiring-people-and-stories/ronald-reagans-berlin-wall-speech/
article28515.html*

THIS HOUSE IS NOT FOR SALE

BY ANDY ROONEY

"One Saturday night, we were sitting around our somewhat shopworn living room with some old friends, when one of them started trying to remember how long we'd lived there. 'Since 1952,' I said. 'We paid off the mortgage eight years ago.' 'If you don't have a mortgage,' he said, 'the house isn't worth as much as if you did have one.' Being in no way clever with money except when it comes to spending it, this irritated me. 'To whom is it not worth as much?' I asked him in a voice that was louder than necessary. 'Not to me, and I'm the one who lives here. As a matter of fact, I like it about 50 percent more than I did when the bank owned part of it.' 'What did you pay for it?' he asked. 'We paid $29,500 in 1952. ' My friend nodded knowingly and thought a minute. 'I'll bet you,' he said, 'that you could get $85,000 for it today....You ought to ask $95,000.'

"I don't know why this is such a popular topic of conversation these days, but if any real estate dealers are reading this, I'll give them some money-saving advice. Don't waste any stamps on me with your offers to buy. You can take me off your mailing list. Our house is not an investment. It is not a hastily erected shelter in which to spend the night before we rise in the morning to forge on farther west to locate in another campsite at dusk. Our house is our home. We live there. It is an anchor. It is a place we go to when we don't feel like going anyplace. We do not plan to move. The last census indicated that 40 million Americans move every year. One out of every five packs up his things and goes to live somewhere else. Where is everyone moving to? Why are they moving there? Is it really better someplace else? If people want a better house, why don't they fix the one they have? If the boss says they're being transferred and have to move, why don't they get another job? Jobs are easier to come by than a home. I can't imagine giving up my home because my job was moving. I have put up 29 Christmas trees in the bay window of the living room, each a little too tall. There are scars on the ceiling to prove it. Behind the curtain of the window nearest my wife's desk, there is a vertical strip of wall four inches wide that has missed the last four coats of paint so that the little pencil marks with dates opposite them would not be obliterated. If we moved, someone would certainly paint that patch, and how would we ever know again how tall the twins were when they were four? My son Brian has finished college and is working and no longer lives at home, but his marbles are in the bottom drawer of his dresser if he ever wants them. There's always been talk of moving. As many as 10 times a year we talk about it—the talk usually brought on by a leaky faucet, some peeling paint or a neighbor we didn't like. When you own a house, you learn to live with its imperfections. You accommodate yourself to them and, like your own shortcomings, you find ways to ignore them. Our house provides me with a simple pleasure every time I come home to it. I am welcomed by familiar things when I enter, and I'm warmed by some ambience which may merely be dust, but it is our dust, and I like it. There are reverberations of the past everywhere, but it is not a sad place, because all the things left undone hold great hope for its future.

"The talk of moving came up at dinner one night 10 years ago. Brian was only half listening, but at one point he looked up from his plate, gazed around the room and asked idly, 'Why would we want to move away from home?' When anyone asks me how much I think our house is worth, I just smile. They couldn't buy what that house means to me for all the money in both local banks. The house is not for sale."

- Andy Rooney, commentator

Reprinted from Wit and Wisdom

FRANKLIN DELANO ROOSEVELT'S FIRST INAUGURAL ADDRESS

MARCH 4, 1933

President Hoover, Mr. Chief Justice, my friends: This is a day of national consecration. And I am certain that on this day my fellow Americans expect that on my induction into the Presidency, I will address them with a candor and a decision which the present situation of our people impels.

This is preeminently the time to speak the truth, the whole truth, frankly and boldly. Nor need we shrink from honestly facing conditions in our country today. This great Nation will endure, as it has endured, will revive and will prosper.

So, first of all, let me assert my firm belief that the only thing we have to fear is fear itself -- nameless, unreasoning, unjustified terror which paralyzes needed efforts to convert retreat into advance. In every dark hour of our national life, a leadership of frankness and of vigor has met with that understanding and support of the people themselves which is essential to victory. And I am convinced that you will again give that support to leadership in these critical days.

In such a spirit on my part and on yours we face our common difficulties. They concern, thank God, only material things. Values have shrunk to fantastic levels; taxes have risen; our ability to pay has fallen; government of all kinds is faced by serious curtailment of income; the means of exchange are frozen in the currents of trade; the withered leaves of industrial enterprise lie on every side; farmers find no markets for their produce; and the savings of many years in thousands of families are gone. More important, a host of unemployed citizens face the grim problem of existence, and an equally great number toil with little return. Only a foolish optimist can deny the dark realities of the moment.

And yet our distress comes from no failure of substance. We are stricken by no plague of locusts. Compared with the perils which our forefathers conquered, because they believed and were not afraid, we have still much to be thankful for. Nature still offers her bounty and human efforts have multiplied it. Plenty is at our doorstep, but a generous use of it languishes in the very sight of the supply.

Primarily, this is because the rulers of the exchange of mankind's goods have failed, through their own stubbornness and their own incompetence, have admitted their failure, and have abdicated. Practices of the unscrupulous money changers stand indicted in the court of public opinion, rejected by the hearts and minds of men.

True, they have tried. But their efforts have been cast in the pattern of an outworn tradition. Faced by failure of credit, they have proposed only the lending of more money. Stripped of the lure of profit by which to induce our people to follow their false leadership, they have resorted to exhortations, pleading tearfully for restored confidence. They only know the rules of a generation of self-seekers. They have no vision, and when there is no vision the people perish.

Yes, the money changers have fled from their high seats in the temple of our civilization. We may now restore that temple to the ancient truths. The measure of that restoration lies in the extent to which we apply social values more noble than mere monetary profit.

Happiness lies not in the mere possession of money; it lies in the joy of achievement, in the thrill of creative effort. The joy, the moral stimulation of work no longer must be forgotten in the mad chase of evanescent profits. These dark days, my friends, will be worth all they cost us if they teach us that our true destiny is not to be ministered unto but to minister to ourselves, to our fellow men.

Recognition of that falsity of material wealth as the standard of success goes hand in hand with the abandonment of the false belief that public office and high political position are to be valued only by the standards of pride of place and personal profit; and there must be an end to a conduct in banking and in business which too often has given to a sacred trust the likeness of callous and selfish wrongdoing. Small wonder that confidence languishes, for it thrives only on honesty, on honor, on the sacredness of obligations, on faithful protection, and on unselfish performance; without them it cannot live.

Restoration calls, however, not for changes in ethics alone. This Nation is asking for action, and action now.

Our greatest primary task is to put people to work. This is no unsolvable problem if we face it wisely and courageously. It can be accomplished in part by direct recruiting by the Government itself, treating the task as we would treat the emergency of a war, but at the same time, through this employment, accomplishing great -- greatly needed projects to stimulate and reorganize the use of our great natural resources.

Hand in hand with that we must frankly recognize the overbalance of population in our industrial centers and, by engaging on a national scale in a redistribution, endeavor to provide a better use of the land for those best fitted for the land.

Yes, the task can be helped by definite efforts to raise the values of agricultural products, and with this the power to purchase the output of our cities. It can be helped by preventing realistically the tragedy of the growing loss through foreclosure of our small homes and our farms. It can be helped by insistence that the Federal, the State, and the local governments act forthwith on the demand that their cost be drastically reduced. It can be helped by the unifying of relief activities which today are often scattered, uneconomical, unequal. It can be helped by national planning for and supervision of all forms of transportation and of communications and other utilities that have a definitely public character. There are many ways in which it can be helped, but it can never be helped by merely talking about it.

We must act. We must act quickly.

And finally, in our progress towards a resumption of work, we require two safeguards against a return of the evils of the old order. There must be a strict supervision of all banking and credits and investments. There must be an end to speculation with other people's money. And there must be provision for an adequate but sound currency.

These, my friends, are the lines of attack. I shall presently urge upon a new Congress in special session detailed measures for their fulfillment, and I shall seek the immediate assistance of the 48 States.

Through this program of action we address ourselves to putting our own national house in order and making income balance outgo. Our international trade relations, though vastly important, are in point of time, and necessity, secondary to the establishment of a sound national economy. I favor, as a practical policy, the putting of first things first. I shall spare no effort to restore world trade by international economic readjustment; but the emergency at home cannot wait on that accomplishment.

The basic thought that guides these specific means of national recovery is not nationally -- narrowly nationalistic. It is the insistence, as a first consideration, upon the interdependence of the various elements in and parts of the United States of America -- a recognition of the old and permanently important manifestation of the American spirit of the pioneer. It is the way to recovery. It is the immediate way. It is the strongest assurance that recovery will endure.

In the field of world policy, I would dedicate this Nation to the policy of the good neighbor: the neighbor who resolutely respects himself and, because he does so, respects the rights of others; the neighbor who respects his obligations and respects the sanctity of his agreements in and with a world of neighbors.

If I read the temper of our people correctly, we now realize, as we have never realized before, our interdependence on each other; that we can not merely take, but we must give as well; that if we are to go forward, we must move as a trained and loyal army willing to sacrifice for the good of a common discipline, because without such discipline no progress can be made, no leadership becomes effective.

We are, I know, ready and willing to submit our lives and our property to such discipline, because it makes possible a leadership which aims at the larger good. This, I propose to offer, pledging that the larger purposes will bind upon us, bind upon us all as a sacred obligation with a unity of duty hitherto evoked only in times of armed strife.

With this pledge taken, I assume unhesitatingly the leadership of this great army of our people dedicated to a disciplined attack upon our common problems.

Action in this image, action to this end is feasible under the form of government which we have inherited from our ancestors. Our Constitution is so simple, so practical that it is possible always to meet extraordinary needs by changes in emphasis and arrangement without loss of essential form. That is why our constitutional system has proved itself the most superbly enduring political mechanism the modern world has ever seen.

It has met every stress of vast expansion of territory, of foreign wars, of bitter internal strife, of world relations. And it is to be hoped that the normal balance of executive and legislative authority may be wholly equal, wholly adequate to meet the unprecedented task before us. But it may be that an unprecedented demand and need for undelayed action may call for temporary departure from that normal balance of public procedure.

I am prepared under my constitutional duty to recommend the measures that a stricken nation in the midst of a stricken world may require. These measures, or such other measures as the Congress may build out of its experience and wisdom, I shall seek, within my constitutional authority, to bring to speedy adoption.

But, in the event that the Congress shall fail to take one of these two courses, in the event that the national emergency is still critical, I shall not evade the clear course of duty that will then confront me. I shall ask the Congress for the one remaining instrument to meet the crisis -- broad Executive power to wage a war against the emergency, as great as the power that would be given to me if we were in fact invaded by a foreign foe.

For the trust reposed in me, I will return the courage and the devotion that befit the time. I can do no less.

We face the arduous days that lie before us in the warm courage of national unity; with the clear consciousness of seeking old and precious moral values; with the clean satisfaction that comes from the stern performance of duty by old and young alike. We aim at the assurance of a rounded, a permanent national life.

We do not distrust the -- the future of essential democracy. The people of the United States have not failed. In their need they have registered a mandate that they want direct, vigorous action. They have asked for discipline and direction under leadership. They have made me the present instrument of their wishes. In the spirit of the gift I take it.

In this dedication -- In this dedication of a Nation, we humbly ask the blessing of God.

May He protect each and every one of us.

May He guide me in the days to come.

http://www.americanrhetoric.com/speeches/fdrfirstinaugural.html 7/17/07

PLANET OF THE YEAR
BY THOMAS A. SANCTON

In the first issue of the new year, TIME magazine publishes its Man of the Year (or Woman of the Year) issue. In its January 2, 1989 issue, instead of naming a Person of the Year, TIME designated our endangered earth as Planet of the Year. (Once before in 1982, TIME named the computer as the Machine of the Year.) Thomas A. Sancton's essay introduced a 33-page package, which included then other essays and a poem entitled "Magnitudes" by Howard Nemerov, commonly regarded as the current poet laureate of the United States. Each of the essays following Sancton's treated in some depth one aspect of the deterioration of our planet. Here is a partial list of the titles of the subsequent essays:

"The Death of Birth" ("Man is recklessly wiping out life on earth.")

"Deadly Danger in a Spray Can" ("Ozone-destroying CFCS {chlorofluorocarbons} should be banned.")

"A Sinking Mess" ("Throwaway societies befoul their land and seas.")

"Too Many Mouths" ("Swarms of People are running out of food and space.")

"Preparing for the Worst." ("If the sun turns killer and the well runs dry, how will humanity cope?")

In the February 13, 1989, issue of TIME, the editors reported that this Planet of the Year issue drew 1,687 letters, "the largest outpouring of mail for a Man of the Year issue since TIME selected the Ayatullah Khomeini in 1979." Judging by that volume of letters to the editor, we would be safe in saying that the topic dealt with in this special issue touched an unusually sensitive nerve in its readers.

"One generation passeth away, and another generation cometh: but the earth abideth forever." –(Ecclesiastes) No, not forever. At the outside limit, the earth will probably last another 4 billion to 5 billion years. By that time, scientists predict, the sun will have burned up so much of its own hydrogen fuel that it will expand and incinerate the surrounding planets, including the earth. A nuclear cataclysm, on the other hand, could destroy the earth tomorrow. Somewhere within those extremes lies the life expectancy of this wondrous, swirling globe. How long it endures and the quality of life it can support do not depend alone on the immutable laws of physics. For man has reached a point in his evolution where he has the power to affect, for better or worse, the present and future state of the planet.

Through most of his 2 million years or so of existence, man has thrived in earth's environment--perhaps too well. By 1800 there were 1 billion humans bestriding the planet. That number had doubled by 1930 and doubled again by 1975. If current birthrates hold, the world's present population of 5.1 billion will double again in 40 more years. The frightening irony is that this exponential growth in the human population-- the very sign of homo sapiens' success as an organism--could doom the earth as a human habitat.

The reason is not so much the sheer numbers, though 40,000 babies die of starvation each day in Third World countries, but the reckless way in which humanity has treated its planetary host. Like the evil genies that flew from Pandora's Box, technological advances have provided the means of upsetting nature's equilibrium, that intricate set of biological, physical and chemical interactions that make up the web of life. Starting at the dawn of the Industrial Revolution, smokestacks have disgorged noxious gases into the atmosphere, factories have dumped toxic wastes into rivers and streams, automobiles have guzzled irreplaceable fossil fuels and fouled the air with their detritus. In the name of progress, forests have been denuded, lakes poisoned with pesticides, underground aquifers pumped dry. For decades, scientists have warned of the possible consequences of all this profligacy. No one paid much attention.

This year the earth spoke, like God warning Noah of the deluge. Its message was loud and clear, and suddenly people began to listen, to ponder what importance the message held. In the US, a three-month drought baked the soil from California to Georgia, reducing the country's grain harvest by 31% and killing thousands of head of livestock. A stubborn seven-week heat wave drove temperatures above 100 degrees F across much of the country, raising fears of the dreaded "greenhouse effect"--global warming as a result of the buildup of carbon dioxide and other gases in the atmosphere--might already be under way. Parched by the lack of rain, the Western forests of the US, including Yellowstone National Park, went up in flames, also igniting a bitter conservationist controversy. And on many of the country's beaches, garbage, raw sewage and medical wastes washed up to spoil the fun of bathers and confront them personally with the growing despoliation of the oceans.

Similar pollution closed beaches on the Mediterranean, the North Sea and the English Channel. Killer hurricanes ripped through the Caribbean and floods devastated Bangladesh, reminders of nature's raw power. In Soviet Armenia a monstrous earthquake killed some 55,000 people. That too was a natural disaster, but its high casualty count, owing largely to the construction of cheap high-rise apartment blocks over a well-known fault area, illustrated the carelessness that has become humanity's habit in dealing with nature.

There were other forebodings of environmental disaster. In the U.S. it was revealed that federal weapons-making plants had recklessly and secretly littered large areas with radioactive waste. The further depletion of the atmosphere's ozone layer, which helps block cancer-causing ultraviolet rays, testified to the continued overuse of atmosphere-destroying chlorofluorocarbons emanating from such sources as spray cans and air conditioners. Perhaps the most ominous of all, the destruction of the tropical forests, home to at least half the earth's plant and animal species, continues at a rate equal to one football field a second.

Most of these evils had been going on for a long time, and some of the worst disasters apparently had nothing to do with human behavior. Yet this year's bout of freakish weather and environmental horror stories seemed to act as a powerful catalyst for worldwide public opinion. Everyone suddenly sensed that this gyrating globe, this precious repository of all the life that we know of, was in danger. No single individual, no event, no movement captured imaginations or dominated headlines more than the clump of rock and soil and water and air that is our common home. Thus in a rare and unprecedented departure from its tradition of naming a Man of the Year, TIME has designated Endangered Earth as Planet of the Year for 1988.

To help focus its coverage, TIME invited 33 scientists, administrators and political leaders from ten countries to a three-day conference in Boulder in November. The group included experts in climate change, population, waste disposal and the preservation of species. In addition to explaining the complexities of these interlocking problems, the specialists advanced a wide range of practical ideas and suggestions that TIME has fashioned into an agenda for environmental action. That agenda, accompanied by stories on each major environmental problem, appears throughout the following pages.

What would happen if nothing were done about the earth's imperiled state? According to computer projections, the accumulation of CO_2 in the atmosphere could drive up the planet's average temperature 3 degrees F to nine degrees F by the middle of the next century. That could cause the oceans to rise by several feet, flooding coastal areas and ruining huge tracts of farmland through salinization. Changing weather patterns could make huge areas infertile or uninhabitable, touching off refugee movements unprecedented in history.

Toxic waste and radioactive contamination could lead to shortages of safe drinking water, the sine qua non of human existence. And in a world that could house between 8 billion and 14 billion people by the mid-21st century, there is a strong likelihood of mass starvation. It is even possible to envision the world so wryly and chillingly prophesied by the typewriting cockroach in Donald Marquis' *archy and mehitabel:* "man is making deserts of the earth/ it won't be long now/ before man will have used it up/ so that nothing but ants/ and centipedes and scorpions/ can find a living on it."

There are those who believe the worst scenarios are alarming and ill founded. Some scientists contest the global-warming theory or predict that natural processes will counter its effects. Kenneth E. F. Watt, professor of environmental studies at the University of California at Davis, has gone so far as to call the greenhouse effect "the laugh of the century." S. Fred Singer, a geophysicist working for the US Department of Transportation, predicts that any greenhouse warming will be balanced by an increase in heat-reflecting clouds. The skeptics could be right, but it is far too risky to do nothing while awaiting absolute proof of disaster.

Whatever the validity of this or that theory, the earth will not remain as it is now. From its beginnings as a chunk of molten rock some 4.5 billion years ago, the planet has seen continents form, move together and drift apart like jigsaw-puzzle pieces. Successive ice ages have sent glaciers creeping down from the polar caps. Mountain ranges have jutted up from ocean beds, and landmasses have disappeared beneath the waves.

Previous shifts in the earth's climate or topology have been accompanied by waves of extinctions. The most spectacular example is the dying off of the great dinosaurs during the Cretaceous period (136 million to 65 million years ago). No one knows exactly what killed the dinosaurs, although a radical change in environmental conditions seems a likely answer. One popular theory is that a huge meteor crashed to earth and kicked up such vast clouds of dust that sunlight was obscured and plants destroyed. Result: the dinosaurs starved to death.

Whether or not that theory is correct, an event of no less magnitude is taking place at this very moment, but this time its agent is man. The wholesale burning and cutting of forests in Brazil and other countries, as one major example, are destroying irreplaceable species every day. Says Harvard biologist E.O. Wilson: "The extinctions ongoing worldwide promise to be at least as great as the mass extinction that occurred at the end of the age of dinosaurs."

Humanity's current predatory relationship with nature reflects a man-centered worldview that has evolved over the ages. Almost every society has had its myths about the earth and its origins. The ancient Chinese depicted Chaos as an enormous egg who separated into earth and sky, yin and yang. The Greeks believed Gaia, the earth, was created immediately after Chaos and gave birth to the gods. In many pagan societies, the earth was seen as a mother, a fertile giver of life. Nature--the soil, forest, sea--was endowed with divinity, and mortals were subordinate to it.

The Judeo-Christian tradition introduced a radically different concept. The earth was the creation of a monotheistic God, who, after shaping it, ordered its inhabitants, in the words of *Genesis*. "Be fruitful and multiply, and replenish the earth and subdue it; and have dominion over the fish of the sea and over the fowl of the air and over every living thing that moveth upon the earth." The idea of dominion could be interpreted as an invitation to use nature as a convenience. Thus, the spread of Christianity, which is generally considered to have paved the way for technology, may at the same time have carried the seeds of the wanton exploitation of nature that often accompanied technical progress.

Those tendencies were compounded by the Enlightenment notion of a mechanistic universe that man could shape to his own ends through science. The exuberant optimism of that world view was behind some of the greatest achievements of modern times: the invention of laborsaving machines, the discovery of aesthetics and vaccines, the development of efficient transportation and communication systems. But, increasingly, technology has come up against the law of unexpected consequences. Advances in health care have lengthened life spans, lowered infant-mortality rates and, thus, aggravated the population problem. The use of pesticides has increased crop yields but polluted water supplies. The invention of automobiles and jet planes has revolutionized travel but sullied the atmosphere.

Yet the advance of technology has never destroyed man's wonder and awe at the beauty of the earth. The coming of England's Industrial Revolution, with its "dark Satanic mills," coincided with the extraordinary flowering of Romantic poetry, much of it about the glory of nature. Many people in this century voiced the same tender feelings on seeing the first images of the earth as seen from the moon. The sight of that shimmering, luminescent ball set against the black void inspired even normally prosaic astronauts to flights of eloquence. Edgar Mitchell, who flew to the moon aboard Apollo 14 in 1971, described the planet as "a sparkling blue-and-white jewel...laced with swirling veils of white...like a small pearl in a thick sea of black mystery." Photos of the earth from space prompted geologist Preston Cloud to write, "Mother Earth will never seem the same again. No more can thinking people take this little planet...as an infinite theater of action and provider of resources for man, yielding new largesse to every demand without limit." That conclusion seems all the more imperative in the wake of the environmental shocks of 1988.

Let there be no illusions. Taking effective action to halt the massive injury to the earth's environment will require a mobilization of political will, international cooperation and sacrifice unknown except in wartime. Yet humanity is in a war right now, and it is not too Draconian to call it a war for survival. It is a war in which all nations must be allies. Both the causes and effects of the problems that threaten the earth are global, and they must be attacked globally. "All nations are tied together as to their common fate," observes Peter Raven, director of the Missouri Botanical Garden. "We are all facing a common problem, which is, How are we going to keep this single resource we have, namely the world, viable?"

As man heads into the last decade of the 20th century, he finds himself at a crucial turning point: the actions of those now living will determine the future, and possibly the very survival, of the species. "We do not have generations, we only have years, in which to attempt to turn things around," warns Lester Brown, president of the Washington-based Worldwatch Institute. Every individual on the planet must be made aware of its vulnerability and of the urgent need to preserve it. No attempt to protect the environment will be successful in the long run unless the ordinary people--the California housewife, the Mexican peasant, the Soviet factory worker, the Chinese farmer--are willing to adjust their life-styles. Our wasteful, careless ways must become a thing of the past. We must recycle more, procreate less, turn off lights, use mass transit, do a thousand things differently in our everyday lives. We owe this not only to ourselves and our children but also to the unborn generations who will one day inherit the earth.

Mobilizing that sort of mass commitment will take extraordinary leadership, of the kind that has appeared before in times of crisis: Churchill's eloquence, galvanizing his embattled countrymen to live "their finest hour," F.D.R.'s pragmatic idealism giving hope and jobs to Depression-ridden Americans. Now, more than ever, the world needs leaders who can inspire their fellow citizens with a fiery sense of mission, not a nationalistic or military campaign but a universal crusade to save the planet. Unless mankind embraces that cause totally, and without delay, it may have no alternative to the bang of nuclear holocaust or the whimper of slow extinction.

Reprinted with permission from Time magazine. Introduction to this discourse is reprinted with permission from Edward P.J. Corbett, Classical Rhetoric for the Modern Student.

The Republic of Silence

By Jean-Paul Sartre

We were never more free than during the German occupation. We had lost all our rights, beginning with the right to talk. Every day we were insulted to our faces and had to take it in silence. Under one pretext or another, as workers, Jews, or political prisoners, we were deported en masse. Everywhere, on billboards, in the newspapers, on the screen, we encountered the revolting and insipid picture of ourselves that our oppressors wanted us to accept. And, because of all this, we were free. Because the Nazi venom seeped even into our thoughts, every accurate thought was a conquest. Because we were hunted down, every one of our gestures had the weight of a solemn commitment. The circumstances, atrocious as they often were, finally made it possible for us to live, without pretense or false shame, the hectic and impossible existence that is known as the lot of man. Exile, captivity, and especially death (which we usually shrink from facing at all in happier times) became for us the habitual objects of our concern. We learned that they were neither inevitable accidents, nor even constant and exterior dangers, but that they must be considered as our lot itself, our destiny, the profound source of our reality as men. At every instant we lived up to the full sense of this commonplace little phrase: "Man is mortal!" And the choice that each of us made of his life and of his being was an authentic choice because it was made face to face with death, because it could always have been expressed in these terms: "Rather death than...." And here I am not speaking of the elite among us who were real Resistants, but of all Frenchmen who, at every hour of the night and day throughout four years, answered no. But the very cruelty of the enemy drove us to the extremities of this condition by forcing us to ask ourselves questions that one never considers in time of peace. All those among us--and what Frenchman was not at one time or another in this situation--who knew any details concerning the Resistance asked themselves anxiously, "If they torture me, shall I be able to keep silent?" Thus the basic question of liberty itself was posed, and we were brought to the verge of the deepest knowledge that man can have of himself. For the secret of a man is not his Oedipus complex or his inferiority complex: it is the limit of his own liberty, his capacity for resisting torture and death.

To those who were engaged in underground activities, the conditions of their struggle afforded a new kind of experience. They did not fight openly like soldiers. In all circumstances they were alone. They were hunted down in solitude, arrested in solitude. It was completely forlorn and unbefriended that they held out against torture, alone and naked in the presence of torturers, clean-shaven, well-fed, and well-clothed, who laughed at their cringing flesh, and to whom an untroubled conscience and a boundless sense of social strength gave every appearance of being in the right. Alone. Without a friendly hand or a word of encouragement. Yet, in the depth of their solitude, it was the others that they were protecting, all the others, all their comrades in the Resistance. Total responsibility in total solitude--is this not the very definition of our liberty? This being stripped of all, this solitude, this tremendous danger, were the same for all. For the leaders and for their men, for those who conveyed messages without knowing what their content was, as for those who directed the entire Resistance, the punishment was the same--imprisonment, deportation, death. There is no army in the world where there is such equality of risk for the private and for the commander-in-chief. And this is why the Resistance was a true democracy: for the soldier as for the commander, the same danger, the same forsakenness, the same total responsibility, the same absolute liberty within discipline. Thus, in darkness and in blood, a Republic was established, the strongest of Republics.

Each of its citizens knew that he owed himself to all and that he could count only on himself alone. Each of them, in complete isolation, fulfilled his responsibility and his role in history. Each of them, standing against the oppressors, undertook to be himself, freely and irrevocably. And by choosing for himself in liberty, he chose the liberty of all. This Republic without institutions, without an army, without police, was something that at each instant every Frenchman had to win and to affirm against Nazism. No one failed in this duty, and now we are on the threshold of another Republic. May this Republic about to be set up in broad daylight preserve the austere virtues of that other Republic of Silence and Night.

http://www.unc.edu/depts/europe/pedagogy/meta/mod5/RepublicofSilence.pdf

APOLOGY

BY SOCRATES

Born in 469 B.C., Socrates belonged to a group of poets, dramatists, philosophers, orators, statesmen, and generals responsible for bringing Athens into its Golden Age in the fifth century B.C. In 399 B.C., at the age of seventy, he was brought to trial in Athens, ostensibly on the charge of corrupting the youth and advocating the worship of new gods. Really, however, he had created problems by questioning the policies and values of the Athenian Establishment. Here he defends himself (apologia means "defense") against the charges leveled against him.

How you, O Athenians, have been affected by my accusers, I cannot tell; but I know that they almost made me forget who I was—so persuasively did they speak; and yet they have hardly uttered a word of truth. But of the many falsehoods told by them, there was one which quite amazed me; mean when they said that you should be upon your guard and not allow ourselves to be deceived by the force of my eloquence. To say this, when they were certain to be detected as soon as I opened my lips and proved myself to be anything but a great speaker, did indeed appear to me most shameless—unless by the force of eloquence they mean the force of truth; for if such is their meaning, I admit that I am eloquent. But in how different a way from theirs! Well, as I was saying, they have scarcely spoken the truth at all; from me you shall hear the whole truth, but not delivered after their manner in a set oration duly ornamented with fine words and phrases. No, by heaven! I shall use the words and arguments which occur to me at the moment, for I am confident in the justice of my cause; at my time of life ought not to be appearing before you, O men of Athens, in the character of a boy inventing falsehoods—let no one expect it of me. And I must particularly beg of you to grant me this favour:—If I defend myself in my accustomed manner, and you hear me using the words which many of you have heard me using habitually in the agora, at the tables of the money-changers, and elsewhere, I would ask you not to be surprised, and not to interrupt me on this account. For I am more than seventy years of age, and appearing now for the first time before a court of law, I am quite a stranger to the language of the place; and therefore I would have you regard me as if I were really a stranger, whom you would excuse if he spoke in his native tongue, and after the fashion of his country:—Am I making an unfair request of you? Never mind the manner, which may or may not be good; but think only of the truth of my words, and give heed to that: let the speaker speak truly and the judge decide justly.

And first, I have to reply to the older charges and to my first accusers, and then I will go on to the later ones. For of old I have had many accusers, who have accused me falsely to you during many years; and I am more afraid of them than of Anytus and his associates, who are dangerous, too, in their own way. But far more dangerous are the others, who began when most of you were children, and took possession of your minds with their falsehoods, telling of one Socrates, a wise man, who speculated about the heaven above, and searched into the earth beneath, and made the worse appear the better cause. The men who have besmeared me with this tale are the accusers whom I dread; for their hearers are apt to fancy that such inquirers do not believe in the existence of the gods. And they are many, and their charges against me are of ancient date, and they were made by them in the days when some of you were more impressible than you are now—in childhood, or it may have been in youth—and the cause went by default, for there was none to answer. And hardest of all, I do not know and cannot tell the names of my accusers; unless in the chance case of a comic poet. All who from envy and malice have persuaded you—some of them having first convinced themselves—all this class of men are most difficult to deal with; for I cannot have them up here, and cross-examine them, and therefore I must simply fight with shadows in my own defense, and argue when there is no one who answers. I will ask you then to take it from me that my opponents are of two kinds; one recent, the other ancient: and I hope that you will see the propriety of my answering the latter first, for these accusations you heard long before the others, and much oftener.

Well, then, I must make my defense, and endeavour to remove from your minds in a short time, a slander which you have had a long time to take in. May I succeed, if to succeed be for my good and yours, or likely to avail me in my cause! The task is not an easy one; I quite understand the nature of it. And so leaving the event with God, in obedience to the law I will now make my defense.

I will begin at the beginning, and ask what is the accusation which has given rise to the slander of me, and in fact has encouraged Meletus to prefer this charge against me. Well, what do the slanderers say? They shall be my prosecutors, and this is the information they swear against me: 'Socrates is an evil-doer; a meddler who searches into things under the earth and in heaven, and makes the worse appear the better cause, and teaches the aforesaid practices to others.' Such is the nature of the accusation: it is just what you have yourselves seen in the comedy of Aristophanes, who has introduced a man whom he calls Socrates, swinging about and saying that he walks on air, and talking a deal of nonsense concerning matters of which I do not pretend to know either much or little—not that I mean to speak disparagingly of anyone who is a student of natural philosophy. May Meletus never bring so many charges against me as to make me do that! But the simple truth is, O Athenians, that I have nothing to do with physical speculations. Most of those here present are witnesses to the truth of this, and to them I appeal. Speak then, you who have heard me, and tell your neighbours whether any of you have ever known me hold forth in few words or in many upon such matters...You hear their answer. And from what they say of this part of the charge you will be able to judge of the truth of the rest.

As little foundation is there for the report that I am a teacher, and take money; this accusation has no more truth in it than the other. Although, if a man were really able to instruct mankind, this too would, in my opinion, be an honour to him. There is Gorgias of Leontium, and Prodicus of Ceos, and Hippias of Elis, who go the round of the cities, and are able to persuade the young men to leave their own citizens by whom they might be taught for nothing, and come to them whom they not only pay, but are thankful if they may be allowed to pay them. There is at this time a Parian philosopher residing in Athens, of whom I have heard; and I came to hear of him in this way:—I came across a man who has spent more money on the sophists than the rest of the world put together, Callias, the son of Hipponicus, and knowing that he had sons, I asked him: 'Callias,' I said, 'if your two sons were foals or calves, there would be no difficulty in finding someone to put over them; we should hire a trainer of horses, or a farmer probably, who would improve and perfect them in the appropriate virtue and excellence; but as they are human beings, whom are you thinking of placing over them? Is there anyone who understands human and civic virtue? You must have thought about the matter, for you have sons; is there anyone?' 'There is,' he said. 'Who is he?' said I; 'and of what country? and what does he charge?' 'Evenus the Parian,' he replied; 'he is the man, and his charge is five minas.' Happy is Evenus, I said to myself, if he really has this wisdom, and teaches at such a moderate charge. Had I the same, I should have been very proud and conceited; but the truth is that I have no knowledge of the kind.

I dare say, Athenians, that someone among you will reply, 'Yes, Socrates, but what is your occupation? What is the origin of these accusations which are brought against you; there must have been something strange which you have been doing? All these rumours and this talk about you would never have arisen if you had been like other men: tell us, then, what is the cause of them, for we should be sorry to judge hastily of you.' Now I regard this as a fair challenge, and I will endeavour to explain to you the reason why I am called wise and have such an evil fame. Please to attend then. And although some of you may think I am joking, I declare that I will tell you the entire truth. Men of Athens, this reputation of mine has come of a certain sort of wisdom which I possess. If you ask me what kind of wisdom, I reply, wisdom such as may perhaps be attained by man, for to that extent I am inclined to believe that I am wise; whereas the persons of whom I was speaking have a kind of superhuman wisdom, which I know not how to describe, because I have it not myself; and he who says that I have, speaks falsely, and is taking away my character. And here, O men of Athens, I must beg you not to interrupt me, even if I seem to say something extravagant. For the word which I will speak is not mine. I will refer you to a witness who is worthy of credit; that witness shall be the god of Delphi—he will tell you about my wisdom, if I have any, and of what sort it is. You must have known Chaerephon; he was early a friend of mine, and also a friend of yours, for he shared in the recent exile of the people, and returned with you. Well, Chaerephon, as you know, was very impetuous in all his doings, and he went to Delphi and boldly asked the oracle to tell him whether—as I was saying, I must beg you not to interrupt—he actually asked the oracle to tell him whether anyone was wiser than I was, and the Pythian prophetess answered that there was no man wiser. Chaerephon is dead himself; but his brother, who is in court, will confirm the truth of what I am saying.

Why do I mention this? Because I am going to explain to you why I have such an evil name. When I heard the answer, I said to myself, What can the god mean? and what is the interpretation of his riddle? for I know that I have no wisdom, small or great. What then can he mean when he says that I am the wisest of men? And yet he is a god, and cannot lie; that would be against his nature. After long perplexity, I thought of a method of trying the question. I reflected that if I could only find a man wiser than myself, then I might go to the god with a refutation in my hand. I should say to him, 'Here is a man who is wiser than I am; but you said that I was the wisest.' Accordingly I went to one who had the reputation of wisdom, and observed him—his name I need not mention, he was a politician; and in the process of examining him and talking with him, this, men of Athens, was what I found. I could not help thinking that he was not really wise, although he was thought wise by many, and still wiser by himself; and thereupon I tried to explain to him that he thought himself wise, but was not really wise; and the consequence was that he hated me, and his enmity was shared by several who were present and heard me. So I left him, saying to myself as I went away: Well, although I do not suppose that either of us knows any thing really worth knowing, I am at least wiser than this fellow—for he knows nothing, and thinks that he knows; I neither know nor think that I know. In this one little point, then, I seem to have the advantage of him. Then I went to another who had still higher pretensions to wisdom, and my conclusion was exactly the same. Whereupon I made another enemy of him, and of many others besides him.

Then I went to one man after another, being not unconscious of the enmity which I provoked, and I lamented. and feared this: but necessity was laid upon me,—the word of God, I thought, ought to be considered first. And I said to myself, Go I must to all who appear to know, and find out the meaning of the oracle. And I swear to you, Athenians,—for I must tell you the truth—the result of my mission was just this: I found that the men most in repute were nearly the most foolish; and that others less esteemed were really closer to wisdom, I will tell you the tale of my wanderings and of the 'Herculean' labours, as I may call them, which I endured only to find at last the oracle irrefutable. After the politicians, I went to the poets; tragic, dithyrambic, and all sorts. And there, I said to myself, you will be instantly detected; now you will find out that you are more ignorant than they are. Accordingly, I took them some of the most elaborate passages in their own writings, and asked what was the meaning of them—thinking that they would teach me something. Will you believe me? I am ashamed to confess the truth, but I must say that there is hardly a person present who would not have talked better about their poetry than they did themselves. So I learnt that not by wisdom do poets write poetry, but by a sort of genius and inspiration; they are like diviners or soothsayers who also say many fine things, but do not understand the meaning of them. The poets appeared to me to be much in the same case; and I further observed that upon the strength of their poetry they believed themselves to be the wisest of men in other things in which they were not wise. So I departed, conceiving myself to be superior to them for the same reason that I was superior to the politicians.

At last I went to the artisans, for I was conscious that I knew nothing at all, as I may say, and I was sure that they knew many fine things; and here I was not mistaken, for they did know many things of which I was ignorant, and in this they certainly were wiser than I was. But I observed that even the good artisans fell into the same error as the poets;—because they were good workmen they thought that they also knew all sorts of high matters, and this defect in them overshadowed their wisdom; and therefore I asked myself on behalf of the oracle, whether I would like to be as I was, neither having their knowledge nor their ignorance, or like them in both; and I made answer to myself and to the oracle that I was better off as I was.

This inquisition has led to my having many enemies of the worst and most dangerous kind, and has given rise also to many imputations, including the name of 'wise'; for my hearers always imagine that I myself possess the wisdom which I find wanting in others. But the truth is, O men of Athens, that God only is wise; and by his answer he intends to show that the wisdom of men is worth little or nothing; although speaking of Socrates, he is only using my name by way of illustration, as if he said, He, O men, is the wisest, who, like Socrates, knows that his wisdom is in truth worth nothing. And so I go about the world, obedient to the god, and search and make inquiry into the wisdom of anyone, whether citizen or stranger, who appears to be wise; and if he is not wise, then in vindication of the oracle I show him that he is not wise; and my occupation quite absorbs me, and I have had no time to do anything useful either in public affairs or in any concern of my own, but I am in utter poverty by reason of my devotion to the god.

There is another thing:—young men of the richer classes, who have not much to do, come about me of their own accord; they like to hear people examined, and they often imitate me, and proceed to do some examining themselves; there are plenty of persons, as they quickly discover, who think that they know something, but really know little or nothing; and then those who are examined by them instead of being angry with themselves are angry with me: This confounded Socrates, they say; this villainous misleader of youth!—and then if somebody asks them, Why, what evil does he practice or teach? they do not know, and cannot tell; but in order that they may not appear to be at a loss, they repeat the ready-made charges which are used against all philosophers about teaching things up in the clouds and under the earth, and having no gods, and making the worse appear the better cause; for they do not like to confess that their pretense of knowledge has been detected—which is the truth; and as they are numerous and ambitious and energetic, and speak vehemently with persuasive tongues, they have filled your ears with their loud and inveterate calumnies. And this is the reason why my three accusers, Meletus and Anytus and Lycon, have set upon me; Meletus, who has a quarrel with me on behalf of the poets; Anytus, on behalf of the craftsmen and politicians; Lycon, on behalf of the rhetoricians: and as I said at the beginning, I cannot expect to get rid of such a mass of calumny all in a moment. And this, O men of Athens, is the truth and the whole truth; I have concealed nothing, I have dissembled nothing. And yet, I feel sure that my plainness of speech is fanning their hatred of me, and what is their hatred but a proof that I am speaking the truth?—Hence has arisen the prejudice against me; and this is the reason of it, as you will find out either in this or in any future inquiry.

I have said enough in my defense against the first class of my accusers; I turn to the second class. They are headed by Meletus, that good man and true lover of his country, as he calls himself. Against these, too, I must try to make a defense:—Let their affidavit be read: it contains something of this kind: It says that Socrates is a doer of evil, inasmuch as he corrupts the youth, and does not receive the gods whom the state receives, but has a new religion of his own. Such is the charge; and now let us examine the particular counts. He says that I am a doer of evil, and corrupt the youth; but I say, O men of Athens, that Meletus is a doer of evil, in that he is playing a solemn farce, recklessly bringing men to trial from a pretended zeal and interest about matters in which he really never had the smallest interest. And the truth of this I will endeavour to prove to you.

Come hither, Meletus, and let me ask a question of you. You attach great importance to the improvement of youth?

Yes, I do.

Tell the judges, then, who is their improver; for you must know, as you take such interest in the subject, and have discovered their corrupter, and are citing and accusing me in this court. Speak, then, and tell the judges who is the improver of youth:—Observe, Meletus, that you are silent, and have nothing to say. But is this not rather disgraceful, and a very considerable proof of what I was saying, that you have no interest in the matter? Speak up, friend, and tell us who their improver is.

The laws.

But that, my good sir, is not my question: Can you not name some person—whose first qualification will be that he knows the laws?

The judges, Socrates, who are present in court.

What, do you mean to say, Meletus, that they are able to instruct and improve youth?

Certainly they are.

What, all of them, or some only and not others?

All of them.

Truly, that is good news! There are plenty of improvers, then. And what do you say of the audience,—do they improve them?

Yes, they do.

And the senators?

Yes, the senators improve them.

But perhaps the members of the assembly corrupt them?—or do they too improve them?

They improve them.

Then every Athenian improves and elevates them; all with the exception of myself; and I alone am their corrupter? Is that what you affirm?

That is what I stoutly affirm.

I am very unfortunate if you are right. But suppose I ask you a question: Is it the same with horses? Does one man do them harm and all the world good? Is not the exact opposite the truth? One man is able to do them good, or at least very few;—the trainer of horses, that is to say, does them good, but the ordinary man does them harm if he has to do with them? Is not that true, Meletus, of horses, or of any other animals? Most assuredly it is; whether you and Anytus say yes or no. Happy indeed would be the condition of youth if they had one corrupter only, and all the rest of the world were their benefactors. But you, Meletus, have sufficiently shown that you never had a thought about the young: your carelessness is plainly seen in your not caring about the very things which you bring against me.

And now, Meletus, I adjure you to answer me another question: Which is better, to live among bad citizens, or among good ones? Answer, friend, I say; the question is one which may be easily answered. Do not the good do their neighbours good, and the bad do them evil?

Certainly.

And is there anyone who would rather be injured than benefited by those who live with him? Answer, my good friend, the law requires you to answer—does anyone like to be injured?

Certainly not.

And when you accuse me of corrupting and deteriorating the youth, do you allege that I corrupt them intentionally or unintentionally?

Intentionally, I say.

But you have just admitted that the good do their neighbours good, and the evil do them evil. Now, is that a truth which your superior wisdom has recognized thus early in life, and am I, at my age, in such darkness and ignorance as not to know that if a man with whom I have to live is corrupted by me, I am very likely to be harmed by him; and yet I corrupt him, and intentionally, too—so you say, although neither I nor any other human being is ever likely to be convinced by you. But either I do not corrupt them, or I corrupt them unintentionally; and on either view of the case you lie. If my offense is unintentional, the law has no cognizance of unintentional offenses: you ought to have taken me privately, and warned and admonished me; for if I had had instruction, I should have left off doing what I only did unintentionally—beyond doubt I should; but you would have nothing to say to me and refused to teach me. And now you bring me up in this court, which is a place not of instruction, but of punishment.

It will be very clear to you, Athenians, as I was saying, that Meletus has never had any care, great or small, about the matter. But still I should like to know, Meletus, in what I am affirmed to corrupt the young. I suppose you mean, as I infer from your indictment, that I teach them not to acknowledge the gods which the state acknowledges, but some other new divinities or spiritual agencies in their stead. These are the lessons by which I corrupt the youth, as you say.

Yes, that I say emphatically.

Then, by the gods, Meletus, of whom we are speaking, tell me and the court, in somewhat plainer terms, what you mean! for I do not as yet understand whether you affirm that I teach other men to acknowledge some gods, and therefore that I do believe in gods, and am not an entire atheist—this you do not lay to my charge,—but only you say that they are not the same gods which the city recognizes—the charge is that they are different gods. Or, do you mean that I am an atheist simply, and a teacher of atheism?

I mean the latter—that you are a complete atheist.

What an extraordinary statement! Why do you think so, Meletus? Do you mean that I do not believe in the god-head of the sun or moon, like the rest of mankind?

I assure you, judges, that he does: for he says that the sun is stone, and the moon earth.

Friend Meletus, do you think that you are accusing Anaxagoras? Have you such a low opinion of the judges, that you fancy them so illiterate as not to know that these doctrines are found in the books of Anaxagoras the Clazomenian, which are full of them? And so, forsooth, the youth are said to be taught them by Socrates, when they can be bought in the book-market for one drachma at most; and they might pay their money, and laugh at Socrates if he pretends to father these extraordinary views. And so, Meletus, you really think that I do not believe in any god?

I swear by Zeus that you verily believe in none at all.

Nobody will believe you, Meletus, and I am pretty sure that you do not believe yourself. I cannot help thinking, men of Athens, that Meletus is reckless and impudent, and that he has brought this indictment in a spirit of mere wantonness and youthful bravado. Has he not compounded a riddle, thinking to try me? He said to himself:—I shall see whether the wise Socrates will discover my facetious self-contradiction, or whether I shall be able to deceive him and the rest of them. For he certainly does appear to me to contradict himself in the indictment as much as if he said that

Socrates is guilty of not believing in the gods, and yet of believing in them—but this is not like a person who is in earnest.

I should like you, O men of Athens, to join me in examining what I conceive to be his inconsistency; and do you, Meletus, answer. And I must remind the audience of my request that they would not make a disturbance if I speak in my accustomed manner:

Did ever man, Meletus, believe in the existence of human things, and not of human beings?...I wish, men of Athens, that he would answer, and not be always trying to get up an interruption. Did ever any man believe in horsemanship, and not in horses? or in flute-playing, and not in flute-players? My friend, no man ever did; I answer to you and to the court, as you refuse to answer for yourself. But now please to answer the next question: Can a man believe in the existence of things spiritual and divine, and not in spirits or demigods?

He cannot.

How lucky I am to have extracted that answer, by the assistance of the court! But then you swear in the indictment that I teach and believe in divine or spiritual things (new or old, no matter for that); at any rate, I believe in spiritual things,—so you say and swear in the affidavit; and yet if I believe in them, how can I help believing in spirits or demigods;—must I not? To be sure I must; your silence gives consent. Now what are spirits or demigods? are they not either gods or the sons of gods?

Certainly they are.

But this is what I call the facetious riddle invented by you: the demigods or spirits are gods, and you say first that I do not believe in gods, and then again that I do believe in gods; that is, if I believe in demigods. For if the demigods are the illegitimate sons of gods, whether by nymphs, or by other mothers, as some are said to be—what human being will ever believe that there are no gods when there are sons of gods? You might as well affirm the existence of mules, and deny that of horses and asses. Such nonsense, Meletus, could only have been intended by you to make trial of me. You have put this into the indictment because you could think of nothing real of which to accuse me. But no one who has a particle of understanding will ever be convinced by you that a man can believe in the existence of things divine and *superhuman,* and the same man refuse to believe in gods and demigods and heroes.

I have said enough in answer to the charge of Meletus: any elaborate defense is unnecessary. You know well the truth of my statement that I have incurred many violent enmities; and this is what will be my destruction if I am destroyed;—not Meletus, nor yet Anytus, but the envy and detraction of the world, which has been the death of many good men, and will probably be the death of many more; there is no danger of my being the last of them.

http://www.sacred-texts.com/cla/plato/apology.htm

Speech on Red Square on Anniversary Celebration of the October Revolution

By Joseph Stalin, November 7, 1941, reprinted in Soviet Russia Today, December, 1941

Comrades, Red Army and Red Navy men, commanders and political instructors, men and women workers, men and women collective farmers, intellectuals, brothers and sisters in the enemy rear who have temporarily fallen under the yoke of the German brigands, our glorious men and women guerrillas who are disrupting the rear of the German invaders!

On behalf of the Soviet Government and our Bolshevik Party I greet you and congratulate you on the 24th anniversary of the great October Socialist Revolution.

Comrades, today we must celebrate the 24th anniversary of the October Revolution in difficult conditions. The German brigands' treacherous attack and the war that they forced upon us have created a threat to our country. We have temporarily lost a number of regions, and the enemy is before the gates of Leningrad and Moscow.

The enemy calculated that our army would be dispersed at the very first blow and our country forced to its knees. But the enemy wholly miscalculated. Despite temporary reverses, our army and our navy are bravely beating off enemy attacks along the whole front, inflicting heavy losses, while our country-our whole country-has organized itself into a single fighting camp in order, jointly with our army and navy, to rout the German invaders.

There was a time when our country was in a still more difficult position. Recall the year 1918, when we celebrated the first anniversary of the October Revolution. At that time three-quarters of our country was in the hands of foreign interventionists. We had temporarily lost the Ukraine, the Caucasus, Central Asia, the Urals, Siberia and the Far East. We had no allies, we had no Red Army-we had only just begun to create it-and we experienced a shortage of bread, a shortage of arms, a shortage of equipment.

At that time 14 states were arrayed against our country, but we did not become despondent or downhearted. In the midst of the conflagration of war we organized the Red Army and converted our country into a military camp. The spirit of the great Lenin inspired us at that time for the war against the interventionists.

And what happened? We defeated the interventionists, regained all our lost territories and achieved victory.

Today our country is in a far better position than it was 23 years ago. Today it is many times richer in industry, food and raw materials. Today we have allies who jointly with us form a united front against the German invaders. Today we enjoy the sympathy and support of all the peoples of

Europe fallen under the yoke of Fascist tyranny. Today we have a splendid army and a splendid navy, defending the freedom and independence of our country with their lives. We experience no serious shortage either of food or of arms or equipment.

Our whole country, all the peoples of our country, are backing our army and our navy, helping them smash the Nazi hordes. Our reserves in manpower are inexhaustible. The spirit of the great Lenin inspires us for our patriotic war today as it did 23 years ago.

Is it possible, then, to doubt that we can and must gain victory over the German invaders? The enemy is not as strong as some terror-stricken pseudo-intellectuals picture him. The devil is not as terrible as he is painted. Who can deny that our Red Army has more than once put the much-vaunted German troops to panicky flight?

If one judges by Germany's real position and not by the boastful assertions of German propagandists, it will not be difficult to see that the Nazi German invaders are facing disaster.

Hunger and poverty reign in Germany. In four and a half months of war Germany has lost four and a half million soldiers. Germany is bleeding white; her manpower is giving out. A spirit of revolt is gaining possession not only of the nations of Europe under the German invaders' yoke, but of the Germans themselves, who see no end to the war.

The German invaders are straining their last forces. There is no doubt that Germany cannot keep up such an effort for any long time. Another few months, another half year, one year perhaps-and Hitlerite Germany must collapse under the weight of its own crimes.

Comrades, Red Army and Red Navy men, commanders and political instructors, men and women guerrillas!

The whole world is looking to you as a force capable of destroying the brigand hordes of German invaders. The enslaved peoples of Europe under the yoke of the German invaders are looking to you as their liberators. A great mission of liberation has fallen to your lot.

Be worthy of this mission! The war you are waging is a war of liberation, a just war. Let the heroic images of our great ancestors—Alexander Nevsky, Dmitri Donskoi, Kusma Minin, Dmitri Pozharsky, Alexander Suvorov, Mikhail Kutuzov—inspire you in this war!

Let the victorious banner of the great Lenin fly over your heads!

Utter destruction to the German invaders!

Death to the German armies of occupation!

Long live our glorious motherland, her freedom and her independence!

Under the banner of Lenin—onward to victory!

http://www.ibiblio.org/pha/policy/1941/411107a.html

A Modest Proposal for preventing the children of poor people in Ireland, from being a burden on their parents or country, and for making them beneficial to the publick.

By Dr. Jonathan Swift. 1729

It is a melancholy object to those, who walk through this great town, or travel in the country, when they see the streets, the roads and cabbin-doors crowded with beggars of the female sex, followed by three, four, or six children, all in rags, and importuning every passenger for an alms. These mothers instead of being able to work for their honest livelihood, are forced to employ all their time in stroling to beg sustenance for their helpless infants who, as they grow up, either turn thieves for want of work, or leave their dear native country, to fight for the Pretender in Spain, or sell themselves to the Barbadoes.

I think it is agreed by all parties, that this prodigious number of children in the arms, or on the backs, or at the heels of their mothers, and frequently of their fathers, is in the present deplorable state of the kingdom, a very great additional grievance; and therefore whoever could find out a fair, cheap and easy method of making these children sound and useful members of the common-wealth, would deserve so well of the publick, as to have his statue set up for a preserver of the nation.

But my intention is very far from being confined to provide only for the children of professed beggars: it is of a much greater extent, and shall take in the whole number of infants at a certain age, who are born of parents in effect as little able to support them, as those who demand our charity in the streets.

As to my own part, having turned my thoughts for many years, upon this important subject, and maturely weighed the several schemes of our projectors, I have always found them grossly mistaken in their computation. It is true, a child just dropt from its dam, may be supported by her milk, for a solar year, with little other nourishment: at most not above the value of two shillings, which the mother may certainly get, or the value in scraps, by her lawful occupation of begging; and it is exactly at one year old that I propose to provide for them in such a manner, as, instead of being a charge upon their parents, or the parish, or wanting food and raiment for the rest of their lives, they shall, on the contrary, contribute to the feeding, and partly to the cloathing of many thousands.

There is likewise another great advantage in my scheme, that it will prevent those voluntary abortions, and that horrid practice of women murdering their bastard children, alas! too frequent among us, sacrificing the poor innocent babes, I doubt, more to avoid the expence than the shame, which would move tears and pity in the most savage and inhuman breast.

The number of souls in this kingdom being usually reckoned one million and a half, of these I calculate there may be about two hundred thousand couple whose wives are breeders; from which number I subtract thirty thousand couple, who are able to maintain their own children, (although I apprehend there cannot be so many, under the present distresses of the kingdom) but this being granted, there will remain an hundred and seventy thousand breeders. I again subtract fifty thousand, for those women who miscarry, or whose children die by accident or disease within the year. There only remain an hundred and twenty thousand children of poor parents annually born. The question therefore is, How this number shall be reared, and provided for? which, as I have already said, under the present situation of affairs, is utterly impossible by all the methods hitherto proposed. For we can neither employ them in handicraft or agriculture; we neither build houses, (I mean in the country) nor cultivate land: they can very seldom pick up a livelihood by stealing till they arrive at six years old; except where they are of towardly parts, although I confess they learn the rudiments much earlier; during which time they can however be properly looked upon only as probationers: As I have been informed by a principal gentleman in the county of Cavan, who protested to me, that he never knew above one or two instances under the age of six, even in a part of the kingdom so renowned for the quickest proficiency in that art.

I am assured by our merchants, that a boy or a girl before twelve years old, is no saleable commodity, and even when they come to this age, they will not yield above three pounds, or three pounds and half a crown at most, on the exchange; which cannot turn to account either to the parents or kingdom, the charge of nutriments and rags having been at least four times that value.

I shall now therefore humbly propose my own thoughts, which I hope will not be liable to the least objection.

I have been assured by a very knowing American of my acquaintance in London, that a young healthy child well nursed, is, at a year old, a most delicious nourishing and wholesome food, whether stewed, roasted, baked, or boiled; and I make no doubt that it will equally serve in a fricasie, or a ragoust.

I do therefore humbly offer it to publick consideration, that of the hundred and twenty thousand children, already computed, twenty thousand may be reserved for breed, whereof only one fourth part to be males; which is more than we allow to sheep, black cattle, or swine, and my reason is, that these children are seldom the fruits of marriage, a circumstance not much regarded by our savages, therefore, one male will be sufficient to serve four females. That the remaining hundred thousand may, at a year old, be offered in sale to the persons of quality and fortune, through the kingdom, always advising the mother to let them suck plentifully in the last month, so as to render them plump, and fat for a good table. A child will make two dishes at an entertainment for friends, and when the family dines alone, the fore or hind quarter will make a reasonable dish, and seasoned with a little pepper or salt, will be very good boiled on the fourth day, especially in winter.

I have reckoned upon a medium, that a child just born will weigh 12 pounds, and in a solar year, if tolerably nursed, encreaseth to 28 pounds.

I grant this food will be somewhat dear, and therefore very proper for landlords, who, as they have already devoured most of the parents, seem to have the best title to the children.

Infant's flesh will be in season throughout the year, but more plentiful in March, and a little before and after; for we are told by a grave author, an eminent French physician, that fish being a prolifick dyet, there are more children born in Roman Catholick countries about nine months after Lent, the markets will be more glutted than usual, because the number of Popish infants, is at least three to one in this kingdom, and therefore it will have one other collateral advantage, by lessening the number of Papists among us.

I have already computed the charge of nursing a beggar's child (in which list I reckon all cottagers, labourers, and four-fifths of the farmers) to be about two shillings per annum, rags included; and I believe no gentleman would repine to give ten shillings for the carcass of a good fat child, which, as I have said, will make four dishes of excellent nutritive meat, when he hath only some particular friend, or his own family to dine with him. Thus the squire will learn to be a good landlord, and grow popular among his tenants, the mother will have eight shillings neat profit, and be fit for work till she produces another child.

Those who are more thrifty (as I must confess the times require) may flea the carcass; the skin of which, artificially dressed, will make admirable gloves for ladies, and summer boots for fine gentlemen.

As to our City of Dublin, shambles may be appointed for this purpose, in the most convenient parts of it, and butchers we may be assured will not be wanting; although I rather recommend buying the children alive, and dressing them hot from the knife, as we do roasting pigs.

A very worthy person, a true lover of his country, and whose virtues I highly esteem, was lately pleased, in discoursing on this matter, to offer a refinement upon my scheme. He said, that many gentlemen of this kingdom, having of late destroyed their deer, he conceived that the want of venison might be well supply'd by the bodies of young lads and maidens, not exceeding fourteen years of age, nor under twelve; so great a number of both sexes in every country being now ready to starve for want of work and service: And these to be disposed of by their parents if alive, or otherwise by their nearest relations. But with due deference to so excellent a friend, and so deserving a patriot, I cannot be altogether in his sentiments; for as to the males, my American acquaintance assured me from frequent experience, that their flesh was generally tough and lean, like that of our school-boys, by continual exercise, and their taste disagreeable, and to fatten them would not answer the charge. Then as to the females, it would, I think, with humble submission, be a loss to the publick, because they soon would become breeders themselves: And besides, it is not improbable that some scrupulous people might be apt to censure such a practice, (although indeed very unjustly) as a little bordering upon cruelty, which, I confess, hath always been with me the strongest objection against any project, how well soever intended.

But in order to justify my friend, he confessed, that this expedient was put into his head by the famous Salmanaazor, a native of the island Formosa, who came from thence to London, above twenty years ago, and in conversation told my friend, that in his country, when any young person happened to be put to death, the executioner sold the carcass to persons of quality, as a prime dainty; and that, in his time, the body of a plump girl of fifteen, who was crucified for an attempt to poison the Emperor, was sold to his imperial majesty's prime minister of state, and other great mandarins of the court in joints from the gibbet, at four hundred crowns. Neither indeed can I deny, that if the same use were made of several plump young girls in this town, who without one single groat to their fortunes, cannot stir abroad without a chair, and appear at a play-house and assemblies in foreign fineries which they never will pay for; the kingdom would not be the worse.

Some persons of a desponding spirit are in great concern about that vast number of poor people, who are aged, diseased, or maimed; and I have been desired to employ my thoughts what course may be taken, to ease the nation of so grievous an incumbrance. But I am not in the least pain upon that matter, because it is very well known, that they are every day dying, and rotting, by cold and famine, and filth, and vermin, as fast as can be reasonably expected. And as to the young labourers, they are now in almost as hopeful a condition. They cannot get work, and consequently pine away from want of nourishment, to a degree, that if at any time they are accidentally hired to common labour, they have not strength to perform it, and thus the country and themselves are happily delivered from the evils to come.

I have too long digressed, and therefore shall return to my subject. I think the advantages by the proposal which I have made are obvious and many, as well as of the highest importance.

For first, as I have already observed, it would greatly lessen the number of Papists, with whom we are yearly over-run, being the principal breeders of the nation, as well as our most dangerous enemies, and who stay at home on purpose with a design to deliver the kingdom to the Pretender, hoping to take their advantage by the absence of so many good Protestants, who have chosen rather to leave their country, than stay at home and pay tithes against their conscience to an episcopal curate.

Secondly, The poorer tenants will have something valuable of their own, which by law may be made liable to a distress, and help to pay their landlord's rent, their corn and cattle being already seized, and money a thing unknown.

Thirdly, Whereas the maintainance of an hundred thousand children, from two years old, and upwards, cannot be computed at less than ten shillings a piece per annum, the nation's stock will be thereby encreased fifty thousand pounds per annum, besides the profit of a new dish, introduced to the tables of all gentlemen of fortune in the kingdom, who have any refinement in taste. And the money will circulate among our selves, the goods being entirely of our own growth and manufacture.

Fourthly, The constant breeders, besides the gain of eight shillings sterling per annum by the sale of their children, will be rid of the charge of maintaining them after the first year.

Fifthly, This food would likewise bring great custom to taverns, where the vintners will certainly be so prudent as to procure the best receipts for dressing it to perfection; and consequently have their houses frequented by all the fine gentlemen, who justly value themselves upon their knowledge in good eating; and a skilful cook, who understands how to oblige his guests, will contrive to make it as expensive as they please.

Sixthly, This would be a great inducement to marriage, which all wise nations have either encouraged by rewards, or enforced by laws and penalties. It would encrease the care and tenderness of mothers towards their children, when they were sure of a settlement for life to the poor babes, provided in some sort by the publick, to their annual profit instead of expence. We should soon see an honest emulation among the married women, which of them could bring the fattest child to the market. Men would become as fond of their wives, during the time of their pregnancy, as they are now of their mares in foal, their cows in calf, or sow when they are ready to farrow; nor offer to beat or kick them (as is too frequent a practice) for fear of a miscarriage.

Many other advantages might be enumerated. For instance, the addition of some thousand carcasses in our exportation of barrel'd beef: the propagation of swine's flesh, and improvement in the art of making good bacon, so much wanted among us by the great destruction of pigs, too frequent at our tables; which are no way comparable in taste or magnificence to a well grown, fat yearly child, which roasted whole will make a considerable figure at a Lord Mayor's feast, or any other publick entertainment. But this, and many others, I omit, being studious of brevity.

Supposing that one thousand families in this city, would be constant customers for infants flesh, besides others who might have it at merry meetings, particularly at weddings and christenings, I compute that Dublin would take off annually about twenty thousand carcasses; and the rest of the kingdom (where probably they will be sold somewhat cheaper) the remaining eighty thousand.

I can think of no one objection, that will possibly be raised against this proposal, unless it should be urged, that the number of people will be thereby much lessened in the kingdom. This I freely own, and 'twas indeed one principal design in offering it to the world. I desire the reader will observe, that I calculate my remedy for this one individual Kingdom of Ireland, and for no other that ever was, is, or, I think, ever can be upon Earth. Therefore let no man talk to me of other expedients: Of taxing our absentees at five shillings a pound: Of using neither cloaths, nor houshold furniture, except what is of our own growth and manufacture: Of utterly rejecting the materials and instruments that promote foreign luxury: Of curing the expensiveness of pride, vanity, idleness, and gaming in our women: Of introducing a vein of parsimony, prudence and temperance: Of learning to love our country, wherein we differ even from Laplanders, and the inhabitants of Topinamboo: Of quitting our animosities and factions, nor acting any longer like the Jews, who were murdering one another at the very moment their city was taken: Of being a little cautious not to sell our country and consciences for nothing: Of teaching landlords to have at least one degree of mercy towards their tenants. Lastly, of putting a spirit of honesty, industry, and skill into our shop-keepers, who, if a resolution could now be taken to buy only our native goods, would immediately unite to cheat and exact upon us in the price, the measure, and the goodness, nor could ever yet be brought to make one fair proposal of just dealing, though often and earnestly invited to it.

Therefore I repeat, let no man talk to me of these and the like expedients, 'till he hath at least some glympse of hope, that there will ever be some hearty and sincere attempt to put them into practice.

But, as to my self, having been wearied out for many years with offering vain, idle, visionary thoughts, and at length utterly despairing of success, I fortunately fell upon this proposal, which, as it is wholly new, so it hath something solid and real, of no expence and little trouble, full in our own power, and whereby we can incur no danger in disobliging England. For this kind of commodity will not bear exportation, and flesh being of too tender a consistence, to admit a long continuance in salt, although perhaps I could name a country, which would be glad to eat up our whole nation without it.

After all, I am not so violently bent upon my own opinion, as to reject any offer, proposed by wise men, which shall be found equally innocent, cheap, easy, and effectual. But before something of that kind shall be advanced in contradiction to my scheme, and offering a better, I desire the author or authors will be pleased maturely to consider two points. First, As things now stand, how they will be able to find food and raiment for a hundred thousand useless mouths and backs. And secondly, There being a round million of creatures in humane figure throughout this kingdom, whose whole subsistence put into a common stock, would leave them in debt two million of pounds sterling, adding those who are beggars by profession, to the bulk of farmers, cottagers and labourers, with their wives and children, who are beggars in effect; I desire those politicians who dislike my overture, and may perhaps be so bold to attempt an answer, that they will first ask the parents of these mortals, whether they would not at this day think it a great happiness to have been sold for food at a year old, in the manner I prescribe, and thereby have avoided such a perpetual scene of misfortunes, as they have since gone through, by the oppression of landlords, the impossibility of paying rent without money or trade, the want of common sustenance, with neither house nor cloaths to cover them from the inclemencies of the weather, and the most inevitable prospect of intailing the like, or greater miseries, upon their breed for ever.

I profess, in the sincerity of my heart, that I have not the least personal interest in endeavouring to promote this necessary work, having no other motive than the publick good of my country, by advancing our trade, providing for infants, relieving the poor, and giving some pleasure to the rich. I have no children, by which I can propose to get a single penny; the youngest being nine years old, and my wife past child-bearing.

On the Horrors of the Slave Trade, 1789

By William Wilberforce (1759–1833)

IN1 opening, concerning the nature of the slave trade, I need only observe that it is found by experience to be just such as every man who uses his reason would infallibly conclude it to be. For my own part, so clearly am I convinced of the mischiefs inseparable from it, that I should hardly want any further evidence than my own mind would furnish, by the most simple deductions. Facts, however, are now laid before the House. A report has been made by his majesty's privy council, which, I trust, every gentleman has read, and which ascertains the slave trade to be just as we know. What should we suppose must naturally be the consequence of our carrying on a slave trade with Africa? With a country vast in its extent, not utterly barbarous, but civilized in a very small degree? Does any one suppose a slave trade would help their civilization? Is it not plain that she must suffer from it; that civilization must be checked; that her barbarous manners must be made more barbarous; and that the happiness of her millions of inhabitants must be prejudiced with her intercourse with Britain? Does not every one see that a slave trade carried on around her coasts must carry violence and desolation to her very center? That in a continent just emerging from barbarism, if a trade in men is established, if her men are all converted into goods, and become commodities that can be bartered, it follows they must be subject to ravage just as goods are; and this, too, at a period of civilization, when there is no protecting legislature to defend this, their only sort of property, in the same manner as the rights of property are maintained by the legislature of every civilized country.

We see then, in the nature of things, how easily the practises of Africa are to be accounted for. Her kings are never compelled to war, that we can hear of, by public principles, by national glory, still less by the love of their people. In Europe it is the extension of commerce, the maintenance of national honor, or some great public object, that is ever the motive to war with every monarch; but, in Africa, it is the personal avarice and sensuality of their kings. These two vices of avarice and sensuality, the most powerful and predominant in natures thus corrupt, we tempt, we stimulate in all these African princes, and we depend upon these vices for the very maintenance of the slave trade. Does the king of Barbessin want brandy? He has only to send his troops, in the night-time, to burn and desolate a village; the captives will serve as commodities, that may be bartered with the British trader.

slave trade, in its very nature, is the source of such kind of tragedies; nor has there been a single person, almost, before the privy council, who does not add something by his testimony to the mass of evidence upon this point. Some, indeed, of these gentlemen, and particularly the delegates from Liverpool, have endeavored to reason down this plain principle; some have palliated it; but there is not one, I believe, who does not more or less admit it. Some, nay most, I believe, have admitted the slave trade to be the chief cause of wars in Africa.

now disposed of the first part of this subject, I must speak of the transit of the slaves to the West Indies. This, I confess, in my own opinion, is the most wretched part of the whole subject. So much misery condensed in so little room is more than the human imagination had ever before conceived.

I will not accuse the Liverpool merchants. I will allow them, nay, I will believe them, to be men of humanity; and I will therefore believe, if it were not for the multitude of these wretched objects, if it were not for the enormous magnitude and extent of the evil which distracts their attention from individual cases, and makes them think generally, and therefore less feelingly on the subject, they never would have persisted in the trade. I verily believe, therefore, if the wretchedness of any one of the many hundred negroes stowed in each ship could be brought before their view, and remain within the sight of the African merchant, that there is no one among them whose heart would bear it.

any one imagine to himself six or seven hundred of these wretches chained two and two, surrounded with every object that is nauseous and disgusting, diseased, and struggling under every kind of wretchedness! How can we bear to think of such a scene as this? One would think it had been determined to heap on them all the varieties of bodily pain, for the purpose of blunting the feelings of the mind; and yet, in this very point (to show the power of human prejudice), the situation of the slaves has been described by Mr. Norris, one of the Liverpool delegates, in a manner which I am sure will convince the House how interest can draw a film over the eyes, so thick that total blindness could do no more; and how it is our duty therefore to trust not to the reasonings of interested men, nor to their way of coloring a transaction.

"Their apartments," says Mr. Norris, "are fitted up as much for their advantage as circumstances will admit. The right ankle of one, indeed, is connected with the left ankle of another by a small iron fetter, and if they are turbulent, by another on their wrists. They have several meals a day—some of their own country provisions, with the best sauces of African cookery; and by the way of variety, another meal of pulse, etc., according to European taste. After breakfast they have water to wash themselves, while their apartments are perfumed with frankincense and lime juice. Before dinner they are amused after the manner of their country. The song and the dance are promoted," and, as if the whole were really a scene of pleasure and dissipation, it is added that games of chance are furnished. "The men play and sing, while the women and girls make fanciful ornaments with beads, with which they are plentifully supplied." Such is the sort of strain in which the Liverpool delegates, and particularly Mr. Norris, gave evidence before the privy council. What will the House think when, by the concurring testimony of other witnesses, the true history is laid open? The slaves, who are sometimes described as rejoicing at their captivity, are so wrung with misery at leaving their country, that it is the constant practise to set sail in the night, lest they should be sensible of their departure. The pulse which Mr. Norris talks of are horse beans; and the scantiness of both water and provision was suggested by the very legislature of Jamaica, in the report of their committee, to be a subject that called for the interference of Parliament.

Norris talks of frankincense and lime juice: when the surgeons tell you the slaves are stored so close that there is not room to tread among them; and when you have it in evidence from Sir George Young, that even in a ship which wanted two hundred of her complement, the stench was intolerable. The song and the dance are promoted, says Mr. Norris. It had been more fair, perhaps, if he had explained that word "promoted." The truth is, that for the sake of exercise, these miserable wretches, loaded with chains, oppressed with disease and wretchedness, are forced to dance by the terror of the lash, and sometimes by the actual use of it. "I," says one of the other evidences, "was employed to dance the men, while another person danced the women." Such, then, is the meaning of the word "promoted"; and it may be observed, too, with respect to food, that an instrument is sometimes carried out in order to force them to eat, which is the same sort of proof how much they enjoy themselves in that instance also.

to their singing, what shall we say when we are told that their songs are songs of lamentation upon their departure which, while they sing, are always in tears, insomuch that one captain (more humane as I should conceive him, therefore, than the rest) threatened one of the women with a flogging, because the mournfulness of her son was too painful for his feelings. In order, however, not to trust too much to any sort of description, I will call the attention of the House to one species of evidence, which is absolutely infallible. Death, at least, is a sure ground of evidence, and the proportion of deaths will not only confirm, but, if possible, will even aggravate our suspicion of their misery in the transit. It will be found, upon an average of all ships of which evidence has been given at the privy council, that exclusive of those who perish before they sail, not less than twelve and one-half per cent. perish in the passage. Besides these, the Jamaica report tells you that not less than four and one-half per cent. die on shore before the day of sale, which is only a week or two from the time of landing. One-third more die in the seasoning, and this in a country exactly like their own, where they are healthy and happy, as some of the evidences would pretend. The diseases, however, which they contract on shipboard, the astringent washes which are to hide their wounds, and the mischievous tricks used to make them up for sale, are, as the Jamaica report says—a most precious and valuable report, which I shall often have to advert to—one principal cause of this mortality. Upon the whole, however, here is a mortality of about fifty per cent., and this among negroes who are not bought unless quite healthy at first, and unless (as the phrase is with cattle) they are sound in wind and limb.

we consider the vastness of the continent of Africa; when we reflect how all other countries have for some centuries past been advancing in happiness and civilization; when we think how in this same period all improvement in Africa has been defeated by her intercourse with Britain; when we reflect that it is we ourselves that have degraded them to that wretched brutishness and barbarity which we now plead as the justification of our guilt; how the slave trade has enslaved their minds, blackened their character, and sunk them so low in the scale of animal beings that some think the apes are of a higher class, and fancy the orang-outang has given them the go-by. What a mortification must we feel at having so long neglected to think of our guilt, or attempt any reparation! It seems, indeed, as if we had determined to forbear from all interference until the measure of our folly and wickedness was so full and complete; until the impolicy which eventually belongs to vice was become so plain and glaring that not an individual in the country should refuse to join in the abolition; it seems as if we had waited until the persons most interested should be tired out with the folly and nefariousness of the trade, and should unite in petitioning against it.

us then make such amends as we can for the mischiefs we have done to the unhappy continent; let us recollect what Europe itself was no longer ago than three or four centuries. What if I should be able to show this House that in a civilized part of Europe, in the time of our Henry VII., there were people who actually sold their own children? What if I should tell them that England itself was that country? What if I should point out to them that the very place where this inhuman traffic was carried on was the city of Bristol? Ireland at that time used to drive a considerable trade in slaves with these neighboring barbarians; but a great plague having infested the country, the Irish were struck with a panic, suspected (I am sure very properly) that the plague was a punishment sent from heaven for the sin of the slave trade, and therefore abolished it. All I ask, therefore, of the people of Bristol is, that they would become as civilized now as Irishmen were four hundred years ago. Let us put an end at once to this inhuman traffic—let us stop this effusion of human blood.

true way to virtue is by withdrawing from temptation; let us then withdraw from these wretched Africans those temptations to fraud, violence, cruelty, and injustice, which the slave trade furnishes. Wherever the sun shines, let us go round the world with him, diffusing our benevolence; but let us not traffic, only that we may set kings against their subjects, subjects against their kings, sowing discord in every village, fear and terror in every family, setting millions of our fellow creatures a-hunting each other for slaves, creating fairs and markets for human flesh through one whole continent of the world, and, under the name of policy, concealing from ourselves all the baseness and iniquity of such a traffic.

will appear from everything which I have said, that it is not regulation, it is not mere palliatives, that can cure this enormous evil. Total abolition is the only possible cure for it. The Jamaica report, indeed, admits much of the evil, but recommends it to us so to regulate the trade that no persons should be kidnapped or made slaves contrary to the custom of Africa. But may they not be made slaves unjustly, and yet by no means contrary to the custom of Africa? I have shown they may, for all the customs of Africa are rendered savage and unjust through the influence of this trade; besides, how can we discriminate between the slaves justly and unjustly made? or, if we could, does any man believe that the British captains can, by any regulation in this country, be prevailed upon to refuse all such slaves as have not been fairly, honestly, and uprightly enslaved? But granting even that they should do this, yet how would the rejected slaves be recompensed? They are brought, as we are told, from three or four thousand miles off, and exchanged like cattle from one hand to another, until they reach the coast. We see then that it is the existence of the slave trade that is the spring of all this infernal traffic, and that the remedy can not be applied without abolition.

, sir, when we think of eternity, and of the future consequences of all human conduct, what is there in this life that should make any man contradict the dictates of his conscience, the principles of justice, the laws of religion, and of God? Sir, the nature and all the circumstances of this trade are now laid open to us; we can no longer plead ignorance, we can not evade it; it is now an object placed before us, we can not pass it; we may spurn it, we may kick it out of our way, but we can not turn aside so as to avoid seeing it; for it is brought now so directly before our eyes that this House must decide, and must justify to all the world, and to their own consciences, the rectitude of the grounds and principles of their decision.

Note 1. From a speech in the House of Commons on May 12, 1789, in support of his own resolution condemning the slave trade, which with the help of Pitt, Burke, and Fox, was carried without a division. Abridged.

http://www.bartleby.com/268/4/8.html#txt1 (7/2/07)

Pope Gregory XI : The Condemnation of Wycliffe 1382 and Wycliffe's Reply, 1384

Bull of Pope Gregory XI, Against John Wycliffe

Gregory, bishop, servus servorum dei, to his beloved sons the Chancellor and University of Oxford, in the diocese of Lincoln, grace and apostolic benediction.

We are compelled to wonder and grieve that you, who, in consideration of the favors and privileges conceded to your University of Oxford by the apostolic see, and on account of your familiarity with the Scriptures, in whose sea you navigate, by the gift of God, with auspicious oar, you, who ought to be, as it were, warriors and champions of the orthodox faith, without which there is no salvation of souls,—that you through a certain sloth and neglect allow tares to spring up amidst the pure wheat in the fields of your glorious University aforesaid; and what is still more pernicious, even continue to grow to maturity. And you are quite careless, as has been lately reported to us, as to the extirpation of these tares; with no little clouding of a bright name, danger to your souls, contempt of the Roman Church, and injury to the faith above mentioned. And what pains us the more, is that this increase of the tares aforesaid is known in Rome before the remedy of extirpation has been applied in England where they sprang up. By the insinuation of many, if they are indeed worthy of belief, deploring it deeply, it has come to our ears that John de Wycliffe, rector of the church of Lutterworth, in the diocese of Lincoln, Professor of the Sacred Scriptures (would that he were not also Master of Errors), has fallen into such a detestable madness that he does not hesitate to dogmatize and publicly preach, or rather vomit forth from the recesses of his breast, certain propositions and conclusions which are erroneous and false. He has cast himself also into the depravity of preaching heretical dogmas which strive to subvert and weaken the state of the whole church and even secular polity, some of which doctrines, in changed terms, it is true, seem to express the perverse opinions and unlearned learning of Marsilio of Padua of cursed memory, and of John of Jandun, whose book is extant, rejected and cursed by our predecessor, Pope John XXII, of happy memory. This he has done in the kingdom of England, lately glorious in its power and in the abundance of its resources, but more glorious still in the glistening piety of its faith, and in the distinction of its sacred learning; producing also many men illustrious for their exact knowledge of the Holy Scriptures, mature in the gravity of their character, conspicuous in devotion, defenders of the Catholic Church. He has polluted certain of the faithful of Christ by sprinkling them with these doctrines, and led them away from the right paths of the aforesaid faith to the brink of perdition.

Wherefore, since we are not willing, nay, indeed, ought not to be willing, that so deadly a pestilence should continue to exist with our connivance, a pestilence which, if it is not opposed in its beginnings, and torn out by the roots in its entirety, will be reached too late by medicines when it has infected very many with its contagion; we command your University with strict admonition, by the apostolic authority, in virtue of your sacred obedience, and under penalty of the deprivation of all the favors, indulgences, and privileges granted to you and your University by the said see, for the future not to permit to be asserted or proposed to any extent whatever, the opinions, conclusions, and propositions which are in variance with good morals and faith, even when those proposing strive to defend them under a certain fanciful wresting of words or of terms. Moreover, you are on our authority to arrest the said John, or cause him to be arrested and to send him under a trustworthy guard to our venerable brother, the Archbishop of Canterbury, and the Bishop of London, or to one of them.

Besides, if there should be, which God forbid, in your University, subject to your jurisdiction, opponents stained with these errors, and if they should obstinately persist in them, proceed vigorously and earnestly to a similar arrest and removal of them, and otherwise as shall seem good to you. Be vigilant to repair your negligence which you have hitherto shown in the premises, and so obtain our gratitude and favor, and that of the said see, besides the honor and reward of the divine recompense.

Given at Rome, at Santa Maria Maggiore, on the 31st of May, the sixth year of our pontificate.

Reply of John Wycliffe to his Summons by the Pope to come to Rome, 1384

I have joyfully to tell to all true men that believe what I hold, and legates to the pope; for I suppose that if my faith be rightful and given of God, the pope will gladly confirm it; and if my faith be error, the Pope will wisely amend it.

I suppose over this that the gospel of Christ be [the] heart of the corpus of God's law; for I believe that Jesus Christ, that gave in His own person this gospel, is very God and very man, and by this heart passes all other laws.

I suppose over this that the pope be most obliged to the keeping of the gospel among all men that live here; for the pope is highest vicar that Christ has here in earth. For moreness of Christ's vicar is not measured by worldly moreness, but by this, that this vicar sues more Christ by virtuous living; for thus teacheth the gospel, that this is the sentence of Christ.

And of this gospel I take as believe, that Christ for [the] time that He walked here, was [the] most poor man of all, both in spirit and in having; for Christ says that He had nought for to rest His head on. And Paul says that He was made needy for our love. And more poor might no man be, neither bodily nor in spirit. And thus Christ put from Him all manner of worldly lordship. For the gospel of John telleth that when they would have made Christ king, He fled and hid Him from them, for He would none such worldly highness.

And over this I take it as believe, that no man should sue the pope, nor no saint that now is in heaven, but in as much as he sues Christ. For John and James erred when they coveted worldly highness; and Peter and Paul sinned also when they denied and blasphemed in Christ; but men should not sue them in this, for then they went from Jesus Christ. And this I take as wholesome counsel, that the pope leave his worldly lordship to worldly lords, as Christ gave them,---and move speedily all his clerks to do so. For thus did Christ, and taught thus his disciples, till the fiend had blinded this world. And it seems to some men that clerks that dwell lastingly in this error against God's law, and flee to sue Christ in this, been open heretics, and their fautors been partners.

And if I err in this sentence, I will meekly be amended, yea, by the death, if it be skilful, for that I hope were good to me. And if I might travel in mine own person, I would with good will go to the pope. But God has needed me to the contrary, and taught me more obedience to God than to men. And I suppose of our pope that he will not be Antichrist, and reverse Christ in this working, to the contrary of Christ's will; for if he summon against reason, by him or by any of his, and pursue this unskilful summoning, he is an open Antichrist. And merciful intent excused not Peter, that Christ should name him Satan; so blind intent and wicked counsel excuses not the pope here; but if he ask of true priests that they travel more than they may, he is not excused by reason of God, that he should not be Antichrist. For our belief teaches us that our blessed God suffers us not to be tempted more than we may; how should a man ask such service? And therefore pray we to God for our Pope Urban the Sixth, that his old holy intent be not quenched by his enemies. And Christ, that may not lie, says that the enemies of a man been especially his home family; and this is sooth of men and fiends.

This text is part of the <u>*Internet Medieval Source Book*</u>. *The Sourcebook is a collection of public domain and copy-permitted texts related to medieval and Byzantine history. http://www.fordham.edu/halsall/ source/1382wycliffe.html*

Progymnasmata
I. Fable
This collection of Fables comes from the following books:

Fun with Aesop Reader, Retold by Paul Tell. Mogadore, Ohio: Tell Publications, 1991.

Aesop's Fables, compiled by Russell Ash and Bernard Higton. San Francisco: Chronicle Books, 1990.

These fables will be used by Rhetoric students in writing exercises. Alternately, students should rewrite one in a shorter version, retaining the meaning and sense of the fable, and then expand another fable, adding detail, description and perhaps dialogue.

II. Dissertation Upon Roast Pig
This story is useful to use as a fable for students to rewrite in 500 words.

Fable
The Crow and the Pitcher
What a hot, dry day, thought Johnny Crow. I think I'll die if I don't get something to drink!

Then Johnny saw a pitcher. It was standing near a well. He jumped up hopefully and stood on its brim. Looking down into it, he saw some water at the bottom.

You could almost hear him thinking: How wonderful that water looks. I must have some. I really must!

But try as he might, Johnny couldn't lean in far enough to reach the water. And all the while he was getting more and more thirsty!

He wasn't strong enough to tip the pitcher, and if he jumped inside he might not be able to fly back out. He thought and thought until he had a plan.

Then he jumped to the ground and picked up a pebble in his beak. He hopped back up and dropped it into the pitcher. He did this again and again, keeping his eye on the water.

He saw the water coming up little by little with every pebble he dropped. Good, he thought, but it's still too far down to reach.

I know what I'll do. I'll keep on dropping in pebbles, more and more of them.

At last, after Johnny had filled the pitcher with many pebbles, the water came up high enough to reach.

Happily he drank until he was full!

Little by little, without stopping, he reached his goal.

239 words

The Bundle of Sticks

One day a father lay sick in bed. He thought about the things he wanted his children to know. There was one important lesson he wanted them to learn. So he called them to his bedside.

He asked the oldest to go and bring back some sticks, one for each of them, and a string.

Wondering what their father would show them, the children waited until the oldest returned. Then, they watched their father take the sticks, count them, and tie them into a bundle.

Starting with the youngest, he asked her to take the bundle and see if she could break it. She tried with all her might but the sticks wouldn't break.

The father then asked the others to take a turn to see who might break the bundle. They all tried, but none of them could break it, not even the oldest.

As they looked at each other and at the bundle, the father told the oldest to untie the sticks, give one to each of his brothers and sisters, and keep the last stick for himself.

"Now," said their father, "try to break them!"

Suddenly, the air filled with a crackling sound as all the sticks broke. Even the youngest was able to break her stick.

"Do you know the lesson this teaches?" asked their father.

Together you are strong; separated you are weak.

228 words

The Donkey and the Lion's Skin

Once upon a time a donkey found a lion's skin which hunters had hung to dry in the sun.

"How exciting it would be to dress up and look like a lion!" said the donkey. Soon he was under the lion's skin and pulled it down over him. As he walked toward the village everyone was afraid and started to run.

"What fun!" cried the donkey.

Feeling very proud of himself, the donkey lifted his head and let out a loud bra-a-a-ay.

Now this is not the sound that lions make, only donkeys!

A fox quickly turned back toward the donkey and said, "I know you by your voice."

Clothes may disguise us, but when we talk, others will know who we really are.

124 words

The Fox and the Grapes

One day a fox was walking through the woods. He saw some grapes hanging from a vine over a tree limb, and his mouth began to water. The grapes looked so good that he decided he must have some.

He jumped and jumped, springing up as high as he could. But try as he might, he couldn't jump high enough to reach them. He quickly looked around to make sure that no one was watching. No fox will admit he cannot do something.

In a final, desperate attempt, the fox started from way back and ran full speed to a new jumping spot. As he reached it he leaped into the air with all his might.

This time he came closer to the grapes, but still not close enough to snatch even one!

Disappointed, he looked around once more just to be sure no one had seen him trying to reach the grapes. Then he walked away saying something to himself.

I didn't really want those grapes. They must be very sour.

172 words

The Goose and the Golden Eggs

There was a farmer who raised a goose. She looked like any other goose. But when she was old enough to nest, the farmer found her first egg was bright yellow.

"How beautiful!" he said, as he held it up and saw it glisten in the sun.

Each day he found his goose had laid another shiny egg, and he would smile.

He soon discovered that these eggs were made of gold, and took them to the market where he sold his grain. The people quickly bought every egg he would bring.

Then one day as the farmer was counting his money he said, "I'm getting rich, but not fast enough."

An idea came to him: If I kill the goose and open it up, I can have all the eggs at once. And I will be the richest person of all!

That was exactly what he did—he killed the goose. But when he opened her up he found no eggs! And his precious goose was gone, never to lay another egg,

By wanting too much, too fast, you may do something wrong and lose what you have.

189 words

A Dissertation Upon Roast Pig

By Charles Lamb

MANKIND, says a Chinese manuscript, which my friend was obliging enough to read and explain to me, for the first seventy thousand ages ate their meat raw, clawing or biting it from the living animal, just as they do in Abyssinia to this day. This period is not obscurely hinted at by their great Confucius in the second chapter of his Mundane Mutations, where he designates a kind of golden age by the term Cho-fang, literally the Cook's Holiday. The manuscript goes on to say, that the art of roasting, or rather broiling (which I take to be the elder brother) was accidentally discovered in the manner following. The swine-herd Ho-ti, having gone out into the woods one morning, as his manner was, to collect mast for his hogs, left his cottage in the care of his eldest son, Bo-bo, a great lubberly boy, who being fond of playing with fire, as youngsters of his age commonly are, let some sparks escape into a bundle of straw, which kindling quickly, spread the conflagration over every part of their poor mansion, till it was reduced to ashes. Together with the cottage (a sorry antediluvian make-shift of a building, you may think it), what was of much more importance, a fine litter of new-farrowed pigs, no less than nine in number perished. China pigs have been esteemed a luxury all over the East, from the remotest periods that we read of.

Bo-bo was in the utmost consternation, as you may think, not so much for the sake of the tenement, which his father and he could easily build up again with a few dry branches, and the labour of an hour or two at any time, as for the loss of the pigs. While he was thinking what he should say to his father, and wringing his hands over the smoking remnants of one of those untimely sufferers, an odour assailed his nostrils, unlike any scent which he had before experienced. What could it proceed from? Not from the burnt cottage: he had smelt that smell before; indeed this was by no means the first accident of the kind which had occurred through the negligence of this unlucky young fire-brand. Much less did it resemble that of any known herb, weed, or flower.

A premonitory moistening at the same time overflowed his nether lip. He knew not what to think. He next stooped down to feel the pig, if there were any signs of life in it. He burnt his fingers, and to cool them he applied them in his booby fashion to his mouth. Some of the crumbs of the scorched skin had come away with his fingers, and for the first time in this life (in the world's life indeed, for before him no man had known it), he tasted *crackling!* Again he felt and fumbled at the pig. It did not burn him so much now, still he licked his fingers from a sort of habit. The truth at length broke into his slow understanding, that it was the pig that smelt so, and the pig that tasted so delicious; and surrendering himself up to the new-born pleasure, he fell to tearing up whole handfuls of the scorched skin with the flesh next it, and was cramming it down his throat in his beastly fashion, when his sire entered amid the smoking rafters, armed with retributory cudgel, and finding how affairs stood, began to rain blows upon the young rogue's shoulders as thick as hail-stones, which Bo-ho heeded not any more than if they had been flies. The tickling pleasure which he experienced in his lower regions had rendered him quite callous to any inconveniences he might feel in those remote quarters. His father might lay on, but he could not beat him from his pig, till he had fairly made an end of it, when, becoming a little more sensible of his situation, something like the following dialogue ensued:

"You graceless whelp, what have you got there devouring? Is it not enough that you have burnt me down three houses with your dog's tricks, and be hanged to you! but you must be eating fire, and I know not what. What have you got there, I say?"

"O father, the pig, the pig! do come and taste how nice the burnt pig eats."

The ears of Ho-ti tingled with horror. He cursed his son, and he cursed himself that ever he should beget a son that should eat burnt pig.

Bo-bo, whose scent was wonderfully sharpened since morning, soon raked out another pig, and fairly rending it asunder, thrust the lesser half by main force into the fists of Ho-ti, still shouting out, "Eat, eat, eat, the burnt pig, father, only taste—O Lord!"—with such-like barbarous exclamations, cramming all the while as if he would choke.

Ho-ti trembled in every joint while he grasped the abominable thing, wavering whether he should not put his son to death for an unnatural young monster, when the crackling scorching his fingers, as it had done his son's, and applying the same remedy to them, he in his turn tasted some of its flavour, which, make what sour mouths he would for a pretence, proved not altogether displeasing to him. In conclusion (for the manuscript here is a little tedious,) both father and son fairly sat down to the mess, and never left off till they had dispatched all that remained of the litter.

Bo-bo was strictly enjoined not to let the secret escape, for the neighbours would certainly have stoned them for a couple of abominable wretches, who could think of improving upon the good meat which God had sent them.

Nevertheless, strange stories got about. It was observed that Ho-ti's cottage was burnt down now more frequently than ever. Nothing but fires from this time forward. Some would break out in broad day, others in the night-time. As often as the sow farrowed, so sure was the house of Ho-ti to be in a blaze; and Ho-ti himself, which was the more remarkable, instead of chastising his son, seemed to grow more indulgent to him than ever. At length they were watched, the terrible mystery discovered, and father and son summoned to take their trial at Peking, then an inconsiderable assize town. Evidence was given, the obnoxious food itself produced in court, and verdict about to be pronounced, when the foreman of the jury begged that some of the burnt pig, by which the culprits stood accused, might be handed into the box. He handled it, and they all handled it; and burning their fingers, as Bo-bo and his father had done before them, and nature prompting to each of them the same remedy, against the face of all the facts, and the clearest charge which judge had ever given—to the surprise of the whole court, townsfolk, strangers, reporters, and all present—without leaving the box, or any manner of consultation whatever, they brought in a simultaneous verdict of Not Guilty.

The judge, who was a shrewd fellow, winked at the manifest iniquity of the decision and when the court was dismissed, went privily and bought up all the pigs that could be had for love or money. In a few days his lordship's town-house was observed to be on fire. The thing took wing, and now there was nothing to be seen but fire in every direction. Fuel and pigs grew enormously dear all over the district. The insurance officers, one and all, shut up shop. People built slighter and slighter every day, until it was feared that the very science of architecture would in no long time be lost to the world. Thus this custom of firing houses continued, till in process of time, says my manuscript, a sage arose, like our Locke, who made a discovery that the flesh of swine, or indeed of any other animal, might be cooked *(burnt,* as they called it), without the necessity of consuming a whole house to dress it. Then first began the rude form of a gridiron. Roasting by the string or spit came in a century or two later, I forget in whose dynasty. By such slow degrees, concludes the manuscript, do the most useful and seemingly the most obvious, arts make their way among mankind.

Made in the USA
Middletown, DE
27 August 2015